MARILYN

DISCOURSES OF
THE VANISHING

MODERNITY,
PHANTASM,
JAPAN

THE UNIVERSITY OF CHICAGO PRESS
CHICAGO AND LONDON

The University of Chicago Press, Chicago 60637
The University of Chicago Press, Ltd., London
© 1995 by The University of Chicago
All rights reserved. Published 1995
Printed in the United States of America
04 03 02 01 00 99 98 97 96   5 4 3 2

ISBN (cloth): 0-226-38832-8
ISBN (paper): 0-226-38833-6

Library of Congress Cataloging-in-Publicaton Data

Ivy, Marilyn.
    Discourses of the vanishing : modernity, phantasm, Japan / Marilyn Ivy.
        p.   cm.
    Includes bibliographical references and index.
    ISBN 0-226-38832-8—ISBN 0-226-38833-6 (pbk.)
    1. Ethnology—Japan.   2. National characteristics, Japanese.
3. Nationalism—Japan.   4. Ethnocentrism—Japan.   5. Culture—Semiotic
models.   6. Japan—Social life and customs.   I. Title.
DS830.I89   1995
306.4'0952—dc20   94-40579
                                                                          CIP

DISCOURSES OF
THE VANISHING

TO MY PARENTS,

BRUNEE AND JAMES IVY

CONTENTS

ACKNOWLEDGMENTS

Books incur debts, both for bibliophiles and for authors. That truism is even truer for books as long in the making as this one. The debts my book and I have incurred are owed not only to my family, but to friends, colleagues, and teachers I have encountered in moving from Oklahoma to Texas to Hawaii, from Ithaca to Tokyo to Chicago to, most recently, Seattle. If indebtedness is the inevitable state of authorship, however, so also is gratitude.

I have come to appreciate the singular importance that teachers have had in my life: J. Wilgus Eberly taught me much about the piano and how music could be connected to a larger world of literature and life. George Tanabe first gave me a sense of the excitement of working with Japanese texts; he was instrumental in my decision to continue graduate studies, as was Charles Collier. My time at Cornell University as a graduate student in anthropology was transformative, and it is to a group of remarkable teachers that I owe much of whatever intellectual awareness I now possess. I want to acknowledge and thank, then: James Boon, for introducing me to the comparative scope of anthropology and the intractability of culture; J. Victor Koschmann, whose engagement with Japanese intellectual history and politics constantly reminded me of the necessity of thinking about Japan as a modern nation-state; Robert Smith, whose wide knowledge of Japan inspired me to keep social conditions and constraints in mind when doing ethnographic research in Japan; and James Siegel, who alerted me to the possibilities of thinking about issues of representation and the logic of the uncanny.

I am inordinately fortunate to have had the anthropologist Yamaguchi Masao as my advisor during my fieldwork in Japan. Rather than insist on my attending university seminars (which he had no duties to teach, in any case), he insisted that I attend and observe kabuki, local festivals, popular theater, avant-garde events, and performances of all kinds. He was the first to suggest that I do fieldwork in Tōno and also introduced me to the popular theater that I analyze in chapter 6 of this book. His encyclopedic knowledge of not only Japanese, but world, expressive forms and performance genres provided me with a truly cosmopolitan intellectual example. I was equally lucky to be affiliated with the Tokyo University of Foreign Studies; I thank the faculty and staff there for their hospitality. In Japan, Asada Akira, Iwasaki Emiko, Kaiwa Fusae, Kaiwa Mitsugi, Nishizawa Haruhiko, Oikawa Sachiko, Okude Naohito, Sasaki Ichirō, Sasaki Momoko, Tatsurō Ishii, Urata Hōichi, Yoshida Kazuyoshi, the employees of the Tōno Museum, and many others provided friendship and assistance to the foreigner in their midst.

My first academic job was in the Department of Anthropology at the University of Chicago; I am grateful to the entire department and to the Japanese Studies faculty for their wonderful generosity. I must particularly thank Andrew Apter, Leora Auslander, Bernard Cohn, Jean Comaroff, John Comaroff, Norma Field, William Hanks, H. D. Harootunian, Tetsuo Najita, Marshall Sahlins, William Sibley, Michael Silverstein, and Sharon Stephens for the friendship they extended to me. Graduate students at Chicago provided rewarding intellectual encounters, and it has been a source of great happiness that many of them have become my friends. Here I want to note my appreciation to Katherine Hall, Esther Hamburger, Thomas LaMarre, Rosalind Morris, Kate Schechter, Susan Seizer, David Slater, Janelle Taylor, and Igarashi Yoshikuni. I also want to register a special debt of gratitude to Arjun Appadurai and Carol Breckenridge for their encouragement, intellectual energy, and friendship; it has been a true pleasure to work on the journal *Public Culture* with them. The Center for Transcultural Studies (formerly the Center for Psychosocial Studies) has allowed me access to a larger world of scholarly exchange, and I particularly credit the director, Benjamin Lee, for the ways he has facilitated that exchange. The Department of Anthropology and the Japan Studies Program at the University of Washington have been generous and welcoming.

Ann Anagnost, Katherine Bergeron, E. Valentine Daniel, Nicholas Dirks, Norma Field, Takashi Fujitani, H. D. Harootunian, Webb Keane, Adela Pinch, Naoki Sakai, Rafael Sanchez, Patricia Spyer, Vicente Rafael, John Treat, and Lisa Yoneyama kindly agreed to hear, read, or comment on portions of this manuscript in its various incarnations. They helped me in many other ways, as well. William Kelly gave me sharp and insightful criticisms as a reader of the manuscript; I thank him and an anonymous reader for their suggestions. I also thank T. David Brent for his editorial attention in producing this book, and Joel Score for his intelligent improvement of my text.

The initial fieldwork on which this book is based was carried out in Japan from October 1982 to August 1985; it was funded by a Fulbright Predoctoral Fellowship for Dissertation Research from 1982 to 1984. Dissertation writing and further research was made possible by a Sage Graduate Fellowship at Cornell University, 1985–1986; an American Association of University Women American Fellowship, 1986–1987; and a postdoctoral fellowship at the Edwin O. Reischauer Institute of Japanese Studies at Harvard University in 1988–1989. Harold Bolitho, director of the institute during my time at Harvard, graciously granted me the freedom to submit my manuscript to presses other than Harvard University Press. I am grateful for his generosity, as well as that of Howard Hibbett. A grant from the Social Sciences Division at the University of Chicago enabled me to do additional research in Japan in 1990.

Brief portions of chapter 2 were previously published in "Tradition and Difference in the Japanese Mass Media," *Public Culture* 1, no. 1 (1988): 21–29. Copyright © 1988 by the Project for Transnational Cultural Studies, University of Pennsylvania. All rights reserved. The photograph of the Exotic Japan poster on page 52 is taken from the book *Ekizochikku Japan: Atarashii tabi no kankaku* (Tokyo: Kōsai Shuppansha, 1985); the photograph on page 62 is the cover of the book *Nyū Japanorojii* (Tokyo: Tatsuki-sha, 1984), designed by Fukawa Michio.

Intellectual friendship is a sublime gift, almost outside the circuits of debt and gratitude I have acknowledged here. My companion and colleague John Pemberton knows more about me and my work than anyone else. His critical engagement with this book has been another sublime gift. Since I can't thank him enough, I would hope that the book itself could stand as a memento of my gratitude. I hope that it will also convey my thankfulness to my sisters, and especially my parents, for their forbearance and support. Of course, in the end, the lapses and shortcomings of the book are mine and mine only.

CHAPTER ONE

National-Cultural Phantasms and Modernity's Losses

The subject of late-twentieth-century Japan confounds the simplicities of world order, whether new or old. Crossing boundaries of race and region, of temporalities and territories established at the foundation of the modern world system, installed everywhere with its enormous reserves of capital, "Japan" appears ubiquitous, nomadic, transnational. Yet at the same time Japan seems to reinscribe the distinction ever more sharply between the "West" and itself.[1] No nation of comparable economic power seems so territorially constricted, so ethnically standardized, so culturally contained: Japanese themselves commonly insist that theirs is a small island country (shimaguni), a homogeneous place. Its economic expansiveness is parried by a national inwardness and a disavowal of internal differences along class or ethnic lines, a disavowal most often laid at the feet of culture. The image of Japan as the great assimilator arises to explain away any epistemological snags or historical confusions: Japan assimilates, if not immigrants and American automobiles, then everything else, retaining the traditional, immutable core of culture while incorporating the shiny trappings of (post)modernity in a dizzying round of production, accumulation, and consumption.

Disclosed in the image of assimilation with its insistence on the final imperviousness of Japanese culture is a profound categorical uneasi-

---

1. The quotation marks around "Japan" and "West" are meant to indicate (as such marks do) the unstable identities that those proper names signify. By claiming that "Japan" is as much a discursive construct as an objective referent (or, rather, that "Japan" has been made objective through discourse), I merely want to emphasize the imaginative and historical dimensions of what we commonly call "Japan"—and what we call the

1

Japan - powerful, transnational
- culturally contained, homogeneous

ness, an uneasiness contained only by keeping the spheres of the economic and the cultural distinct. Americans know that the Japanese are technologically and economically modern—with factory robots, electronic toys, and megabanks—but culturally, Japan is "an exclusive, homogeneous Asian ocean-and-island realm, tribal, intricately compact, suppressive, fiercely focused."[2] Tribal? This description, from *Time* magazine, reveals the popular extent to which Americans perceive Japanese as culturally not modern, a nonmodernity sustained by patterns of social organization and symbolic production that persist no matter what goes on in the fabulous realms of advanced capitalism.

The stereotypical dimensions of this perception of Japan are not confined to the American popular press. What is striking is the extent to which essentialized images of Japan resonate with many Japanese self-descriptions: everyday, academic, and mass-market. An entire publishing genre has developed to categorize such reflections: *Nihonjinron*, "discourses on the Japanese." Immensely popular works in this genre—written in Japanese by Japanese for Japanese—assert, for example, that the Japanese language is the most difficult in the world, that Japanese are not logical, that Japanese selves are sheerly "relational," and that the Japanese are a homogeneous race.[3] Whether these works put a positive or negative spin on their conclusions, they assert with numbing repetition the uniqueness of Japan, a uniqueness constituted as the particularized obverse of the West (with the United States its exemplary representative).

Keeping Japanese culture intact allows the anxiety Japan provokes to be controlled, if not overcome—for nation-identified Japanese as well as Americans. Yet maintaining this intactness has its costs. Despite the absorption of the foreign in everything from cooking to philosophy, a feeling of isolation haunts many in Japan. Karatani Kōjin, one of Japan's most compelling literary critics, addresses the lack of exteriority *(gaibu)* and of fundamental *kōtsū* (traffic; intercourse) with the outside world.[4] The problem of otherness is here confronted, as the foreign can only operate as a commodified sign of reassurance. That

---

"West." I will generally not use quotation marks around these terms in the rest of this book, now that they have been marked.

2. Lance Morrow, "Japan in the Mind of America," 16.

3. For a critique of these writings, see J. Victor Koschmann, "Nihonjinron in Postwar Japanese History"; see also Harumi Befu's essay "Nationalism and *Nihonjinron*," as well as Peter Dale, *The Myth of Japanese Uniqueness,* and Yoshino Kosaku, *Cultural Nationalism in Contemporary Japan: A Sociological Enquiry.*

4. For example, Karatani Kōjin states that "Japan will remain for the West a place of exteriority rather than being what in fact it is: a discursive space filled with complacency

is, the foreign—because of its very threat—must be transformed into a manageable sign of order, a transformation indicated most clearly by what, in Japan, is perhaps the dominant political concept of the past ten years: internationalization *(kokusaika)*. While internationalization elsewhere implies a cosmopolitan expansiveness (even while retaining the national frame), the Japanese state-sponsored version tends toward the domestication of the foreign. Schemes to internationalize the communications industry, education, and the citizenry index the pressures on the state to give the appearance, at least, of openness, while carefully circumscribing the problem of identity and difference. As many observers, both domestic and foreign, have noted, kokusaika is a conservative policy that reflects the other side of a renewed sense of Japanese national pride, if not nationalism. It has thus been remarked that instead of opening up Japan to the struggle of different nationalities and ethnicities, the policy of internationalization implies the opposite: the thorough domestication of the foreign and the dissemination of Japanese culture throughout the world.[5] A bumper sticker seen on Tokyo taxis in the early 1990s said, if not all, quite a bit: Import Now! The ubiquitous sticker appeared as part of the state's campaign to step up imports in response to international pressure. But it was written in English, thereby not only ensuring that many Japanese would initially be unable to read it, but emphasizing that the imperative to "open up" once again emanated from the outside, from the western foreign, which the English language generically indexes.

What these moments of cultural anxiety and category trouble designate is the dialectically entwined status of the United States (as the paradigm of the West) and Japan as national-cultural imaginaries. By hyphenating "national" and "cultural," I want to indicate the inextricable linkage of culture with the idea of the nation, such that it is

---

and almost totally lacking in exteriority." He is pointing here to the difficulty for modern Japanese of imagining otherness, since an emphasis on national uniqueness tends to incorporate signs of difference as merely exotic or, alternatively, to disavow difference through exclusion. This refusal of national-cultural alterity is, in fact, hardly different from the forms of chauvinism familiar to Europeans and Americans. But certain exacerbating factors are present in the Japanese case, where a limited territorial domain coincides with the relative physical rarity of "non-Japanese," a global economic presence, and ample domestic wealth, which allows Japanese to consume the signs and products of otherness. Karatani, "One Spirit, Two Nineteenth Centuries," 271.

5. James Fujii has explored some of the dimensions of this discourse on kokusaika, particularly as it relates to the state's formation of the International Research Center for Japanese Studies in Kyoto (Nichibunken, in abbreviated Japanese) to consolidate the importance of Japanese culture in the world. See Fujii, "Culture, Political Economy and Japan's Discourse of Internationalization."

misleading to talk about Japanese "culture" without immediately thinking of the question of the nation (and implied within that is yet another linkage, that with the state). By using the idea of the imaginary, I am pointing to the element of phantasm that lies at the basis of national-cultural communities. There are at least four configurations of the imaginary that resonate, in different ways, with my use: Benedict Anderson's "imagined communities" as the basis for the modern nation-state; Cornelius Castoriadis's "social imaginary," which operates almost as an analogue to culture as theorized by structural anthropologists, as the codified ground for the social production of meaning; Claude Lefort's "imaginary community," which he links with modern ideologies and the rise of mass media; and Lacan's "imaginary" as the phantasmatic basis for the human subject's early, presymbolic identification with the image.[6] It is the intertwining of these imaginaries within the United States, for example, and Japan that I find compelling, but therein lies the historical rub. Japan is literally unimaginable outside its positioning vis-à-vis the West. Like other colonized or near-colonized polities, Japan as a *nation-state* was instaurated in response to the threat of domination by European and American powers in the mid–nineteenth century. It is arguable that there was no discursively unified notion of the "Japanese" before the eighteenth century, and that the articulation of a unified Japanese ethnos with the "nation" to produce "Japanese culture" is entirely *modern*.[7]

What I mean by modern—as if one could simply define it—indicates not only the urban energies, capitalist structures of life, and mechanical and electrical forms of reproduction that came into sharpest

6. For these four configurations, see Benedict Anderson, *Imagined Communities: Reflections on the Origin and Spread of Nationalism;* Cornelius Castoriadis, *The Imaginary Institution of Society;* Claude Lefort's collected essays, *The Political Forms of Modern Society: Bureaucracy, Democracy, Totalitarianism,* especially his "Outline of the Genesis of Ideology in Modern Societies"; and the works of Jacques Lacan: for example, the classic "The Mirror Stage as Formative of the Function of the I" in his *Écrits: A Selection* and *The Four Fundamental Concepts of Psycho-Analysis.*

7. Naoki Sakai claims that Japanese language and culture as recognizable discursive unities emerged in the eighteenth century, but he recognizes the difference between this eighteenth-century unification and the modern, post-Meiji configuration. This difference is intimately entwined with the rise of the nation-state, in which "the unity of the Japanese and the 'interior' were equated to the existing language and community without mediation. . . . The Japanese language and its ethnos were brought into being and made to exist in the present and were thereby transformed into unobjectionable certainties as if they were entities observable in experience. Thus the Japanese were resurrected from the dormant past and, as a nation, began to play the role of the subject to and for the modern state. . . . Needless to say, this was the process in which the modern nation-state of Japan was appropriated into the nineteenth-century discourse of global colonialism,

MODERN

relief in the Japan of the 1920s.[8] It indicates the problem of the nation-state and its correlation with a capitalist colonialism that ensured Japan would be pulled into a global geopolitical matrix from the mid-nineteenth century on. It indicates as well the changes effected in identities and subjectivities, through the emergence of individualism and new modes of interiority; in relationships to temporality, through the emergence of "tradition" as the background against which progressive history could be situated; and in institutional procedures, through what Foucault has called individualization and totalization: bureaucratic rationalisms, Taylorized modes of production, novel forms of image representation, mass media, scientific disciplines.[9] In their historical specificity, these modes, procedures, and apparatuses constitute a discursive complex which I think of as modern. What I want to underline, however, is the co-occurrence—the coevalness—of the problem of Japanese modernity with that of modernities elsewhere, and the shared temporality that implies.[10]

That coevalness does not imply the collapsing of differences within

cultural essentialism, and racism." Sakai, *Voices of the Past: The Status of Language in Eighteenth-Century Japanese Discourse*, 336.

8. Historian Miriam Silverberg has written with great insight about Japanese modernity, modernism, and mass culture, particularly during the interwar years. See her *Changing Song: The Marxist Manifestos of Nakano Shigeharu*, "Constructing the Japanese Ethnography of Modernity," and "Remembering Pearl Harbor, Forgetting Charlie Chaplin, and the Case of the Disappearing Western Woman: A Picture Story" for a range of arguments about the distinctiveness of Japanese modernity (as opposed, say, to conflations of the "modern" with the "western"). Late-twentieth-century Japan poses other problems for a rethinking of the modern.

9. The names of Marx, Weber, Freud, Foucault, and Habermas (not necessarily in that order) hardly need to be invoked as essential theorists of modernity. I would also like to note the inescapable importance of three other names to my thinking about modernity and its phantasms: Adorno, Benjamin, and de Certeau. The sustained energy that Japanese intellectuals have brought to encountering the dilemmas of modernity is humbling: Kobayashi Hideo, Maruyama Masao, Miki Kiyoshi, Nishida Kitarō, Takeuchi Yoshimi, and Yoshimoto Takaaki are just a few of those intellectuals. The working through of modernity's contradictions by Japanese artists and writers constitutes another vast domain of inquiry.

10. Thus the insistence of Karatani, in his afterword to the English edition of his *Nihon kindai bungaku no kigen*—published in translation as *The Origins of Modern Japanese Literature*—that, in the realm of literature, "as long as a work is seen as the 'expression' of the 'self' of an 'author,' that work is already located within the apparatus of modern literature, no matter how antimodern and anti-Western it may be" (p. 192). Thus, no matter what the thematic content of Japanese literary works from the Meiji period on, they are modern because of their concern with expression and the interiority of the self—a concern he states was absent from pre-Meiji literature. Karatani works to locate Japan fully within a world-historical context, arguing that Japan's "nearness to origins" (the origins of modernity, that is) links it to other nation-states that came to power in the late nineteenth century.

an undifferentiated global modernity, although I would argue that we ignore the homogenizing trajectories of advanced capitalism at our peril. Japan is not merely the same as other nation-states within this global order by virtue of its modernity, nor is it just a variation on the larger modernization theme, a divergence (modernization debates are often couched as choices between "divergence" and "convergence"). Neither, however, would I want to insist on the radical nature of Japanese difference and thus to displace the shared historical burdens of modernity and its underlying modes of production in favor of a specifically *cultural* incommensurability (with Japan, as with other nonwestern nations, difference is often laid at the feet of culture: Japanese management practices are so different from American ones, the argument goes, because Japanese culture is so different). Instead, I prefer to emphasize the contradictions that always accompany the ruptures of modernity, such that the very formulation of the notion of "culture" as that which could bear the burden of difference is unthinkable outside the transformations of the twentieth century. If Japan is incommensurable, it is incommensurable in ways commensurate with other modern nation-cultures in the historical specificity of its modern entanglements.

In warding off the intrusions of the colonial powers after Perry's 1853 arrival, the newly instituted Japanese state bent all efforts toward rapid industrialization and the formation of a unitary polity, a process that often entailed brutal force and violent exclusions. The formation of a modern nation-state demanded the repression of internal differences in the service of what Slavoj Žižek has called the "National Thing," one that could stand apart and up to the powers of the West (*seiyō*).[11] An obscure emperor was restored and positioned as an absolute paternal subject reigning over a totalized national body (or "body politic," *kokutai*) comprised of individuated (through education, conscription, and moral discipline) imperial subjects (*shinmin*) who were simultaneously constructed as modern citizens (*shimin*). That specific history has determined the fatefully dense articulation of the Japanese national imaginary with the fantasies of the West.

Recent works on colonialism and nationalism have tried to account for the working of mimetic desire in colonial discourses; in Homi

---

11. Slavoj Žižek, "Eastern Europe's Republics of Gilead." By "National Thing" Žižek means the nexus of national identification that is organized around what he calls "enjoyment" (from Lacan) and bears a particular relationship to the problem of national others. Žižek leans on Lacan and his notion of the "Thing," which derives from his anatomy of demand and desire and their emergence from an irrevocable lack within human sub-

→ *Marx's bourgeois*

Bhabha's terms, the colonized responds to colonial domination via a
complex "mimicry," a mimicry that can never succeed in effacing the
difference between the western original and the colonized copy. Colonized mimics remain as "not white/not quite" in Bhabha's formulation.[12] Is it any wonder that Japanese have been both extolled and denigrated as adept mimics, good at copying but lacking originality? Or
that the South African government at one time officially designated
Japanese as "honorary whites" (in deference to Japan's status as South
Africa's primary trading partner)? Yet in Bhabha's formulation the mimetic attempts of the colonized also contain an element of menace
because of their dangerous doubling and uneasy proximity to the colo-   *uncanny*
nizer's position: there is always an excess, a slippage that reveals mimicry as something more (and less) than the object of mimesis. It is no
doubt Japan's (some would say presumptuous) entry into geopolitics
as an entirely exotic and late-modernizing nation-state instead of as an
outright colony that has made its mimicry all the more threatening. As
the only predominantly nonwhite nation to have challenged western
dominance on a global scale during World War II—and to have done
so by becoming colonialist, imperialist, and (some would say) fascist—
Japan, in its role as quasi-colonized mimic, has finally exceeded itself:
now it is American companies, educators, and social scientists who
speak of the necessity of learning from Japan in the hope of copying its
economic miracles, its pedagogical successes, its societal orderliness. If
a modernity often imagined as American is installed in the interior of
the Japanese national imaginary, "Japan" conversely indicates a loss at
the heart of American self-perceptions: "The Cold War is over, and
Japan won." Japan's very devastation in World War II has allowed it to
emerge belatedly victorious in the current wars of trade. Japan's martial loss thus prefigured a victory, a deferred victory that now marks
the defeat of the United States. In the American national rhetoric of
deficit, Japan marks out a nation-space of excess operating as the
nameable supplement of the United States, the defeated term that
comes both to add to and invasively supplant the victorious one (even
American cars are made with Japanese parts).

The excesses of mimicry remarked by both westerners and Japanese   *excess*
indicate the instabilities that founded the difference between quasi-

jects. That lack means that the object of desire is always the desire of the other. But that
desire is a "non-object"; it can never be specified as such but is always displaced. This
non-object, this residuum of desire, is what Freud first referred to as *das Ding*, the
"Thing." It is related to the idea of the "uncanny," which I develop in chapter 3.

12. Homi Bhabha, "Of Mimicry and Man: The Ambivalence of Colonial Discourse."

colonial original and quasi-colonized copy in the first instance. They point as well to the impossibility, in a radical sense, of instituting a sheer difference between Japan and the West, although attempts to do so are far from abating. As Naoki Sakai points out, in an essay on modernity and its critique in *prewar* Japan:

> Perhaps the most crucial point the [Japanese] philosophers of world history did not realize was that Japan did not stand *out-side* the West. Even in its particularism, Japan was already implicated in the ubiquitous West, so that neither historically nor geopolitically could Japan be seen as the *outside* of the West. This means that, in order to criticize the West in relation to Japan, one has necessarily to begin with a critique of Japan. Likewise, the critique of Japan necessarily entails the radical critique of the West.[13]

[margin handwritten note: unfamiliar + familiar]

It is only through a realization, finally, of the coincidences of modernity that anything politically powerful (or interesting) can be said about a Japan that is, in the end, a representation coeval, if not identical, with the sensibility of the modern in the putative West.[14] Although an initial insistence on clearly delineated cultural otherness can constitute the first step in the recognition of historical domination and orientalism, it can hardly stand as the *final* step in a truly critical anthropology (or history, or literary analysis). Indeed, it is increasingly crucial to recognize—with as much complexity and delicacy as possible, but still to recognize—the coincident modernity of Japan and the West. And that recognition entails rejecting the fetishized simplicities of sheer cultural relativism: what are imagined as the specificities of Japan or Japanese culture can never be unilaterally deployed as unexamined critical tools to undo presumed western hegemonies.[15]

13. Naoki Sakai, "Modernity and Its Critique: The Problem of Universalism and Particularism," 113–14.

14. See Rey Chow's essay "Seeing Modern China: Toward a Theory of Ethnic Spectatorship," in her *Women and Chinese Modernity: The Politics of Reading Between West and East,* for a critique of unexamined cultural relativism.

15. Subaltern theorists writing about the colonization of India and the struggles of nationalism have provided compelling revelations of the dangers and seductions of using a nonwestern "culture" to critique the West, when the non-West is inextricably bound up with originally western discourses (of modernity, of nationalism, of revolution). Partha Chatterjee's *Nationalist Thought and the Colonial World: A Derivative Discourse* is one of the emblematic works of these theorists. See also Dipesh Chakrabarty's essay "Postcoloniality and the Artifice of History: Who Speaks for 'Indian' Pasts?" on the question of the "lack" of modernity in India. Nicholas Dirks has written of the critical place that history occupies in any rethinking of modernity. See his "History as a Sign of the Modern."

European and American attempts to place Japan as unassimilably alter and Japanese attempts to live up to—to assert—its difference cannot thus be easily dissociated, despite numerous efforts to maintain the distinction between the two geohistorical unities. The efforts to sustain that difference have never been without remainders, losses, and violences, not only within the "island nation" but outside: violences enacted not only on Japanese but by them. The hybrid realities of Japan today—of multiple border crossings and transnational interchanges in the worlds of trade, aesthetics, science—are contained within dominant discourses on cultural purity and nondifference, and in nostalgic appeals to premodernity: what makes the Japanese so different from everyone else makes them identical to each other; what threatens that self-sameness is often marked temporally as the intrusively modern, spatially as the foreign. Although those discourses are being altered by the effects of advanced capitalism (the need for cheap labor, which has led to growing numbers of illegal "guest workers"; the pressure to increase imports from the United States; international tourism; consumerism; mass-mediated spectatorship; and market differentiation), they have proved to be remarkably resilient as they haunt the possibilities for a postnationalist consciousness in contemporary Japan.[16]

That supplemental relationship and the vicissitudes of history—the temporal deferral that retrospectively inscribes Japan as the winner in the global market wars, for example—point to a way to begin to loosen the entanglements of Japanese modernity. *Discourses of the Vanishing* traces remainders of modernity within contemporary Japan. Traversing genres, temporalities, and topoi, I examine how Japan's national successes have produced—along with Corollas and Walkmans—a certain crucial nexus of unease about culture itself and its transmission and stability. This anxiety indicates, conversely, a troubling lack of success at the very interior of national self-fashioning, a recurring motif of critical import in thinking about the instabilities of what is often depicted as uncannily stable. That is, there is widespread recognition in Japan today that the destabilizations of capitalist modernity have

16. The writings of Arjun Appadurai theorize the transnationally disjunctive relationships between and among diasporas, global flows of capital and information, and cultural dispersions. See in particular his "Disjuncture and Difference in the Global Cultural Economy." On foreign workers in Japan, see Komai Hiroshi, "Tan'itsu minzokushugi wa koerareruka: Nihon ni okeru tabunkashugi no kanōsei." Komai claims that there were, at the time of his writing, some 250,000 foreign workers who had "overstayed their visits" (*chōka taizaisha*) and were working illegally in Japan. The increasing presence of such foreigners in Japan has led to widespread speculation about the possi-

decreed the loss of much of the past, a past sometimes troped as "traditional"; at the same time, there is a disavowal of this recognition
through massive investment in representative survivals refigured as
elegiac resources. Through tourism, folklore studies, education, and
mass media—and through everyday moments of national-cultural in-
terpellation and identification—Japanese of all generations seek a recognition of continuity that is coterminous with its negation. As culture
industries seek to reassure Japanese that everything is in place and all
is not lost, the concomitant understanding arises (sometimes ob-
scurely) that such reassurance would not be necessary if loss, indeed,
were not at stake. Thus the consuming and consumable pleasures of
nostalgia as an ambivalent longing to erase the temporal difference
between subject and object of desire, shot through with not only the
impossibility but also the ultimate unwillingness to reinstate what was
lost. For the loss of nostalgia—that is, the loss of the desire to long
for what is lost because one has *found* the lost object—can be more
unwelcome than the original loss itself. Despite its labors to recover
the past and deny the losses of "tradition," modernist nostalgia must
preserve, in many senses, the sense of absence that motivates its desires.[17]

The linkage of recognition and disavowal describes what in psychoanalytic criticism is known as the logic of the fetish, the denial of a
feared absence through its replacement with a substitute presence.[18]
But this very replacement inevitably announces the absence it means
to cover up, thus provoking anxiety. This concurrent recognition and

---

bility of Japanese multiculturalism, which in the standard portrayals of Japan would
seem oxymoronic: Japan is nothing if not monocultural.

17. The peculiarities of nostalgic desire—a desire that subsists in the insistence on an
unbridgeable distance between the subject and ostensible object of desire—is explored
with great delicacy and precision in Susan Stewart's *On Longing: Narratives of the Miniature, the Gigantic, the Souvenir, the Collection*. Stewart's densest meditations concern narrative nostalgia. Take, for example, these reflections: "Nostalgia, like any form of narrative,
is always ideological: the past it seeks has never existed except as narrative, and hence,
always absent, that past continually threatens to reproduce itself as a felt lack. Hostile
to history and its invisible origins, and yet longing for an impossibly pure context of
lived experience at a place of origin, nostalgia wears a distinctly utopian face, a face that
turns toward a future-past, a past which has only ideological reality. *This point of desire
which the nostalgic seeks is in fact the absence that is the very generating mechanism of desire*"
(p. 23; emphasis added). Kathleen Stewart evokes the imponderables of class and nostalgia in West Virginia; see, for example, her "Nostalgia—A Polemic."

18. Freud's classic essay on fetishism—although he repeatedly addressed the issue
throughout his career—is (not surprisingly) entitled "Fetishism." The peculiar workings
of the notion of fetishism—the correlate display and disavowal of absence through a

disavowal can only be sustained by a certain splitting of the subject, a topological segregation of the subject who knows (something is missing) and the subject who (fixed on the replacement of absence) doesn't. Anxiety appears as the symptomatic effect of a self-sameness that can only be different from itself.[19]

The movements of national-cultural self-fashioning often retrace the lines of fetishistic investment in the most general sense. In Japan, refined high culture is one such site, where, for example, Noh theater, tea ceremony, and Kyoto politesse attain the realm of desirable banality for the domestic bourgeoisie and approved export status as icons of Japaneseness. Another locus we might call the generalized, customary everyday, where chopsticks, kimono, and sushi materially demarcate the Japanese "thing." Yet another asserts the sublimity of the Japanese language and opposes the inscrutabilities of Japanese selves to western logocentric individuals.[20] Allied with this are the varieties of state-

---

substitute—is of course put into the register of the economic in Marx's commodity fetishism. Recent work has pushed the fetishistic dynamic into new realms of analysis. See, for example, the volume *Fetishism as Cultural Discourse*, edited by Emily Apter and William Pietz. See "Fetish," a special issue of the *Princeton Architectural Journal.*

19. Žižek, following Octave Mannoni, states: "We could thus say that the formula of fetishism is "'I know but nevertheless . . .' ('I know that Mother doesn't have a penis, but nevertheless . . . [I believe that she has]')." There is thus a movement of identification that exists only in difference, described as a split between knowledge and belief. Žižek, *For They Know Not What They Do: Enjoyment as a Political Factor*, 245.

20. Works included within the Nihonjinron genre usually assert such diametrical opposition to western individualistic selves. The genre finds its provenance in many of the prewar texts of Japanese philosophy, which probed the distinctiveness of a Japanese national subjectivity in the face of western domination. The difficulties of asserting difference from the West lay, of course, in the dialectical terms predicating those assertions. That is, in a necessity well known to critics of orientalism and colonialism, the colonized must always assert its difference *in relation to* the West, and as such even its difference is dependent on the other term. This dilemma has often led to an ever-greater hypervaluation of difference. Postwar reconfigurations of these assertions of difference in the social sciences, in state policies, and popular discourses have deeply disturbed many Japanese who have tried to think through new forms of resistant subject formation and nonauthoritarian forms of community (the political theorist Maruyama Masao is merely the most emblematic of such modernist thinkers). One of the most disturbing effects of these reconfigurations is their attempt to deny the anxieties of modernity, with its rationalizing technologies, individualizing procedures, and totalizing apparatuses. An anthropology of Japan that has not been sufficiently attuned to the political valences of these historical dimensions has tended to validate many of the claims of cultural essentialists and has in turn been reappropriated to serve as evidence for Japanese uniqueness. Ruth Benedict's *Chrysanthemum and the Sword* is of course a classic example, originally anti-racist in inspiration, of how shifting historico-political terrain can lead to reversed readings. A psychologically oriented anthropology is always in danger of unwittingly ignoring the contingencies of history.

approved anthropological arguments for Japan as a household *(ie)* society.[21] Arguably the most charged topos of all is that of the emperor, who, despite his postwar denial of divine status and his placement as a powerless symbolic monarch, still remains a deified icon for nationalists, literally embodying the logic of fetishistic denial, with all its disturbing political effects.[22] These registers of investment are of course not mutually exclusive; rather, they are interimplicated in the formation of Japan as a national-cultural unity.

My interests linger primarily, however, on discourses and practices where ethnos, voice, and nation-culture problematically coincide: the register of what is sometimes called the folkloric, sometimes temporalized as the essentially "traditional," concurrently located as the "marginal."[23] Neither lodged in the repetitions of metropolitan everyday practice nor infused with high cultural capital, the instances I seek to engage are explicitly entangled in rhetorics of loss and recovery. Located in the ever-receding countryside *(inaka)* or on the edges of advanced capitalist prosperity—that is, distanced in some fashion from central, metropolitan sites of representation—these practices compel as recalcitrant spectacles of the elegiac, as allegories of cultural loss that Japanese often link, viscerally, with personal loss. Whether the embodied search for an authentic locus of Japaneseness (chapter 2), the discovery of Japanese folktales *(minwa)* in the early twentieth century or their current renarrativization (chapters 3 and 4), the recalling of the dead by blind female spirit mediums (chapter 5), or the staging of class and gender differences in itinerant theater (chapter 6), the instances I encounter are all effected in discourses that evoke the vanishing auratic in an age of electronic reproduction. Through the powers of mass-mediated dissemination and spectatorship, a revived folk festival, for example, not only becomes a local representation of a cultural

21. See Murakami Yasusuke, Kumon Shunpei, and Sato Seizaburō, *Bunmei toshite no ie shakai* (Household Society as Civilization).

22. Norma Field locates the dangers of the "harmless" symbolic emperor through stories of contemporary Japanese who have relinquished the comforts of the imperial fetish in her powerful *In The Realm of a Dying Emperor: Japan at Century's End.*

23. I use the notion of discourse in ways inspired by Foucault: discourse as a mode of language use articulated with forms of power, institutional and otherwise. I am also indebted to Michel de Certeau, who is acutely attuned not only to discourses as orders of representation, but also to the problem of alterity: that which is not representable. Discourses are constituted as much by their relationship to the nonrepresentable as by their status as representations. That is why the question of the irrational and the logics of psychoanalysis particularly engage de Certeau as a theorist of the "heterological" dimensions of modern discourses. See in particular his collection of essays *Heterologies: Discourse on the Other.*

world where such festivity had its place but also becomes generically representative; that is, it generically reminds Japanese of what such festivals (*matsuri*) used to signify. At the same time it consoles them with what still undeniably lives—representatively.[24] Representative value becomes a mobile sign, detachable from locale but dependent on perpetually evoking it. Such instances lend themselves to allegorical displacement, to highlighting the difference between what is enacted and what is not, to the distinction between the literal and the figural, the grammatical and the rhetorical. The events, rituals, texts, stories, and performances I address enact a difference from the past as they seek to reduce that difference. They thematize loss in a variety of ways as they work inevitably to recover that loss. That work sometimes takes the guise of mourning, sometimes of recursive repetition, sometimes of rememoration or memorialization. And it also appears in the mode of forgetting, through moments of fetishistic disavowal.

Eric Santner outlines two dimensions of mourning tasks in his moving work *Stranded Objects: Mourning, Memory, and Film in Postwar Germany*: particular, historical tasks of mourning; and mourning for those "'catastrophes' that are inseparable from being-in-language," what Santner refers to as "structural" loss.[25] Language reveals a movement of loss and recovery, of difference and repetition. There is something within the production of a text that allows for its coming apart, its difference from itself, and its elegiac reinscription. Texts often allegorize this "something," and this something is nothing other than the movement of desire in language: that which is not reducible to what language intends to say and which returns to trouble the surface of

24. William Kelly has written sensitively of the complexities of the rationalization of the countryside (and the complexities of the nostalgia it provokes) in "Rationalization and Nostalgia: Cultural Dynamics of New Middle-Class Japan"; his "Japanese No-Noh: The Crosstalk of Public Culture in a Rural Festivity" takes this sort of argument further by focusing on how Kurokawa Noh (the masked dance-drama of the Kurokawa region) has become a focus for Japanese preoccupations with archaic "tradition" (which in turn has led to complex reconfigurations of local identities and practices surrounding this performance). Similarly, Jennifer Robertson's *Native and Newcomer: Making and Remaking a Japanese City* traces the history and contemporary deployments of issues of local identity and place in a suburban city near Tokyo, and locates those deployments within current Japanese ideologies of identity (she includes a concise discussion of the notion of *furusato* in Japan today, a word she translates as "native place"). Yet another anthropological work that deals with issues of tradition and identity, Theodore Bestor's *Neighborhood Tokyo*, is a careful analysis of the social alliances, organizations, and events that sustain a Tokyo neighborhood's corporate sense of itself as traditional. And Brian Moeran's *Lost Innocence: Folk Craft Potters of Onta, Japan* addresses issues of loss and nostalgia among "traditional" craft practitioners.

25. Eric Santner, *Stranded Objects: Mourning, Memory, and Film in Postwar Germany*, 29.

meaning.[26] Yet to dwell in this structural realm is to displace, potentially, the historical and discursive production of another realm of difference. The unbinding of texts and the undoings of history are not
mutually exclusive; nor are they sheerly contradictory. To linger exclu-
sively on one or the other would be to return to a binary opposition
that would scarcely do justice to the complex workings of memory,
history, and language. Santner instead calls for a "sedimentation" of
mourning tasks, a working through of the past—which, in the postwar
German case, requires coming to terms with what he calls the "poi-
soned legacy" of fascism in ways that renounce the simple, affirmative
narcissisms of nostalgia in favor of more renunciatory modes and strategies of engagement.[27]

Santner's call for a postmodern politics of mourning grounds itself
in the specific situation of postwar Germany and the trauma of the
Holocaust. How is it possible to speak of German culture, tradition, or
heimat after Hitler? The parallels with Japan are instructive. World War
II also left Japanese with an enormity of mourning tasks, but they have
never been as unambiguously recognized (even by way of denial) as
the German ones. Japan's invasion of Asia, the massacres perpetrated
there, and the oppression of minorities within Japan have not attained
the status of the Holocaust; Japanese fascism, in its reactive articulation with western colonialism, has never seemed quite as horrendous
as Germany's (although the comparative hierarchization of horror is
never a plausible labor). Yet, the metatrope for loss in Japan, as in Germany, is World War II. That war resulted in both external destruction
and interior losses, the most emblematic being the atomic bombings
of Hiroshima and Nagasaki and the emperor's renunciation of divinity
immediately after the war. Insofar as the war marked the apotheosis
in Japan of what Jeffrey Herf, writing about Germany, has called "reactionary modernism"—the coincidence of capitalist and technological
modernity with a totalizing drive to reunite its disunities within an

26. "Desire in language" is a phrase most commonly linked to Julia Kristeva, who
has tried to articulate a "translinguistics" (with Bakhtinian precedents) by tracing out
the poetic effects of language—those effects that can never be the object of a scientific
linguistics. See the essays in her *Desire in Language: A Semiotic Approach to Literature and
Art.*

27. "The error of Paul de Man in this historical series was, I suggest, that he sought
to *displace* and *disperse* the particular, historical tasks of mourning which for him, as is
now known, were substantial and complex, with what might be called structural mourning, that is, mourning for those 'catastrophes' that are inseparable from being-in-
language. . . . The more difficult labor would have been, of course, to *sediment* these tasks
of mourning, to explore the ways in which they might, in the long run, mutually enlighten one another." Santner, *Stranded Objects*, 29.

archaic, continuous, and harmonious culture—the defeat and the American Occupation meant the presumed purging of reactionary elements in a newly purified democratic modernity.[28] Only that chastened modernity and a corresponding miracle could heal the losses (of empire, of divine emperorship, of life). Fortunately, a miracle dutifully developed: the so-called economic miracle, which allowed the manic overcoming of war's trauma through the displacement of memories in the routines of overwork.[29]

Yet that overcoming and the drive for economic superpowerdom could not quite account for all the remainders of the past, could not quite eliminate all residues of national-cultural fear. Anxieties increased in the 1960s and 1970s in the wake of pollution scandals and global economic uncertainties. Accompanying those anxieties came new yet familiar attempts at recovery, both utopian and reactionary. Citizens' movements (shimin undō), examinations of the democratic possibilities of indigenous communities, and experiments with communal forms resonated with the rediscovery of Japanese folklore studies, "tradition," and nature.[30] Many of these attempts corresponded to the "homeopathic renunciations" that Santner finds necessary for the deep reconsideration of the past, but others repeated the atavistic gestures of the prewar period, now in the considerably expanded modes of affluent consumer capitalism. A little nostalgia goes a long way, for deeper identifications with loss—denser, local rememorations of the traumas of modernity, renunciations that could lead to extended mournings—are not conducive to the everyday business of Japan, or of any advanced industrial polity.

The moments engaged by this study overleap the now-fading trauma of Japan's militaristic modernity and its devastating results. They indicate a return to modernity's before within the future anterior after of increasingly dominant (post)modern regimes of signification, repertoires of consumption, and modes of information.[31] Not strictly

28. See Jeffrey Herf, Reactionary Modernism: Technology, Culture, and Politics in Weimar and the Third Reich.

29. Santner locates this dimension of mania in Germany's "economic miracle" as well.

30. Many of these attempts tried to find forms of community that could somehow escape the negative association with dangerous prewar romanticizations of the communal (romanticizations so often linked with the emperor system and fascism). For two essays which grapple with the dilemmas of community and autonomy, see Sakuta Keiichi, "The Controversy over Community and Autonomy," and Irokawa Daikichi, "The Survival Struggle of the Japanese Community."

31. I have written about Japanese regimes of consumption and the possibilities of politics in "Critical Texts, Mass Artifacts: The Consumption of Knowledge in Postmodern Japan"; I have also traced a history of postwar transformations in these regimes in

confined to the enclosure of the pastoral (although located most paradigmatically there), they index the investment in the survival of a continuous communality, guaranteed by the thought of tradition (dentō)
as unbroken transmission. This transmission is assured by the redemptive mode of the dialogic presumed in its most unmediated form: that
of the "voice." Michel de Certeau, writing of the intimate linkage of
voiced speech and *nostos*, the desire for origins, asserts that all returns
to the past are a return to the voice.[32] But not just any voice will do.
Much of this study follows Japanese attention to the "grain of the
voice"—the pungency of dialects in a world of standardized speech,
the discovery of folktales, the voiced recallings of the dead by spirit
mediums—and how it moves through other registers of national-
cultural desire.[33] Clearly, the "voice" in its reductive singularity here
stands for the heterogeneity of all voices threatened by the homogenizing trajectory of modern nation-statehood. To the extent that these
voices—along with a multitude of material practices, artifacts, and
their associated social forms—were disrupted and marginalized by
that trajectory, their reappearance in the late twentieth century as *instances* of the now-traditional marginal points to the ways in which the
materiality of diverse voices becomes spectacularized. As Foucault

"Formations of Mass Culture." Tessa Morris-Suzuki provides a critical exposé of the
Japanese "information society"—what she prefers to call "information capitalism"—in
her informative *Beyond Computopia: Automation and Democracy in Japan,* and Mark Poster
considers new forms of simulation and mass images (moving from Jean Baudrillard's
insights) in *The Mode of Information: Poststructuralism and Social Context.*

32. Much of de Certeau's work concerns the impossible "quest for lost and ghostly
voices" in modern, "scriptural" societies, impossible because those voices can only be
heard, retrospectively, from the other side of modern formations of knowledge. "It is thus
useless to set off in quest of this voice that has been simultaneously colonized and mythi-
fied by recent Western history. There is, moreover, no such 'pure' voice, because it is always
determined by a system . . . and codified by a way of receiving it. . . . Thus we must give up
the fiction that collects all these sounds under the sign of a 'Voice,' of a 'Culture' of its
own—or of the great Other's. Rather orality insinuates itself, like one of the threads of
which it is composed, into the network—an endless tapestry—of a scriptural economy"
(p. 132). De Certeau thus theorizes the discovery of the "voice" as unthinkable without its
prior repression. Although he relinquishes the comforting possibility of a return to (premodern) voices, he fully understands the loss and the concomitant work of mourning that
accompanies such a refusal, as he retains the possibility of the phantasmatic "insinuation"
of fugitive voices within the discourse of modernity: thus his interest in traces, ephemerali-
ties, fragments, marginalities, excess—the signifiers of the heterological moments of modernity. De Certeau, *The Practice of Everyday Life,* 131–32.

33. "Grain of the voice" is Roland Barthes's phrase, one he used to describe the materiality of the voice in itself (rather than what the voice signifies). See his remarks in the
interview entitled "The Phantoms of the Opera," in his *The Grain of the Voice: Interviews
1962–1980,* 183–87.

and recent interpreters have shown, one of the critical features of modernity is the way its subjects are organized within regimes of representation of which the visual is the model.[34] From another perspective, the question of the imaginary itself—most typically with its Lacanian resonances—is often framed in the realm of the visual.[35] My intention is not to set up a dichotomy between speech and sight; Johannes Fabian has argued for such a dichotomy, as have those theorists of orality who sheerly oppose it to (spatially deployed, thus visual) writing.[36] One of my concerns is to show how nonstandard Japanese practices of the voice have become spectacularized as the singularly representative voice of the nation-culture. I am thus concerned with the scenic deployment of this now-singularized voice: its theatricalization in modes that work to reassure spectators, auditors, and performers of their places within a Japan that can encompass such constitutive signs of difference. Yet I am equally concerned to indicate how a plurality of voices unravels to exceed the bounds of its enframing discourses. If the practices and discourses I engage speak of the powers of recuperation and appropriation in late-twentieth-century Japan (which they do), they attest as well to the perdurability of local forms and practices

34. Bentham's panoptical apparatus is only the most striking of the visual metaphors Foucault links to modernity. *The Order of Things* also traces a progression through visualities, finding in Velázquez's *Las Meninas* the spatial playing out of the forms of subjectivity that come to be called modern. Martin Jay extends these reflections to a larger consideration of modernity and vision in his "Scopic Regimes of Modernity." Jonathan Crary undertakes a history of the "seeing body" in modernity and the various prosthetic devices that allowed a standardization of vision at the same time the observer was made into an autonomous subject of sight in his *Techniques of the Observer: On Vision and Modernity in the Nineteenth Century.*

35. The dynamics of phantasm link the book with at least four configurations of the imaginary that I have mentioned earlier in the text. What they all point to is the element of the phantasmatic in communities, nations, and subjects. Lauren Berlant has enabled the thinking of nationalism and fantasy in *The Anatomy of National Fantasy: Hawthorne, Utopia, and Everyday Life*, in which she develops the idea of the "National Symbolic" as the space for the linked production of desire and regulation through "national fantasy."

36. Johannes Fabian critiques visualism in anthropology, opposing it to a notion of coevalness that he locates in the realm of dialogue. Although he takes pains to abjure any simplistic rejection of the visual per se—and his political analysis of anthropological knowledge is very acute—he still maintains a notion of spoken communication that is based on an idea of unmediated cotemporality, as if language (spoken or otherwise) does not always imply deferral, difference, and miscommunication. See, for example, his claim that "the temporality of speaking . . . implies cotemporality of producer and product, speaker and listener, Self and Other," in *Time and the Other: How Anthropology Makes Its Object*. Walter Ong has furthered some of these premises by demarcating a sharp division between the spoken and the written in *Orality and Literacy: The Technologizing of the Word*, 164. Derrida's work provides some of the most intractable rejoinders to a too-quick valorization of voice or spoken dialogue as unmediated communication.

and to the strength of memory and desire in the midst of modernity's depredations.

Japanese culture industries and institutions have tended to locate these practices of the voice among the "folk" (*jōmin*, in the canonical Japanese folklore studies terminology, or *minzoku*), the "abiding people," the everyday Japanese folks who have existed outside history because their existence is not archival; that is, they are not dependent on history.[37] Indeed, their presumed embodiment of the dialogical, of the communal, functions as a negation of the archive. The notion of tradition itself already refers to unmediated cultural transmission, and transmission through the voice is the exemplary means of knowledge production within the familial community (*kyōdōtai*) of the nation-culture.[38]

These notions of unmediated transmission have been incorporated into state-sponsored theories of Japan as a "holonic society," for example. H. D. Harootunian has shown how, in what has been called since the 1970s the "age of culture" (*bunka no jidai*), ideologues have refined for the twenty-first century the notion of a *volkisch* unity defined by a near-telepathic, transparent, harmonious communication between Japanese, in a "culture" untainted by history or conflict (thus

---

Other than *Of Grammatology*, perhaps the most powerful work in this regard is "Signature Event Context" in his *Margins of Philosophy*.

37. The extraarchival nature of the essential Japanese community was a premise of the folklore studies of Yanagita Kunio, Japan's most famous folklorist (or nativist ethnologist). The most direct Japanese precedents to Yanagita's notions of orality, national-cultural identity, and authenticity are found in the nativist studies (*kokugaku*) of the Tokugawa period. H. D. Harootunian's *Things Seen and Unseen: Discourse and Ideology in Tokugawa Nativism* is a powerful revelation of Tokugawa nativist philosophies and their quest for the restoration of authentic Japanese language, life, and labor.

38. In a provocative discussion of the concept of tradition, Raymond Williams etymologically unravels the word to show that, in English, "tradition" entails both the sense of "handing something down" and of something "age old." This handing down is linked specifically to spoken transmissions of knowledge. Extensions of this core of meaning have led to a wide range of nuances; for example, "traditional" can also mean "conventional" or "authoritative." The concept of continuous, repetitive transmission through time is central to most current definitions of tradition. But Williams also uncovers two archaic definitions of tradition as "betrayal" and "surrender." He states that "the word moves again and again towards *age-old* and towards ceremony, duty, and respect. Considering only how much has been handed down to us, and how various it actually is, this, in its own way, is both a betrayal and a surrender." Williams, *Keywords: A Vocabulary of Culture and Society*, 259. Williams is pointing to the selective nature of what is known as tradition, that which is handed down but which also betrays the past. In Japanese, a similar range of meanings surrounds the term *dentō*, often translated as "tradition." In particular, the notion of an unmediated, spoken transmission inheres in the word.

the toxic implications of *bunka*—"culture"—in contemporary Japan).[39]
Some of the most compelling attempts to grapple with modernity and
its ruptures occurred in the prewar period; perhaps the most famous
of these was the famous symposium of 1942 devoted to "overcoming
the modern" *(kindai no chōkoku)*, in which the questions of historical
change and Japan's place within a westernized world order were confronted. The more recent state attempts to "conquer the modern" by
returning to an "age of culture" is frighteningly ahistorical in its implicit reference to the prewar symposium, without even the earlier attempt's recognition of the existence of conflict and change. Instead,
the virtues of indigenous relationism *(aidagarashugi)* and harmony have
been resurrected yet again from the archive of unique Japanese cultural traits to obscure the contradictions that exist.

In this vision, the transparent communication that Japanese share in
their relational culture models itself on the dream of unimpeded, face-
to-face dialogue: an interpenetration of voices. But nothing could be
further from the radical inflection of Mikhail Bakhtin's conception of
dialogism, for example, which starts from the assertion of radical otherness, otherness that might then begin to be recognized in dialogue.[40]
It is crucial to recall that Bakhtin's dialogism does not primarily refer
to face-to-face interchange between two interlocutors. As Bakhtin reveals, it is rather the dialogic encounter of different *discourses* that frees
up the possibility of politics.[41] It is this discursive dialogism that is
sometimes foreclosed in the romanticization of intercommunicating

39. H. D. Harootunian performs a genealogical critique of the idea of culture *(bunka)*
and the "holonic society" in contemporary Japan in his "Visible Discourses/Invisible
Ideologies." By holonic society is meant a society in which the totality is present in its
parts, thus moving toward what might be thought of as a "holographic" society.

40. This is a crucial notion for Bakhtin, which he calls "exotopy," or alterity.

41. As V. N. Volosinov (who I will take to be analogous, if not identical, to Bakhtin)
states: "Dialogue, in the narrow sense of the word, is, of course, only one of the forms—
a very important form, to be sure—of verbal interaction. But dialogue can also be understood in a broader sense, meaning not only direct, face-to-face, vocalized verbal communication between persons, but also verbal communication of any type whatsoever. A
book, i.e., a *verbal performance in print*, is also an element of verbal communication. . . .
Thus the printed verbal performance engages, as it were, in ideological colloquy of large
scale: it responds to something, objects to something, affirms something, anticipates
possible responses and objections, seeks support, and so on." Volosinov, *Marxism and
the Philosophy of Language*, 95. As Bakhtin's translators have explained, dialogism refers
to the "constant interaction of meaning"; a "word, discourse, language or culture under-
goes 'dialogization' when it becomes relativized, deprivileged, aware of competing
definitions for the same things." Caryl Emerson and Michael Holquist, in M. M. Bakhtin,
The Dialogic Imagination, 426–27.

Japanese voices (and is often foreclosed in certain reductive versions
of so-called dialogic anthropology).[42]

To call Japan a "holonic society" presumes the identity of the totality
in the merely provisional difference of its constituents. It is the wish
for an unmediated return to origins, for the identity of difference, and
for culture as unity (for which the voice becomes the medium) that
makes this collective formation so dangerously regressive. Yet the desire for return, in its longing to mark a difference from what is, speaks
also of a redemptive impulse, even if that impulse is cannily channeled
by the apparatuses of the state and the media, a utopian wish in the
midst of what is often bluntly ideological.[43] In her mother's praise for
Bertolucci's portrayal of China in *The Last Emperor*, Rey Chow found "a
fetishizing imagining of a 'China' that never is"; yet she realized that
"in that response also lies the wish that is the last residue of a protest
against that inevitable 'dismemberment' brought about by the imperi-
alistic violence of westernization."[44] Repeated, fetishized assertions of
Japanese cultural unity uncover the fragmenting processes of modern
westernization itself and the necessity for Japanese subjects to bring
together—to suture—those fragments. The residual protest of that suturing occurs most compellingly around moments of loss and their
imaginary reconstitution as survivals.

An organizing theme of this study is that of the vanishing, which
(dis)embodies in its gerund form the movement of something passing
away, gone but not quite, suspended between presence and absence,
located at a point that both is and is not here in the repetitive process
of *absenting*. How is that moment—if it can be called that—made to
signify? What marks it as founding entire regimes of authentication?
The vanishing can only be tracked through the poetics of phantasm,
through attentiveness to the politics of displacement, deferral, and originary repetition. Practices and discourses now situated on the edge
of presence (yet continuously repositioned at the core of the national-
cultural imaginary) live out partial destinies of spectacular recovery.
Their status is often ghostly. And it is through the ghosts of stories and
(sometimes) stories of ghosts that I work, disclosing an economy of

[margin annotation: wish-image to central dismemberment]

42. An exemplary set of essays in contemporary anthropology that uses the notion of
dialogism with its full political and critical weight is Michael Fischer and Mehdi Abedi's
Debating Muslims: Cultural Dialogues in Postmodernity and Tradition.
43. Fredric Jameson has elaborated this interplay of ideology and utopia (which
Frankfurt school theorists, particularly Adorno and Horkheimer, had recognized) in
"Reification and Utopia in Mass Culture."
44. Chow, "Seeing Modern China," 27.

the appropriated marginal, of lacunae in representation at the center of the dominant. Through a tracing of supplementary logics—of things that don't quite add up even as they add to—of temporal deferrals and recursions, and of uncanny repetitions, I unfold narratives of revenant knowledge, displacing Japanese "culture" as a stable signification.

Are efforts at recovering the past based on sheer invention or do they seek to recover actual losses? The question is wrongly posed. My approach sharply distinguishes itself from the "invention of tradition" mode of analysis, although some of the local instances may be provisionally subsumed under that category.[45] It is not possible to rest easy with the by now common critique of the invention of tradition: that is, that all tradition is invented. To say that all tradition is invented is still to rely on a *choice* between invention and authenticity, between fiction and reality, between discourse and history. I find myself here in resonance with Michael Taussig's working through of the implications of mimesis: "As the nature that culture uses to make second nature, mimesis cannot be outside of history, just as history cannot lie outside of the mimetic faculty. Here we take odds with the fashionable theses of construction, that nature itself is a social construction, just as we take odds with the converse, that history itself can be reduced to an essential nature."[46] The assertion "All tradition is invented" is akin to the too facile (and often bizarrely undertheorized) claim, for example, that there is nothing outside discourse: "It's all discursive." I would argue that to claim there is no prediscursive reality is to redraw the boundary lines of a totality that operates as metaphysically as any unreformed theory of truth ever did. And I would argue that enclosing any such totality (such as discourse) produces a supplement (the pre- or nondiscursive) that returns to trouble its stability.[47] The relationship between the historical erasures effected by industrial capitalism since the late

45. The invention of tradition was most famously thematized in a volume edited by Eric Hobsbawm and Terence Ranger, entitled *The Invention of Tradition.*

46. Taussig, "With the Wind of World History in Our Sails," in his *Mimesis and Alterity: A Particular History of the Senses,* 70. Taussig's notion of mimesis draws close to other theories of the image and of the imaginary, positing the mimetic faculty as that capacity without which symbolization (and thus culture) would be impossible. He repeatedly tempers his reading of mimesis, however, with evocations of historical specificity highly resonant with the writings of Walter Benjamin.

47. It seems to me that much of Derrida's work demonstrates the possibility of accounting for the surplus that such (now-naturalized) notions as "discourse" and "culture" produce as excessive supplements (for example, the "prediscursive" and "nature"). The reverse would also apply: any unmediated appeal to a prediscursive reality will contain within it the possibility of its supplement—discourse.

nineteenth century in Japan and the ongoing reinscriptions of those lost differences as identities is, instead, phantasmatic.

By stating that this relationship is phantasmatic I am not saying that it is fictional. Rather, I am gesturing toward a body of work on phantasm and the event that reveals how an originary event can never be grasped in its punctual thusness, but can only emerge as an event across a relay of temporal deferral (what is sometimes called "deferred action" or *Nachträglichkeit*).[48] The second event—when the originary moment emerges as an event to consciousness—is thus the *first* instance: the origin is never at the origin; it emerges as such only through its displacement. The event, the origin (or the origin as event)—what we might imagine as the substratum of the real—is thus embedded in a structure of phantasm, if phantasm is understood as an epistemological object whose presence or absence cannot be definitively located. The event never simply exists as such, but produces its effects only after the fact, in a repetition that becomes its own spectral origin.[49]

To say, for example, that Japanese investments in the continuity of tradition disclose a phantasmatic structure is not to say that there is nothing to tradition. But it is to say that phantasm—in the sense I have discussed it—is all that is available to gesture towards the displaced origins that the invocation of tradition would call up. To say that the pervasive longing to return to present origins—even in the quotidian sense of a return to one's own rural "hometown," or *furusato*—is phantasmatic does not mean that people are nostalgic for no good reason, that no "real" losses have been incurred in the rapid industrialization of the countryside, for example. It means rather that loss can never be known simply *as* loss, as originary loss.

My thinking about loss and recuperation, practices of the voice, and the status of the vanishing thus follows the rhetoric of phantasm and its operations within Japanese modernity. That is why the workings of

48. Freud used this term repeatedly in his writings, and it became particularly salient in his analysis of the famous "Wolf Man" case. But it was Lacan who brought serious attention to the notion and developed it further. "Deferred action" (or "deferred interpretation") refers most fundamentally to the way subjects revise "past events at a later date *(Nachträglich)* and that it is this revision which invests them with significance and even with efficacity or pathogenic force." This idea of deferral opens the way for a consideration of lived temporality as retroactive, of origins as events known only in their later construal. The quote is from the indispensable work by J. Laplanche and J.-B. Pontalis, *The Language of Psychoanalysis,* 112.

49. The question of phantasm and the event becomes the subject of an intense meditation by Foucault on Deleuze's attempts to grapple with the materiality of the incorporeal, to think the event, in his essay "Theatrum Philosophicum." This essay is often ignored by those more interested in using Foucault as a theorist of power, rather than as a philos-

doubles, of ghostliness, of death and memory as figures for representation, wind their way through this study. Those workings I will later situate as the "uncanny," referring to the strangeness of that which is most familiar: the uncanny as place out of place.

In looking for what haunts cultural consolation, I start from the interior of certain identities and then reveal the marks of their difference. There are, of course, other ways to contest the interior certainties of Japanese culture. One is to examine instances of difference that is generally acknowledged as difference, cases of people explicitly recognized as deviating from Japaneseness: foreigners, *burakumin* (so-called outcastes, or discriminated-against "special status" people), guest workers, Okinawans.[50] Another strategy would be to uncover the alienating gestures of everyday life and language; to do so would also necessarily entail critiquing disciplinary discourses (like anthropology) that organize the themes of cultural Japaneseness.[51] These strategies intersect and in no way exclude each other. This labor has long been under way, both in Japan and elsewhere.[52] My strategy, however, is to

opher of the event. See "Theatrum Philosophicum," as well as "Nietzsche, Genealogy, History," in Foucault, *Language, Counter-Memory, Practice: Selected Essays and Interviews.*

50. Anthropologist Emiko Ohnuki-Tierney has analyzed the structural implications of marginal status in Japan. See both her *Illness and Culture in Contemporary Japan: An Anthropological View* and *The Monkey as Mirror: Symbolic Transformations in Japanese History and Ritual.*

51. I find troubling the way the anthropological use of the notion of relationality replicates much of the Nihonjinron literature, which also relies on a notion of Japanese relationality (an idea already found in prewar culturalist philosophy). Watsuji Tetsurō (1889–1960), in particular, is credited with developing the notion of *aidagara*, or human "relationality" as the basis for a totalized analysis of Japanese culture. It is no accident that the Heideggerian Watsuji is often linked with Japanese ultranationalism. Because of this history, it is problematic to assume that an embedded cultural relationality can be used in any direct way to critique a presumed nonrelational, logocentric western singular self. As I am arguing here, any such sheer opposition between "Japan" and the "West" is in danger of ignoring the deep historical imbrication of those two discursive unities, and of ignoring as well the cross-cutting *individualizing* modalities of capitalist modernity that have already made it quite impossible to insist on purely relational or situational selves in contemporary Japan (the obverse, that American selves are *not* relational—even if the ideology of American selfhood is all that is considered—is equally impossible). Naoki Sakai has written a dense set of reflections on Watsuji's "anthropology" *(ningengaku)*, his notions of relationality and the nation, and the dangers of "communalist identification" that mark his thinking (and have made Watsuji's writings attractive to postwar nationalists and culturalists). He demonstrates, in the end, that "Watsuji's ethics of '*nakayoshi*' (being on good terms) transformed itself into the ethics of '*ichioku gyokusai*' (the total suicidal death of one hundred million.)" Sakai, "Return to the West/ Return to the East: Watsuji Tetsuro's Anthropology and Discussion of Authenticity," 190.

52. Edward Said's *Orientalism* provided the original terms for the discussion of the colonial legacy in area studies. Masao Miyoshi's *Off Center: Power and Culture Relations between Japan and the United States* is a strong indictment of Japanology, nationalism, and

work from the interior of dominant discourses of national-cultural
identification, and to show the critical difference discursively embodied in that very interior. An example that has been developed by Japanese theorists concerns the place of the emperor. Although the emperor may be seen as the very epitome of the Japanese "thing," in that
he appears to embody the unbroken transmission of Japanese culture,
there is much evidence to show that the line of emperors originated
in Korea—Japan's colonized, denigrated national other—and various
features of emperorship as an institution lead back to China. To show
how the most authoritative interior sign of native Japaneseness is originally foreign points to an essential alienation at the national-cultural
core.[53] While the emperor may merely be the most spectacular and at
the same time most banal example of this alien interiority, the entire
national-cultural fantasy of Japan—indeed of any nation—must form
itself around such foreign irritants. Furthermore, it is no accident that
Korea constituted Japan's premier colony during its imperialist stage.
The modernity of Japan is not separate from its formation as a nation-
state *and* the colonizing project that nation-statehood inevitably entails. Etienne Balibar's claim that "every modern nation is a product of
colonization: it has always been to some degree colonized or colonizing, and sometimes both at the same time" proves compellingly apt
for Japan.[54] This internal alienation—what Lacan termed *extimité* in the
realm of the individual subject—is at the core of what Fanon recognized as the "occult instability" of the nation; I extend the premise into
the realm of Japanese culture seen as a displacement from considerations of national power.

Extimité is nothing if not intimate. Rather than focus on high instances of extimité (like the emperor, although one cannot ignore that
presence in talking about modern Japan), I look at formations of what
I call the "public intimate": the warmth of tales told around the hearth
(*irori*), the poignancy of rituals and festivals of village solidarity, the
spirituality of travel, the familial appeal of proletarian theater. Small-
scale enactments or practices have, by their very retention of the
intimate, become beautifully susceptible to public representation.

capitalist culture in both Japan and the United States. Dorinne Kondo's *Crafting Selves:
Power, Gender, and Discourses of Identity in a Japanese Workplace* questions the role of the
ethnographer in producing anthropological knowledge of Japan.

53. Karatani Kōjin speaks of the emperor as an embodiment of the "nothingness" of
Japanese culture, which he links to the historical fact of the emperor's original foreign-
ness. See his "Ri no hihan: Nihonshisō ni okeru puremodan to posutomodan."

54. Etienne Balibar, "The Nation Form: History and Ideology," in his *Race, Nation,
Class: Ambiguous Identities*, 89.

Through their marginality-turned-traditional and their (vanishing) preservation of a world before the destruction of communal solidarities, these enactments occur in the space between us (*entre nous*), where "us" (in this case) means "us Japanese." Claude Lefort elaborated the notion of the entre nous to account for the binding power that modern ideologies and national culturalisms exercise over disparate groups and diverse interests.[55] It is through the entre nous that nation-cultures imaginarily cohere.

The attempt to represent the communally intimate through the publicity of the televisual apparatus, for example, configures the paradoxes already attendant on the reversal of the public and the private, the outside and the interior. Intimacy is stretched to cover the entire reach of all Japanese (as Žižek has shown, only people with the same national "thing" share the same forms of enjoyment): what could be more intimate than the telepathies of the holonic society? Yet the alienated origins of this intimacy within the discourses of modernity and its posts are obscured. This alienation has a historical genesis: the double movement whereby that which was marginalized by the advent of nationalist modernity in the Meiji period (1868–1912)—peasant practices, superstitions, the folkloric—was in the same movement objectified as most essentially traditional. This double inscription—as both superfluous and essential, marginal and traditional—is necessary for loss to emerge as recoverable. Parallel to the dynamics of fetishistic disavowal and identification, the belated consciousness of Japanese modernity emerges only through the temporal process of representation.[56] The cultural reversals that occur—that *must* occur—attest to the disavowals that operate here, in which losses emerge as excessive survivals.

What positions these in this double way are the regnant discourses and institutional matrices of Japanese interpretation and dissemination: the discipline of folklore studies, advertising, national tourism, civic reconstruction, high theory, and mass culture. These are registers in which loss becomes harder to deny because it is both foregrounded and displaced more frontally. These are points at which modernity creates a sharper displacement, rendering the consolations of culture and the comforts of tradition more difficult to accept at the same time that

55. Claude Lefort speaks of the "incantation of familiarity" and the "hallucination of nearness" in the electronically facilitated ideologies of industrial nations. Lefort, "Outline of the Genesis of Ideology in Modern Societies," in his *The Political Forms of Modern Society: Bureaucracy, Democracy, Totalitarianism*, 228.

56. "Belated consciousness" is a phrase used by Rey Chow, which we can read as not unrelated to deferred interpretation. See Chow, "Seeing Modern China," 26.

they seem to be more readily proffered. These events, spaces, and narrated landscapes serve to resituate Japanese as modern national-
cultural subjects as they locate Japanese in a legacy, a genealogical
succession. Mass cultural and statist rhetorics of recovery constitute an
undiscovered Japan (more precisely, a lost Japan) as an object of
knowledge.

 Japan emerges as the armature of intense preoccupations with essential national-cultural identity, continuity, and community that mark
and remark it with the signs of totality. The effort to sustain this totality
announces itself in every tourist advertisement, every appeal to
"home" (furusato), every assertion that "we Japanese are modern, but
we have kept our tradition," every discourse on public (Japanese) harmony. This effort to maintain the self-sameness of Japanese culture
thus exposes itself by its denial of social difference—race, ethnicity,
class. This denial is not sheerly ideological, for the policies of the Japanese state and historical contingencies have determined that in fact
those differences *are* reduced: less than 1 percent of the population of
Japan are non-Japanese citizens, so say the official statistics. There are
strong structural, institutional, and legal denials and controls of ethnic
and racial differences; there are refusals of heterogeneity at many levels. While anthropologists and historians attempt to find difference,
resistance, and ambiguity in Japan—and of course any polity as vast
and affluent as Japan must generate differences, if only by negation—
there is an equal necessity to come to terms with what is a powerfully
normalizing and standardizing nexus of institutional, legal, and socio-
cultural apparatuses.[57]

Modernity and its margins and remainders are thus my preoccupations in this book, the result of some years of engagement with Japanese thought, texts, and persons and an equally long engagement with
anthropology and affiliated disciplines. As much a product of my encounters with theory and politics as of a delimited period of fieldwork,
the book does not rest squarely within the boundaries of what is called
ethnography (although ethnography is much of what it is about). I
have been deeply impressed by the calls for new forms of ethnographic
writing and the possibilities of anthropology as cultural critique, as
well as the concerns with authorial reflexivity that any politically aware
anthropologist must share. Going against the grain of many so-called
reflexive ethnographies, however, I have tended not to announce rhe-

---

57. Any number of recent writings in English have disclosed the contours of these
apparatuses, including works by Field, Harootunian, Miyoshi, Morris-Suzuki, and
others.

torically my positions, my subjectivities, or my default identities in the text; nor have I expressly lingered on my experiences as a fieldworker (neither have I excised them).[58] Maurice Blanchot, writing of writing, notes that

> the writer, it is said, gives up saying "I." Kafka remarks, with surprise, with enchantment, that he has entered literature as soon as he can substitute "He" [or "It"]. . . . If to write is to surrender to the interminable, the writer who consents to sustain writing's essence loses the power to say "I."[59]

I do not have the extraordinary capacity to be a writer in Blanchot's sense (although I have often felt a "surrender to the interminable" when writing this book). Yet I think I understand what he is saying. Far from attempting to control the position of the authorial "I" by announcing it as such, a writer (in Blanchot's sense) accepts a certain privation (which nevertheless is enchanting) in giving up on the "I" and letting the work and the implications of the text emerge otherwise. Not that any text is free from its own rhetorical entanglements; quite the contrary. But it is my own distinct preference as a reader to unfold through reading, however slowly and furtively, the promises and possibilities of a text—without undue authorial interruptions, apostrophes, and proclamations (such as these).

By all means, writers should reflect ceaselessly and critically on the terms of their interests in particular subjects or objects. But I tend to be more fully persuaded (or moved, or engaged, or inspired) by writers who embody such reflection in the very texture of their writing, where it may be discovered by reading. That readerly preference has undoubtedly shaped my writerly choices. The question remains: Where does reflexivity lie? In the writing of a text? A chapter? A paragraph? A comma? A hyphen? Perhaps a specific hyphen in all its par-

58. Still the most comprehensive interrogation of anthropology's promises and premises in the late twentieth century is George Marcus and Michael Fischer's *Anthropology as Cultural Critique: An Experimental Moment in the Human Sciences.* The authors recognize a number of different modalities in accomplishing politically, aesthetically, and theoretically moving anthropological works; the genre often known as "reflexive" ethnography is only one of the possibilities they discuss. Marcus has also written an incisive analysis of the relationship of contemporary ethnographic practice and problem of modernity; see his "Past, Present, and Emergent Identities: Requirements for Ethnographies of Late Twentieth-Century Modernity Worldwide."

59. Maurice Blanchot, *The Space of Literature,* 26–27. I originally discovered this quote from Blanchot in a footnote in Naoki Sakai's *Voices of the Past,* where he discusses the notion of the "subject" in the Japanese language, a language which (as language) can never, as he says, "be transparent; it is always 'broken,' so that one never totally belongs to it, and no body, no body of the enunciation . . . is ever exhaustively at home there." Sakai, *Voices of the Past,* 336.

ticularity can embody more reflexivity, more experience, and more real politics than all the enframed *assertions* of politics ever could. E. Valentine Daniel has written of the metaphor of interclusion in ethnography and the more "spartan form of reflexivity" that then becomes visible:

> I am thinking of the ultimate in intercluding marks, the hyphen. Reflexivity in ethnography can be brief, small, a particle in flight or a fleeting particular, a crepuscular detail; hyphenlike: holding together and holding apart, maintaining continuity and creating a breach, uniting and separating, estranging and binding, and most importantly, dividing but also compounding.[60]

I have tried to effect writerly displacements of the comforts of identification, displacements that also help to open up the kinds of solid (even if presumably multiple) identifications that operate in Japanese and Euroamerican cultural nationalisms. By showing the uncanny effects generated by modern Japanese discourses on the nation-culture, I have argued that those effects are not outside the discourses that I am compelled to inhabit as a presumed westerner. And I have tried to effect these displacements through a range of generic and thematic crossings—textual, ethnographic, national, historical, and otherwise—and through attention to momentary particulars and metaphors of interclusion. It is only with the assumption of inhabiting a world that exceeds the binary simplicities of cultural relativism, and with help from colleagues in Japan and elsewhere, that I can offer this book as an encounter with the phantasms of our (and I use the pronoun reflexively) modernity.

60. E. Valentine Daniel, review of *A Crack in the Mirror: Reflexive Perspectives in Anthropology*, ed. J. Ruby, 247.

CHAPTER TWO

Itineraries of Knowledge:
Trans-Figuring Japan

How might one traverse the itineraries of high theory, marketing texts, touristic rhetoric, and autoethnologizing, outlining crucial figurations of national-cultural phantasm in contemporary Japan? To historicize such figurations is to begin to map one crossing through Japan as object of knowledge in the late twentieth century and to mark out public parameters for that knowledge. One of the most enduring and paradigmatic attempts to fix these parameters was Japan National Railway's tourism campaign entitled "Discover Japan," which developed a securely nativist project of national (re)discovery emblematic of the 1970s. That discourse was seemingly overcome in the railways' advertising campaign of the 1980s, tellingly subsumed under the slogan "Exotic Japan." The difference between these two national discourses reflects changing valences in popular perceptions of national-cultural identity over a span of almost twenty years. Seemingly assimilable to one variety of the modernist/postmodernist divide, this distinction has replayed itself in a range of affiliated contexts. The fantasy of Japan as an archive of exotic commodity forms finds parallels in marketing texts that speak of retro "neo-nostalgia" and the ascendance of the "neo-Japonesque" as a commodifiable style; parallels also cross the domains of academic theory, where the momentary emergence of "new Japanology" recapitulated the rise of the "neo" in other spheres. Yet despite the efflorescence of "neos" in Japanese popular and quasi-academic writings, I argue that the various itineraries traced keep returning home to Japan as originary source and destination, even when they seem to escape from its domesticating pull.

That travel and its contemporary generalization in mass tourism should become a primary medium for a return to origins, to a national-cultural home, sharply foregrounds the contradictions of identity and difference, loss and discovery. The very idea of leaving home—traveling—to find home has not gone unremarked by those caught up in following the figure of the journey and the ways in which it redoubles the narrative trajectory of the will to knowledge.[1] "Home" marks the necessary starting point and point of return without which travel is unimaginable. Travel to discover Japan, for example, presumes both that one's point of departure, one's home, is *not* Japan, and that the Japan motivating travel is incomplete, not fully locatable: there would be no need to travel if one were at the destination, no impetus for a journey if what one sought to discover had already been found.

The powers of travel and its links to Japan as a displaced yet originary home and destination parallel the epistemological quest for Japan as origin and telos of national-cultural knowledge. Georges Van Den Abbeele has marvelously traced the labyrinthine implications of travel:

> If, however, a voyage can only be conceptualized economically in terms of the fixity of a privileged point *(oikos)*, the positing of a point we can call home can only occur retroactively. The concept of a home is needed (and in fact it can only be thought) only *after* the home has already been left behind. In a strict sense, then, one has always already left home, since home can only exist as such at the price of its being lost. The *oikos* is posited *après-coup*. Thus, the voyage has always already begun.[2]

But if the voyage has already begun then it is inexplicably anterior to what Van Den Abbeele calls the *oikos* or "home"—that point which is the necessary *precedent* of the notion of travel. How can something precede the precedent? It can do so only through the workings of supplementation that Derrida, for example, has elaborated in his writings on writing.[3] Any opposition (home/travel) unravels itself in its own

1. Much of James Clifford's recent work has been concerned with the intersections of travel and theory. One representative example of this writing is his "Notes on Travel and Theory" (in a special issue of *Inscriptions* entitled "Traveling Theories: Traveling Theorists"). Clifford's reflections focus particularly on the movements of theories and theorists across bordered frontiers, as he addresses in particular the predicaments of postcolonial intellectuals and first-world anthropologists.

2. Georges Van Den Abbeele, *Travel as Metaphor: from Montaigne to Rousseau*, xviii–xix.

3. Derrida produces the idea of the supplement in the chapter in *Of Grammatology* entitled "... That Dangerous Supplement ... ," where he examines the entanglements of Rousseau's writings on nature and writing. Derrida, *Of Grammatology*, 141–64.

supplementarity. To restitch that unraveling is to produce a stable binarism that allows the opposition to be thought. Van Den Abbeele continues:

> What is commonly called "travel" is but an attempt to contain that other prototravel [the travel that would precede "home" as origin] through a kind of reverse denegation that denies travel precisely by affirming it. When I say I am taking a trip, I feel confident in my ability to define it according to an itinerary between points. This "definition" is a containment of travel which allows it then not only to be thought but to be thought as a narrative.[4]

The containments of travel facilitate the narrative bounding of Japan as object of knowledge, as an object that constantly threatens to overrun its borders and thus must be policed. The common figure of travel—and its standardized dissemination via tourism—both demands and domesticates the desire for a return to the starting point. This originary telos, this home, is troped in the ubiquitous appeals of the *furusato; furusato* is sometimes translated as "native place" but perhaps should be rendered more colloquially as "hometown," with resonances not unlike its American parallel.[5]

I am initially concerned with remarking the textual place that travel occupies in the representation of the Japanese thing in the new folklore studies; it emerges repeatedly as a topos for the discussion of Japanese national-cultural constitution.[6] In a parallel fashion, the commodification of travel in institutional tourism emerges as a way to think about the implied identity of Japan as narrative oikos. Travel (as a difference that allows home to be thought) and home (as a deferred origin that allows travel to take place) emerge as phantasmatic constituents of Japanese identity.

There are, of course, powerful material and institutional forces that articulate with these rhetorics of travel. The interlinked industries of tourism, transportation, advertising, mass media, and publishing have created institutional circuits that channel local eccentricities into a standardly pluralized nation-culture. These industries have leveled re-

4. Van Den Abbeele, *Travel as Metaphor*, xix.
5. A number of recent writers have remarked on the salience of the furusato notion in postwar, and particularly contemporary, Japan. See in particular William Kelly's "Rationalization and Nostalgia" and "Japanese No-Noh." See as well Jennifer Robertson's "The Culture and Politics of Nostalgia: *Furusato* Japan" and *Native and Newcomer.*
6. Another recent example of the transformation of Japanese folklore studies is *Kore wa "minzokugaku" de wa nai: shinjidai minzokugaku no kanōsei* (This Is Not "Folklore Studies": Possibilities for Folklore Studies in the New Era), ed. Komatsu Kazuhiko.

gional differences, stabilized diverse pasts, and—perhaps most significantly—made them accessible to Japanese cultural consumers.
Tourism is that sector of the Japanese culture industries which perhaps
most powerfully articulates Japanese place with the formation and circulation of Japanese national-cultural subjects.[7]

There is, of course, a history to all this. There have long been circuits
for the dissemination of knowledge about Japanese place. Travel existed in the pre-Tokugawa period primarily as a form of religious practice or an occupational necessity: a variety of ascetics, healers, and
saintly figures wandered throughout Japan, as did peddlers, artistes,
beggars, occupational specialists, and ritual performers. (One person
often played several of these roles.)[8] These wanderers and travelers
recited songs or told stories around the theme of wandering itself, reflecting on their own existential condition.

Travel and place became highly stressed literary themes. Poetic top-
onyms *(utamakura)* densely punctuate Japanese poetry, and travel diaries *(kikō)* constitute a genre in and of themselves.[9] The theme of the
wandering stranger-god is one of the most important literary, theatrical, and religious motifs in Japan. Exile and exclusion, travel and return, visitation and withdrawal form pairs of significant thematic oppositions in Japanese literature.

Traveling as a form of tourism became widely popular, however,
only in the Tokugawa period (1603–1868). The rise of a market economy and an urban protobourgeoisie led to the florescence of pilgrimage circuits and routes to distant shrines, temples, and sacred mountains. Widely distributed illustrated guidebooks *(meisho zue)* and
woodblock prints helped standardize itineraries and sights; one of the
most famous of these was the *Edo meisho-zue* (Illustrated Guide to Famous Places of Edo), published in seven volumes between 1830 and
1840.[10] In the following Meiji period (1868–1912), the building of railroads, the development of Tokyo as a modern attraction, with its inter-

7. Dean MacCannell's social analyses of tourism have illuminated the way touristic
rhetorics and practices rework distinctions that are embodied in modernity itself: tourism as the very cutting edge of modernity. See MacCannell, *The Tourist: A New Theory of
the Leisure Class.*

8. These peregrinating nonagriculturalists *(hinōgyōmin)* are the provocative focus of
the work of Amino Yoshihiko, in what has been hailed as some of the most significant
historical writing in Japan today. See Amino, *Muen, kugai, raku: Nihon chūsei no jiyū to
heiwa.*

9. Four travel diaries of the Japanese middle ages are the subject of English translations by Herbert Plutschow and Hideichi Fukuda, *Four Japanese Travel Diaries of the Middle Ages.*

10. *Kodansha Encyclopedia of Japan,* s.v. "meisho zue."

national exhibitions and Imperial Palace, and the popularity of school field trips (shūgaku ryokō) helped codify the sights and scenes of Japan as well as create new meisho (noted places). Indeed, in the Meiji drive to incorporate diversity under state supervision, marginal sites and events were selectively either held up as paragons of Japanese culture—such as kabuki—or stigmatized, such as "folk" practices associated with a backward countryside.[11] This stigmatization later reached another plateau, becoming the object of a scholarly discipline (folklore studies) and of literary nostalgia. Much of the cultural policy of the Meiji state and after must also be seen in relation to Japanese efforts to present selected images of its culture in relation to Euroamerican nations, to fix public presentations of high culture and to downplay or eradicate those aspects at odds with western mores and morality. To this day, the Japanese National Tourist Organization hesitates to distribute information about Japan's phallic festivals to foreign tourists.[12]

For the contemporary domestic audience, however, no place is too remote, no festival too salacious, no group too impoverished or marginal to be featured in a guidebook or spotlighted on television. Tourism, publishing, Japan Broadcasting Corporation (Japan's public television network, known as NHK), railways, the discipline of folklore studies, and the camera industry all have a stake in discovering and purveying striking remnants of a purer, more pristine Japan. While the history of this interest in origins can be traced back in ever-receding loops, it is in the postwar era (particularly in the late 1960s and after) that it has become a truly national, pervasive, mass phenomenon.[13]

11. See Edward Seidensticker, Low City, High City: Tokyo from Edo to the Earthquake, 107, for his vivid description of General Ulysses S. Grant's triumphant visit to Tokyo in 1879 and his evening at kabuki—a confirmation that the formerly disreputable theater of actors, townsmen, prostitutes, and samurai on the sly had officially made it.

12. One such festival that has become a sort of underground phenomenon in recent years is the Jibeta Matsuri of the Kanayama Shrine in Kawasaki, a city on the outskirts of Tokyo. The deity of the shrine is a metal phallus; the shrine has long been used as a place of supplication for prostitutes and their customers, and more recently by massage-parlor workers in this heavily industrial and working-class area. In order to attract more visitors to its annual spring festival, which features the metal phallus in a raucous portable-shrine procession, the shrine started staging a "phallic costume" contest with free beer, directed towards foreigners. Publicity was distributed through the weekly English language tourism papers in Tokyo and through the grapevine, but the JNTO refused to allow any publicity in its office. I attended the festival in 1983.

13. The intersections of the dynamics of tourism and the logics of nostalgia have been usefully summarized by John Frow, "Tourism and the Semiotics of Nostalgia." Frow ranges over the work of many authors who address tourism and its associated practices, from Dean MacCannell to Susan Stewart (whose On Longing includes a treatment of the souvenir and the postcard).

My point, however, is not to linger on travel and tourism per se (one of the most stubbornly banal of topics); rather I want to think about why the trope of travel arises when Japanese national-cultural identity is at stake and, further, why there is always an invocatory return to the discipline of Japanese folklore studies (minzokugaku, which I also translate as "nativist ethnology") and its ostensible objects: originary voices and their unmediated transmission as "tradition." Along the way, I canvass an array of antinomies that arise when Japanese identity and subjects are linked to the theme of the journey and consider how this theme is operationalized through different sectors of the culture industries.

The media blitz that most clearly used this obsession with origins in the postwar period was the Discover Japan (Jisukabā Japan) campaign of Japan National Railway. Launched in 1970 by Dentsū, the world's largest advertising agency (or second largest, depending on the year), Discover Japan became the most successful advertising campaign in Japanese history, as the phrase itself condensed the longings of up-wardly and outwardly mobile Japanese.[14] By the early 1970s, rapid industrial growth had led to high levels of pollution and urban sprawl, as well as rural devastation and depopulation. Discover Japan was the first highly visible, mass campaign urging Japanese to discover what remained of the premodern past in the midst of its loss.

Travels of the Nation-Culture

Discover Japan summed up the longings of an entire decade, that of the 1970s. The phrase took on a resonance far exceeding its pragmatic function as a publicity slogan for the national railways, as it came to symbolize a generation's desire to escape to its origins. At the same time, it generated vocal opposition from a range of environmental groups, local citizens, and intellectuals. Anti–Discover Japan move-ments appeared.[15] The critic Tsumura Takashi has written of the con-

14. Armand Mattelart, *Advertising International: The Privatisation of Public Space*, 15. When Karel van Wolferen heard me refer to Dentsū as the world's largest advertising agency, he remarked that calling Dentsū the world's largest ad agency is like calling IBM the world's largest maker of electric typewriters.

15. As Tsumura Takashi discusses, Discover Japan, in conjunction with the popular girl's magazine *An An* and others, helped disseminate the idea of consumption in and of itself as a positive good. Consumption could bring about "another self"—thus the campaign's slogan: "Let's discover another self" (*Mō hitori no jibun o mitsukeyō*). Tsumura finds a range of small-scale oppositions to these incorporative movements, not only in local citizen's groups but in a developing weariness with consumption itself (exempli-

solidation of the masses under the guise of differentiated consumption in what he calls contemporary Japan's "techno-fascism." He cites the Discover Japan moves of the 1970s as part of the increasing capacity of the large public relations and advertising firms to incorporate and "internalize" (naibuka) those areas of Japan that were marginal and "external" (gaibu). This internalization of locales into a larger Japan was of course dependent on their status as consumable. Through the years the campaign inundated Japanese with hundreds of condensed images of authentic Japan, generically imagined and presented, as it encouraged an encounter with the reterritorialized terrain of this newly discoverable Japan.

The impact of Discover Japan capitalized on personal dramas of encounter unfolded along classically narrativized points of separation, quest, encounter, and return. Rather than the rush to view and photograph famous sights collectively (as Japanese group tourism—and mass tourism globally—encourages), Discover Japan advocated a solitary, small-scale form of travel, in which landscapes became settings for miniature dramas of national-cultural and subjective discovery. The landscapes and places depicted and promoted were not the famous icons of Japanese natural beauty and civilization, but obscure, often unnamed scenes: a forest here, a mountain temple there. These scenes were paradigmatically populated with young urban women. (That young women operated as the mobile place of suture between the contemporary and the originary, the urban and the rural, indicates yet again how female gender often emerges to close the disjunctures in consumerist discourses of authenticity.)

The impact of this long-running appeal to Japanese was immense; its effectiveness can be gauged partly by its duration. Far exceeding the typical six-month life span of an advertising campaign, Discover Japan ran for eight years, only to be followed by Discover Japan II. The national railways' theme of discovery lasted over ten years, finally supplanted by a new slogan in 1984: Exotic Japan (Ekizochikku Japan). Following the privatization and break-up of the national railways, Exotic Japan devolved into Exotic Japan II and various regional campaigns, recalling the logic of serialization at work in Hollywood blockbuster movies (where Rocky is followed by Rocky II, Rocky III, and so on).

We can gain some insight into the aims and intentions of Discover

---

fied by "do-it-yourself" types throughout Japan). Tsumura, "Gendai Nihon ni ariuru fuashizumu wa nanika."

Japan as advertising, for the creator of the campaign has written a book as well as articles about his role in the project. Fujioka Wakao has been a high-level advertising executive, a powerful culture broker and image purveyor who scans the fringes of Japan's youth culture and publishes pronouncements about the future of Japanese consumer society. Part of neither the new wave of Japanese copywriters nor the old guard, he has been spectacularly successful in turning emerging tendencies into full-fledged trends through his canny advertising blitzes. By far his greatest coup was Discover Japan.

Discover Japan was formulated in 1970, a crucial year in Japan's postwar history. It was the peak of high-level economic growth, the year of Expo '70 (the first world's fair held in an Asian country), and the year when pollution became a national issue.[16] Expo '70 had a great impact on the national economy, particularly on the transportation infrastructure. One out of every two Japanese visited the Osaka exposition, using the *shinkansen* (the so-called bullet train), expanded local railway lines, and the improved national highway network.[17] One of the major problems faced by Japan National Railway and related industries in the wake of Expo '70, however, was to maintain the level of travel and freight traffic the fair had stimulated. The problem set for the Dentsū advertising team, then, was to boost domestic travel in the anticipated post-Expo slump, and a team was formed within Dentsū for this purpose, with Fujioka as its account executive.[18]

The planning began with a series of musings about the definition of travel itself. There are several words in Japanese for travel: *ryokō* is a common Sinified compound that means "trip" or "travel," used in referring to journeys of all sorts. *Kankō*, another Sinified compound, indicates "tourism." The word *tabi*, however, has an aura of the antique about it. *Tabi* is a non-Sinified Japanese lexeme (not a compound), and, as is true of many such indigenous terms, it portrays an aesthetic and affective concept Japanese feel is uniquely theirs. Recreational travel or tourism only became widely popular in the Edo period, although

16. Tatsurō Uchino, *Japan's Postwar Economy*, 165.
17. Sasaki Shun'ichi, "Banpaku to Jisukabā Japan," 25.
18. Fujioka Wakao's revelations in his book *Kareinaru shuppatsu: Jisukabā Japan* (Magnificent Departure: Discover Japan), his other writings, and my interview with him in July 1985 provide glimpses into the production of national meaning. Part confession, part manual for would-be ad executives, Fujioka's book discloses the contradictions inherent in framing tradition as a series of touristic images, destinations of travel, or recoverable, discoverable origins. The book can be read precisely as a guide for the production of an imaginary Japan, activated through the guise of discovery via the sign of mobility itself: travel.

flower- and moon-viewing expeditions, visits to scenic spots, and the-
atergoing as forms of sightseeing *(kenbutsu)* had long existed in Japan.[19] Before that, tabi meant travel undertaken for a specific purpose,
often religious, sometimes occupational.[20] In the premodern period,
there were also categories of ritual specialists, performers, peddlers,
and artisans who were truly itinerant—who "wandered" *(hyōhaku
suru,* in the phrase popular with Japanese historians). Tabi, unlike wandering, involves a departure and a return, a separation from "home"
and a reincorporation. As the team stated, tabi should have something
old *(furui)* about it. Tabi brings up associations of solitary pilgrims
traversing remote mountains; it is a word appropriate for describing
the journeys of Japan's famous spiritual poet-travelers, the monk Sai-
gyō and the haiku master Bashō. By concentrating on the nuances of
tabi, the team stressed the "traditional" aspects of journeys. Yet in the
Japan of the 1970s, the team concluded that few people had ever em-
barked on a "real" trip *(tabirashii tabi),* a trip that would embody all
those aspects of spiritual self-discovery implied in tabi. On closer inspection, however, it became obvious that people could travel if they
really desired to, despite the restrictions on vacation time and the limited budgets of most industrial workers. The crux of the problem lay
in stimulating the desire for travel: people had to be made to travel, to
feel that they *must* travel.

It is remarkable how quickly the account team turned their strategy
to the subject of women, as they decided that "travel is for young
women" *(tabi wa wakai josei no mono).*[21] In a reversal of the classicized
notions of tabi they seemed to be promoting—wherein the prototypical travelers are solitary, often poetically inclined, men—Fujioka and
his colleagues determined that in postindustrial Japan only young
women initially had the time and the ease for travel. Far from stopping
there, however, the team realized that by concentrating on young
women they would gain entrance to a larger market; for young women
in Japan get married, and after their discovery of "Discover Japan"
they would demand tabi from their mates as well. The willingness to

19. Judith Adler persuasively claims that the now-dominant intimate relationship between travel and sight developed after the European Renaissance. In Japan, however,
travel—even the poetic travel of classic literary and historical figures—has long been
intimately linked with viewing conventionally demarcated important sights. The Japanese word *kenbutsu* also contains nuances of theater viewing, thus linking travel as sightseeing with the viewing of performance. See Adler, "Origins of Sightseeing."

20. See Gorai Shigeru, "Yūkai to junrei," 6–8.

21. Fujioka, *Kareinaru,* 30. All translations and summaries from the Japanese are mine
unless otherwise noted.

travel would become one of the prerequisites for a prospective husband.

Throughout Fujioka's revelations there is a linkage between travel, the losses of modernity, and young women as marginal points of entry into the market. In his sociology, the youth market is the most profitable one for mass advertising. Youth are not completely enclosed by rule-bound working society; they can transgress and traverse societal boundaries that working men cannot. If youth are therefore freer than adults, how much more so are young women. For women do not have to enter society at all, he asserts. Instead, they operate as hidden manipulators in the comfort of their homes, making decisions and controlling their husbands. Moreover, Fujioka continues, women are perfectly aware of their control: where women go, men follow.

The team's strategy, then, targeted what they considered to be the weakest, most manipulable sector of the market, and characterized this sector through a series of deferrals and reductions. It focused on women as creatures of desire—therefore manipulable—who in turn, through these very desires, could seduce and manipulate the more resistant members of society, that is, men. There is a relay of desire from the lure of the commodity, through the mediation of women, and finally to men—and thence to the society-wide possibility of national-cultural discovery.

Travel becomes equated with sexuality in Fujioka's calculations. Tabi, he states, implies overnight stays; until recently parents would not let their young daughters travel, he claims. The age of a woman's first overnight trip parallels the age of the first sexual encounter: travel as sexual discovery. The freedom of women to travel secures the eroticization of the trip—and Japan—with a doubled sense of discovery.

The task remained, then, to sell tabi to young women by determining what would appeal to their specific psychology. Fujioka depicts women as *kusemono*, "rouges" or "rascals," by which he means they do not know their own intentions: women do not know their own minds and are easily manipulated. The early market surveys conducted by the team reinforced this analysis. In these surveys, questioners asked groups of young women where they would like to travel in Japan. With few exceptions, their answers fell into three categories: remote regions or distant islands; places where the old Japan (*furui Nihon*) remains; places for recreation.[22] What united these answers was the fact that all the places named had already been popularized by the mass media

22. Ibid., 38.

(*masu komi*, also meaning "mass communication"). The account team thus concluded that these women were highly influenced by the mass media.

It is perhaps not surprising that advertising executives would believe so firmly in the power of the mass media to shape desires and devise images that promise to fulfill those desires. Yet Fujioka goes even further with his faith in benign media power: the word he uses to describe the actions of the mass media is *sōsa*—a word more often used by critics of the media, connoting manipulation or "management"—rather than the softer *eikyō* (influence) that ad agencies usually prefer.

In an attempt to get beyond the already canonized set of travel destinations that young women invoked, Dentsū conducted in-depth interviews. The results led the account team to make a larger leap, connecting the peculiarities of feminine psychology with the seductions of real travel. In the women's descriptions of their trips, they appeared "just like movie heroines," actresses on a stage, and what they revealed in their stories was the self (*jibun*), a self that nobody knew, completely different from the everyday self.[23] As Fujioka put it, travel operates as a stage apparatus (*daidōgu*) or stage (*butai*) for forming this extraordinary jibun. In travel, women want to become a different self, and, at the same time, they want to be seen: "for a woman, nothing is as bad as not being seen" (*onna ni totte, mirarenai to iu koto hodo tsurai koto wa nai*).[24] He goes even further, stating that for a woman, "not being seen is as bad as death." The narcissistic desire to be seen, to be an object of sight, to be discovered, merges with the desire to discover Japan in a conflation of psychosexual and national-cultural trajectories.

In a series of moves that parallels the always destabilized relationship of travel to that which it would traverse—that is, home as both origin and final destination—Japanese women, as figures of feminine plenitude identified with the home, now become the mobile operators through which home is seen to be essentially lacking: lacking both in the satisfaction necessary to keep women at home (and thus not traveling) and in the resources necessary to actualize "woman" as the desirable object of a generalized male gaze. A woman must leave home, realize home as essentially lacking, in order to display and thus discover herself in the eyes of the other. Yet the self discovered is left open to further operations of difference, to further desires: one always

23. Ibid., 39.
24. Ibid., 40.

returns home from the sheerly partial pleasures of travel, but the home (and by extension the everyday self) to which one returns is thereby different. And, if "travel that is really travel" has taken place, then one must reactualize those desires, repeatedly, in further travels.

In these descriptions, then, travel becomes a literalized narrative in which women perform as selves other than the everyday selves associated with "home." Display is conflated with sightseeing: the sights to be seen become the women themselves, with landscapes reduced to stage settings for dramatized moments of double discovery and recognition by the onlooking male traveler.

Discovering "Myself"

Fujioka defines tabi in negative terms: in tabi, a separation from society occurs. Tabi is everything that society is not: it is the natural, the free, the rural, the humane, the nonordinary. In travel there is the promise of a retrieval of everything lost in the current age. In the midst of these musings about travel, he states that the word *hakken* (discovery) suddenly came to him. *This* was the "campaign concept" *(kyanpein konseputo)* he had been waiting for:

> For discovering, there is no need for nature or scenery or people. Discovery is really one's own self. "Discover myself," I said to myself. The self of travel, the discovery of myself, traveling through myself.... "Discover myself" *[jisukabā maiserufu]* had become our campaign concept.[25]

Discovery thus becomes an epistemological imperative, divorced from "nature or scenery or people." What remains, simply, is myself (maiserufu), as both the desiring consumer-discoverer and the object of discovery, in a solipsistic internalization of the circuits of travel. The elimination of the scene of the journey—no need for nature or other people—within a perfectly individualized "myself" could not of course sustain an actual tourism campaign. Self-discovery had to be rearticulated with the national-cultural object of Japan, the discovery of "myself" mapped onto the terrain of the Japanese archipelago, now colonized by this expansive ego.[26]

25. Ibid., 48–49.
26. The extent to which Fujioka insisted on the centrality and originality of touristic self-discovery is striking. In my interview with him in July 1985, he repeatedly insisted that Discover Japan really had little to do with the nostalgic search for national-cultural origins; instead, it had everything to do with "discovering myself," he claimed. This

Yet what is this "myself" that can so readily be conflated with Japan? The previous revelation that women want to discover another self in travel became complicated by this revelation: the campaign's core concept that in tabi one "discovers myself" (jisukabā maiserufu), a self that is authentic, but lost. Travel is the means to rediscover and recover this lost self: "Discover Myself" becomes the equivalent of Discover Japan. Travel and that which it discovers—a lost personal self, a culturally authentic Japan—become the antitheses of the contemporary, urban everyday. Travel (of course, via the national railways) becomes a disciplinary apparatus, if a pleasurable one, for producing individuated Japanese subjects.

In the descriptions of both the traveling woman's creation of another self and the (implied) Japanese everyman's discovery of his lost authentic self, travel operates as a line of escape from the everyday. But whereas the female traveler creates a romantic, alternate persona who uses travel as a stage device (one is reminded of the stage journeys— *michiyuki*—of Noh drama and bunraku puppet theater), the traveler in the second phase of Dentsū's planning discovers a *true* "other self." In the first case, travel allows a fictional self to emerge; in the second, an authentic one to be recuperated. Somewhere along the way, the traveler has shifted from the female actress to a generic (and thus, implicitly, male) subject in search of authentic origins (*moto no tokoro*). Images of fictionality and authenticity waver between the poles of the feminine and the masculine, the non-native and the native.

It is telling that the Discover Japan campaign, which evoked the possibility of a return to native origins and ethnically true selves, had as its point of departure the falsity of the female traveler's self. The process of semantic elimination outlined by the campaign's creator first established tabi as something for young, frivolous, easily manipulated, narcissistic, seductive women, a means for discovering and displaying another woman in a different scene. It ended with a Japanese self (re)discovering its authenticity by moving through originary landscapes. The gendered aspect of this rhetoric was overlaid on a landscape already binarized in terms of national-cultural authenticity and falsity. Because the figure of the young woman threatened to tip the rhetorical balance in the direction of falsity, it became necessary to authenticate her as truly Japanese by inducing her to travel domestically; the duplicitous feminine could thus be shifted

concept, he argued, set Discover Japan apart from the derivative rhetoric of the then-current Exotic Japan campaign.

to the ethnic authentic, in the figure of the generalized Japanese subject-traveler.

Discover Japan played on the most reified and consumable distinction between national self (in its at least double senses) and other. There is no doubt that this other fundamentally implied the rationalized American other. The campaign appealed to nostalgia for origins, and, in its creator's ideology, Americanized rationalism and materialism are the antitheses of the Japanese *kokoro*, or "heart"—that much-invoked concept in both advertising and ethnic theorizing, which is also equated with the place of return: that which is uniquely Japanese and native.[27] In this theory of travel and origins, the self equals an original Japanese self, which equals the authentic kokoro, which in turn equals the rural, remote, non-American, and nonrational. Travel is the operator which connects the terms by allowing the displacement of discovery, as it permits a temporary recovery of a lost self.

Fujioka narrates his discovery of discovery—of self, of Japan—as a sudden, indigenous revelation. Yet what he fails to mention are the foreign origins of this most native of concerns. Far from being an original slogan for a quest for origins, Discover Japan directly mirrored that of a national domestic tourism campaign in the United States only three years earlier: Discover America. Fujioka in fact coauthored a book about this campaign entitled (not surprisingly) *Jisukabā Amerika* (Discover America).[28] Although he would later claim that the motivations behind the two campaigns were completely different—in the American case, advertising aimed to keep tourists and their dollars at home; in Japan, it attempted to keep demand high for Japan National Railway after the 1970 exposition—both were massive appeals for domestic travel.

Discover Japan was in fact a direct transfer from Discover America. It copied not only the copy, but also the graphics of Discover America, transforming its trademark weathervane arrow into a stylized, foreshortened one. Discover Japan is a perfect example of the transnational flows of marketing techniques and advertising stratagems, signaling from its inception its place within an entirely global, advanced capitalist economy: Discover Japan and its insistence on the natively local presents the strongest evidence possible for the delocalization promoted by an American-led transnational capitalism. Perhaps even

27. Brian Moeran has discussed the ubiquity of the keyword *kokoro* in advertising and its relationship to the larger semantic domain of *seishin* (spirit). Moeran, "Individual, Group and *Seishin:* Japan's Internal Cultural Debate."
28. Fujioka Wakao and Nakai Kōichi, *Jisukabā Amerika: Amerika no kankō kyanpein.*

more striking for a campaign based on a valorization of native Japaneseness, the slogan was usually written in unadorned English, "Discover Japan," not transliterated in the script commonly used for rendering foreign words into approximations of Japanese, *katakana*. In Japanese the campaign was prevalently known as *Nihon no saihakken*, which literally means "*re*discover Japan," perhaps a more accurate rendition of the sentiments that Dentsū and the national railways were promoting. Adding the prefix already locates the movement of appropriation in a repetitive structure: one can only *re*discover what one has already discovered before. Yet the desire to rediscover implies a loss, a forgetting of the object of knowledge, and thus the need for the repetition of discovery.

Since it is "myself" that is discovered in travel, the direct selling of approved scenic destinations suddenly seemed obsolete (for this advertising mode, at least). Instead of using its posters to present famous scenes, scenery that the traveler could buy, Discover Japan stressed the interaction of the traveler with nature *(shizen)* and tradition; by touching *(fureau)* nature and tradition, Japanese would discover themselves as Japanese.

For example, one of the first of the campaign's famous series of posters depicted several young women raking autumn leaves deep in the mountains. It was a photograph of Nikkō, one of Japan's most famous travel destinations, but this fact was not readily discernible from either the picture or the minute logo at the bottom of the poster. To the planners, this poster was a negation of advertising that merely enticed tourists to buy scenery without any discovery. Natural beauty in and of itself was not the issue; what was important was the encounter, the contact *(fureai)* between the quotidian and the nonordinary:

> What we were trying to do in our campaign was to promote, in this day and age, the discovery of the self that money cannot buy, through the kind of travel that money cannot buy. . . . By coming in contact with beautiful nature and tradition we also discover our own nature. To do this, we must travel in a way that conserves the environment, in which nature and tradition are allowed to exist, beautifully. Therefore, if beautiful scenic photographs function merely to entice people to travel, we must negate that function itself. . . . What Mr. Matsuda of our project team decided on as the Discover Japan poster motif was not scenic beauty, but rather "the beauty and sadness of 'contact.'" The contact of the everyday and the non-everyday, the present and the past, the artificial and the natural, the so-

phisticated and the primitive; or, in a different sense, the
brushing past [surechigai] [of these opposites].[29]

The task of the photographers was to capture the instant of contact,
the moment when different worlds touched. Posters in the series had
one or two modern young women encountering a fragment of tradition
or nature: an old monk at a mountain temple, the slow approach of a
farmer on a country road, the massive wooden doors of an eighteenth-
century gatehouse.

What the rhetoric and the photographic images indicate is the rediscovery of the subject in travel. Landscape is no longer an object pas-
sively viewed by the distanced observer; landscape itself takes on renewed subjective qualities, as the repository of fureai. Travel is an
occasion—perhaps *the* occasion—for the rediscovery of the self, as
landscapes become settings for haiku-like moments of encounter.

The campaign's submotto highlighted this newly reconsidered relationship between Japanese landscape and Japanese person: "Beautiful
Japan and Myself" (*Utsukushii Nihon to watakushi*), a slightly askew citation of novelist Kawabata Yasunari's Nobel Prize acceptance speech,
"Utsukushii Nihon *no* watakushi." Kawabata's 1968 speech is also conventionally translated as "Beautiful Japan and Myself," yet the posses-
sive *no* indicates a self modified by "beautiful Japan" rather than separated from it. Dentsū's introduction of the conjunction *to*, translated
here as "and," discreetly yet firmly keeps apart the poetic unity of Kawabata's place and person. Although Discover Japan promised a return
of the authentic Japanese self in the midst of truly traditional landscapes, a fusion of self and scene was forestalled—for it was actual
travel, with all its associations, that would provide the means for momentary discovery and completion. If both "beautiful Japan" and "myself" could be discovered in a purely poetic mode, without ever leaving the confines of one's urban prison, then tabi would no longer be
necessary.

In the stereotypical pre–Discover Japan mode, Japanese considered
travel as sightseeing—the viewing, often seasonal, of culturally ac-
claimed landscapes and sites: the cherry blossoms of Yoshino, the autumn leaves of Lake Towada, snow-clad Mount Fuji. Travel to these
landscapes was an exercise in confirmation: the sightseer (in the strict
sense) expected no unusual encounters, no solitary experience (*keiken*).
The express purpose of travel was to see what one was supposed to
see, to view an already culturally valued scene, and to acquiesce in the

29. Ibid., 104–5.

general opinion.[30] The desire to encounter people of the locale and have meaningful exchanges with them grew, according to many observers, with the experiences Japanese had at Expo '70. There, pavilions and personnel from previously little-known countries encouraged Japanese visitors to participate (sanka suru) in an experience with the unknown. Discover Japan intended to develop this desire for contact by pointing the way from the passive social confirmation of scenic beauty to the active, personal appropriation of experience within travel, alluding to earlier forms of pilgrimage and poetic peregrination that relied on the solitary, experiencing subject. It did this through an array of techniques and a guiding philosophy called deadvertising (datsukōkoku), which represented, to Fujioka, a break with past marketing approaches. He asserted that Discover Japan was not an attempt to incorporate and promote all of an older Japan as touristic commodities, but rather the altruistic presentation of the Japanese spirit, divorced from any taint of the profit motive. According to this philosophy, advertisements should not exist merely to sell things; advertisers are responsible for including cultural and social value (kachi) as well. And in deadvertising, which embodies this philosophy of value, ads no longer primarily serve business or the producer, but rather social and cultural consciousness:

> Advertisements should not serve business or commodities as their masters. If we use the word "serve," then what advertising must serve is contemporary cultural and social thought and consciousness ["gendai no bunka ya shakai shisō ya ishiki ni tsukaeru"]. In order to do that, advertisements must be conceived of not from the perspective of business or commodities, but rather by asking what society or the masses are searching for—by asking what will appeal to society or the masses. If that something is not information about a business or a commodity, then we can no longer call it an advertisement, according to existing conceptions. The reason that I call this kind of phenomenon deadvertisement is because [its rules] are absolutely different from the rules of advertising.[31]

Fujioka is deft in countering objections to his notion of deadvertising. He likens those who claim that businesses pour money into advertising only to get a proportionate return in sales to people who do kindnesses to others only in expectation of reward. He insists that his

30. See Sasaki Shun'ichi, "Banpaku to Jisukabā Japan."
31. "Ningen to bunmei," Māketingu to Kōkoku, November 1970, as cited in Fujioka, Kareinaru, 88–89.

motivation is altruistic, that he does not calculate profit but dispenses general information of cultural and social value solely for the edification of the masses. Fujioka cites the Ningen to Bunmei (Humanity and Civilization) series he designed in 1970 for Fuji Xerox Corporation as a transparent example of deadvertising, with its full-page newspaper (de)advertisements presenting the public with "information of value" (kachi aru jōhō); he cites as well Mōretsu kara Byūtifuru e (From Gungho to Beautiful), another campaign for the same corporation. In the latter campaign, the word byūtifuru was used, not in the sense of the Japanese word utsukushii (usually translated as "beautiful"), but in the sense of humane and relaxed. This newly created "beautiful"—again revealing the penchant in Japanese advertising for transformations of English—contrasted with mōretsu, a word appropriate to the heavily stressed, intense Japanese worker of the period of high economic growth. The Fuji Xerox ad announced a shift in priorities in the post-Expo period: from a life devoted solely to work to one in which leisure, culture, and travel would have their roles. This new kind of corporate advertising, according to its promoters, seeks only to present disinterested information; the return is not in monetary terms, but in affective ones. There is no promotion of a specific commodity or service; even the name of the sponsor (suponsā) is downplayed. Instead, these deadvertisements are euphemistically called feeling advertisements (fuiringu kōkoku), as if the appeal to feeling could automatically negate the function of advertising in a capitalist economy.

Discover Japan was included in this new advertising genre—or rather, antigenre. Instead of directly encouraging travel to specific locations, the campaign tried to induce a generalized ambience signifying travel. The railway stations and trains themselves were transformed into galleries filled with a succession of posters in which the Japanese self was variously imagined.[32] The place names of the scenes depicted were often buried in a lower corner of the posters, whose task was to create a general desire for tabi. These posters, far from being an ancillary part of the campaign, were at the forefront of a strategy which targeted train stations as ready-made sites for massive advertising, complete with a captive audience of daily commuters.

Travel posters before this campaign had usually declaimed the beauties of known locations; name and scene adhered in the Japanese concept of the meisho, a "noted place," a "place with a name." Mount

32. Sasaki Shun'ichi, "Banpaku to Jisukabā Japan," 26.

Fuji is perhaps the most famous of these, but there was an almost limitless number of notable named sites, many of which had been grouped in numbered circuits or itineraries: three famous scenes of Japan *(Nihon sankei)*, fifty-three way stations of the Tōkaidō *(Tōkaidō gojūsan tsugi)*, three holy places of Japan *(Nihon sandai reijō)*. These numbered and grouped rankings of scenes codified specific associations for specific sites. In Discover Japan, however, the appeal was nonspecific, to a Japan in general—unnamed, yet somehow recognizable. The encounter of young women—marginal to the workaday world—with natural beauty and rusticated "tradition" (also marginal to the urban centers of Japan) created a repertoire of standard images of a Japan timelessly held in reserve for the traveler, ready to be discovered.

In previous domestic travel advertisements, a poster or a television commercial depicting a resort, a famous landscape, or an historical site had a specific, direct appeal. There was no necessary linkage between their specificity and a traditional Japan writ large, although undoubtedly those associations were made in the case of especially potent natural symbols of Japaneseness, like Mount Fuji. In the new campaign's strategy, however, the trope of synecdoche dominated, with parts of Japan, almost always vaguely identified, standing for Japan itself in all its native purity. Similarly, the (re)discovered "myself" also operated as a synecdoche of an essentially coterminous Japan.

Although this Japan was billed as native and original, it was a Japan in many ways unknown to its young urban travelers. The valorization of the native capitalized on its remoteness, its mystery for mainstream Japanese. Nevertheless, Japan beckoned as something strangely familiar: the native remote. If the truly Japanese had receded, it was yet rediscoverable, recoverable, if one could only touch it.

At the same time that Discover Japan led to a return to the native in the 1970s, the age of mass overseas tourism brought Japanese into unprecedented contact with the foreign. Yet expanding affluence, increasing imports, foreign travel, and the innovative work of Japanese designers and producers in fabricating and selling western-style consumer goods brought much of the material exotic within domestic purview. America and Western Europe, at both the symbolic and the object level, began to lose their snob appeal. Non-Japanese Asia, the third world, and—for the younger generation of the 1980s—prewar Japanese mass culture became new boundaries of the exotic. The growing cosmopolitanism and wealth of many Japanese were accordingly echoed and amplified in all areas, including advertising. If Discover

Japan created a practicable, profitable strategy for incorporating the rustic margins as quintessentially native for the 1970s, Exotic Japan presented a different Japan for the 1980s.

Exotic Japan

The 1984 appearance of Exotic Japan finally supplanted the official nostalgia of Discover Japan. This campaign reversed the terms of the former one: instead of urging the (re)discovery of native Japan, it enticed travelers with images of non-native Japan. In the imaginings of author Itsuki Hiroyuki, the creative force behind this Japan National Railway campaign, domestic monuments to continental culture constituted the exotic within Japan. Mount Kōya, seat of the esoteric Shingon sect and great repository of Buddhist riches from Central Asia and China, became the first representative of this internal exotic. The choice of Mount Kōya was undoubtedly related to the explosion of interest in esoteric Buddhism accompanying the 1,150th anniversary celebration of the death of Kōbō Daishi, one of the most revered figures in Japanese history.[33]

On the literal level of text and images, Exotic Japan built on the continuing fascination with the non-Japanese Orient, the Orient of the Silk Road (known as *shiruku rōdo*)—of Samarkand, Kashmir, T'ang China, Korea—the route for diffusion of both continental treasures and continental Buddhisms. The Silk Road became, in the late 1970s, a metaphor for Japan's ancient, tenuous, and winding connections with a greater world of cultural and material splendor and a ubiquitous object of artistic and media attention, including synthesizer wizard Kitarō's Silk Road record cycle and NHK television's hugely popular *Silk Road* series.

The inaugurating television commercial for the campaign, however, did not play up the Silk Road motif. Instead, it brought out one of Japan's pop idols, Go Hiromi, dressed in kabuki-inspired sci-fi costume and singing an Exotic Japan refrain. This television spot was a fantastic pastiche, incorporating both high-tech futurism and stereotypical Japanese high culture as signifiers of the exotic. Later commercials, how-

---

33. Kōbō Daishi (773–835), also known as Kūkai, is one of the most renowned saints in Japanese history, a worker of miracles, reputed to be alive even today within his mausoleum on Mount Kōya. See Joseph Kitagawa, *Religion in Japanese History*, 63–66, for a brief history of Kōbō Daishi.

ever, repeated the visual and verbal motifs of the railway posters, which, by virtue of their sheer ubiquity, had had a great impact on popular perceptions. These advertising posters referred more directly to the exotica of the continental East, but in a complex fashion that undercut any simple opposition between Japan and others.

Instead of the standard Discover Japan scene of two girls in jeans making contact with a local person in an unspecified rustic setting, Exotic Japan posters created a photographic swirl around a trendily clad young woman, conspicuously alone. The Mount Kōya presentations arrayed gilded phoenixes, wrathful bodhisattvas, brocades, and pagodas in a montage from which emerged the pale, meditative visage of a young urbanite. Other posters in this campaign featured Nagasaki, with its Chinese-derived festivals, and Kyoto's Gion Matsuri, with its floats (dashi) of Persian provenance.

In none of these is the model set within a unified landscape, identified or otherwise. Rather, she is located—or dislocated—within an array of parts that indicate the exotic within Japan. The dominant rhetorical trope is metonymy—a contiguous linking of related objects—but the linkages do not constitute a narrative; the parts are not unified to form a totality, to tell a story. Exotic Japan is described by the elements it contains, its fragments, as the exotic is reduced to the level of objects. No longer is there the lure of tabi as self-discovery and holistic encounter with the scenic native, but rather the seductiveness of rare objects within a fragmented yet sumptuous space.

The Discover Japan images were quotations of tourist photography without the usual souvenir snapshot's overt reference to place. They sought to convey an artless, natural reflection of experience in integral, bounded images. The Exotic Japan works, however, are artful; their use of montage explicitly announces their fabrication. No longer is there an appeal to the transparent simulacrum of the photograph. Instead, there is a foregrounding of the work of the advertisement itself, its fictive, textual quality, through the use of photographic fragments.

Unlike Discover Japan's peripheralizing of captions for its photographs, Exotic Japan integrates text into its montage, rather than relying on a seemingly unmediated photographic message. Exotic Japan, written in katakana, is centrally superimposed over the montage in a facsimile of dot matrix print, thus indicating the computerization of writing that has revolutionized Japanese life since the 1980s (theretofore, Japanese was either handwritten, typed with a Rube Goldberg–esque contraption, or printed after equally cumbersome typesetting). Other elements of the text, however, are printed in a spidery handwritten style. The core phrase of the campaign "Ima Nihon wa, dokidoki suru hodo shigekiteki da: aa, Ekizochikku Japan!" (Japan now—so thrilling it makes your heart pound: Ah, Exotic Japan!) is followed by the name "Itsuki Hiroyuki" written in the same script. We are thus clearly led to infer that Itsuki's name is in fact his signature, and that the slogan exalting Japan as exotic is his authorial creation, written in his own hand. This sets up an opposition—between the high-tech Japan with its anonymously generated, standardized computer writing and a Japan of individual, authorial handwritings—that comments on other oppositions established by the ensemble of images, textual messages, and writing; this ensemble displays a complex interplay of rhetorical modes and subject positions in relation to national-cultural self and other.

Unlike the phrase Discover Japan, which was taken directly from the Discover America tourism campaign and written in English (although pronounced in Japanese fashion), Exotic Japan is here written in katakana, the script used to transcribe foreign languages, as if "Japan" had been introjected as the foreign, as something that entered from the outside.[34] There is a double movement here: because Exotic Japan is written in katakana, it is marked as foreign, as non-native. Foreign, that is, to Japanese, since in the everyday state of things, non-Japanese are not expected to be able to read katakana. By definition, from a Japanese national perspective, that which is exotic is not Japan; place names that are written in katakana conventionally mark the non-Japanese. On the level of script, then, Ekizochikku Japan establishes Japan as elsewhere, as other: the non-Japanese seen through Japanese eyes. Yet the message, Exotic Japan, is an almost comically stereotypical description of Japan as seen by westerners (specifically English-speaking westerners). The phrase calls up visions of the triumvirate of the Japanese exotic—geisha, cherry blossoms, and "Fujiyama" (the western mispronunciation of Fuji-san, Mount Fuji)—and refers to the whole panoply of guidebooks and travelogues promising to reveal Japan as exotic. There is a contradiction between the script of the text and what the text suggests. The message appropriates Nihon from the perspective of a foreigner looking at Japan; its scripting indicates the subject location of a Japanese looking at the foreign. This latter position is understandable, since the author indeed intended to point to what

34. Katakana has other uses as well—to express surprise, to render the pronunciation of Chinese characters, to emphasize—but it is also the script used to "Japanize" non-Japanese languages.

was exotic—derived from the outside—in Japan. But from the perspective implied by the message "ekizochikku Japan" *all* of Japan—whether pristinely native or recently imported—becomes exoticized.

At issue is the notion of an other, itself in relation to what might be imagined as a self within a dialectic of identity and difference. Any claim to radical self-identity turns into a claim for radical alterity. For what is radically self-identical is set apart, imagined as noncomparable and thereby different, other. All ethnocentrisms operate by this logic: an encapsulation of identity that thereupon guarantees its difference, its otherness from others.[35] In the savvy rhetorical and textual strategies of Exotic Japan, however, one does not sense the anguished sorting out of self and other that occupies the vast Japanese literature on national character, although its explicit theme is (once again) the Japanese thing. Instead, there is a distancing, as it encourages Japanese to play with all differentiations without guilt or concern. Exotic Japan presents Japanese difference from and identity with both the Occident and the Orient as a matter of style.

Discover Japan attempted to present different worlds touching by capturing narrative moments: the moment when the aged priest walks past or when the farmer hands the traveler an eggplant, accompanied by an exchange of gazes. From these moments a whole discourse of discovery could be reconstructed. Exotic Japan implies a counternarrative strategy: Japan is represented as a montage of exotic objects—brocades, statuary, paintings—around a New Wave teenager who looks enigmatically out from the montage, appearing herself as an object among objects. In her black-and-white (mostly black) *fuasshon* (fashion) she reflects the resolute asceticism of the leading avant-garde designers of the Japanese 1980s, Kawakubo Rei (of Commes des Garçons) and Yamamoto Yohji. In one poster the motif of black cape and white shirt is repeated by a crowd of young monks in black habit and white underkimono; the association with asceticism strikes all the stronger, since Kawakubo and Yamamoto—with their uncompromising severity and taciturnity—are known for their almost mystical renunciation. The ascetic monochromaticism of the model and the young practitioners is in starkest contrast with the brocaded golds and crimsons of Buddhist exotica: not a dialectic, but a serial reversal of renun-

35. Much of Tokugawa nativist scholarship was equally concerned to define the native as unique. Western intrusion, however, exacerbated this tendency. What must be studied are the actual ways in which the dominant position of the western powers was introjected and the complex sorts of claims to cultural uniqueness that emerged in Japanese self-descriptions.

The inaugural 1984 poster for Exotic Japan

ciation and desire, of acerbic consumer stylishness and archaic religious excess.

On the denotative level, text and image refer us immediately to continental culture as exotic. But their wider connotative possibilities refer
not only to tantric paraphernalia or Indic gods. The world of avant-
garde fashion in itself defines another boundary of desire for (young)
Japanese, and it is its coupling with a stereotypically conceived domestic alterity that defines a more comprehensive vision of the exotic. We
are led to believe that what is really exotic is a Japan that can montage
such disparities with such exciting aplomb. The seemingly indiscrimi-
nate cultural mixing and matching that some have taken as the hallmark of modern Japan becomes, in the global matrix of advanced capitalism, the stylish prerogative of an affluent nation.

In perhaps the strongest advertising statement of the ekizochikku
approach, a Victorian doll with pale hair and eyes stands on a beach,
looking out at the viewer. At her feet is a shattered mirror, which
throws back fragments of her reflection. To the left is written in Japanese *Nihon wa gaikoku desu:* "Japan is a foreign country." Designed to
promote tourism to Hiroshima (much could be said about *that* site as
exotic), the poster asserts that antique dolls arrived in Hiroshima in
the nineteenth century, that they are waiting for the traveler, and—not
the least of its assertions—that Japan is "just like" a foreign, exotic
country, not only to Japanese but also to those long-dead "dollmakers
across the sea." A certain seductive conflation of national self and other
reflects itself in the eerie juxtaposition of mute doll and broken mirror,
placed even further into the register of the phantasmatic by the claim
that Japan is *just like* an exotic country (whereby the danger of Japan
as an *actual* foreign country, announced by the statement "Japan is a
foreign country," is softened). In the assertion of Japan as just like a
foreign country we can detect the rhetoric of the simulacrum so prominent in contemporary thought and fiction. One thinks of the stunningly salable fictions of Yoshimoto Banana, intended primarily for the
same young women that Exotic Japan targeted, and intended to evoke
the so-called *shōjo* (young girl) aesthetic. Throughout her works the
logic of the "just like" is replayed, repeatedly.[36] The phantasmatic
claims of the "just like" articulate seamlessly with that of the "neo,"

36. John Whittier Treat skillfully reveals the complicitous intersections of nostalgia,
simulacra, and popular culture in "Yoshimoto Banana Writes Home: *Shōjo* Culture and
the Nostalgic Subject."

the notion of the (ever-)new as nothing more than the repetitive insistence of the (re)marketed commodity body.[37]

The Neo-Japonesque

In his role as ostensible author of Ekizochikku Japan, Itsuki tried originally to appeal to the Silk Road fascination, locating it at its eastern terminus, Japan itself. But as is the wont of texts in general and mass-mediated mantras in particular, Exotic Japan took on dimensions far exceeding its author's expressed intentions. Marketing teams and advertising agencies, as well as the popular and quasi-academic press, expanded the possibilities of Exotic Japan, redefining it for the young. As the meaning of exotic slipped from "foreign" to "(just) like the foreign," from the actual alien and nonindigenous to the simply strange and unfamiliar, Exotic Japan came, then, to imply not only the foreign lodged within the native (Persian floats, Victorian dolls) but the native itself as the foreign: "Japan is a foreign country." Japan is no longer searched for in the vanishing forms of the native; there is no attempt at nostalgic recuperation. There is a thus a literal inversion of Discover Japan, with its search for the authentic.

Exotic Japan's advertising rhetoric focused on the non-Japanese Orient. But to marketing strategists, Exotic Japan refers to more than just Indic or Sinic influences. For the generation born after 1955, Japan itself, they insist, has become exotic. What is familiar to this generation is Americanized life itself. Rather than equating the unfamiliar with the imported—with the classically exotic—this younger generation, reared in the lap of westernized luxury, finds the thrill of the unfamiliar in lost aspects of Japanese life.

These conclusions were put forth in a wide-ranging set of reflections on postwar Japan published by the avant-garde of Japanese marketing, the Parco Company (a subsidiary of the giant department store corporation, Seibu). In a popular text devoted to predicting patterns of future consumption, the Parco editors divide the postwar populace into three distinct generations based on their attitudes toward *wayō*, "Japan and the West."[38] It calls the current age the "profligate age" or "age of

---

37. Max Horkheimer and Theodor Adorno relentlessly expose the repetitions of identity in the culture industry's production of difference in "The Culture Industry: Enlightenment as Mass Deception." For example: "Freedom to choose an ideology—since ideology always reflects economic coercion—everywhere proves to be freedom to choose what is always the same" (pp. 166–67).

38. *Gekkan Akurosu* Henshū Shitsu, ed., *Ima, chōtaishū no jidai*, 43–51.

dissipation" *(hōtō eiji)*, in which performance and novelty outweigh the concern for status and quality which occupied the previous postwar generations. In a history based on consumption patterns, the first post-war generation (those who came of age in the 1940s) found itself confronted with the overwhelming wealth of the occupying Americans; America and American products were the salient symbols of status and wealth, imported goods intrinsically valuable. The second generation grew up in the rapidly expanding economy of the 1960s, in which western products already occupied standard niches. Basic material needs fulfilled, they looked to satisfy burgeoning desires for style and individuality. Brand-name goods—one is tempted to say the brand names themselves—crystallized concerns for quality: Gucci and Hermes became household words. Imported goods per se no longer automatically conferred status; imported *luxury* items did. The overseas travel boom of the early 1970s further accustomed Japanese to the ubiquity of the foreign. Imported goods lost their essential mystique; the search for quality and style was on, whether in foreign or indigenous products.

Now, the third postwar generation—what the Japanese press has lately come to call *shinjinrui* (new humans) or *shin Nihonjin* (new Japanese)—has grown up in an Americanized, affluent state in which certain things Japanese appear more exotic than products of western civilization. Unlike the 1960s generation, which initiated a double reappraisal of Japanese "tradition"—the high and the low of elite fine arts and artless folk crafts—the shinjinrui are inspired by what might be called mass culture, particularly the popular products of the Taishō (1912–1926) through early Shōwa (1926–1989) periods. Games, toys, fashion—what are commonly called *fūzoku* (manners and customs)—and hobbies such as *bonsai* cultivation pique their interest. They are fascinated by the minutiae of daily lives now gone, and copywriters have echoed this quotidian fascination in their citations and reproductions of advertisements from different historical periods, particularly the 1920s and early 1930s. The object of nostalgia subsists, in short, in the emergent forms of Japanese modernity and its mass culture.

These objects when commodified are called "nostalgia products" *(nosutarujii shōhin)* and the ads "nostalgia advertisements" *(nosutarujii kōkoku)* by people in the trade. Yet the ads primarily target not people who grew up in the 1920s but young people who know nothing of prewar Japan. This nostalgia differs from the varieties invoked by Discover Japan and expressed through the various community-building and regional movements of the sixties and seventies (and even today).

No explicit appeal to return, no acute sense of loss, and no reference to embodied memory mars the glib evocation of vanished commodity forms. One could wonder, then, if nostalgia, with its stubborn implications of loss and desire, is really the appropriate notion here. Yet we are recalled to it by the explicit terms of this modality of consumption: the products *are* after all termed nosutarujii shōhin. The use of 1920s typography and design or the actual reproduction of period pieces evokes, however, not a historical period but a free-floating past. Stripped of any tangible historical context, these cited moments of style operate as novel elements in the image repertoire of hip Japan.

Why have the everyday objects and commodities of modernity past become the site for such reproductive nostalgia? Commodity forms offer themselves as easily appropriated repositories of discrete style elements; their status as already circulated and advertised forms provides the requisite distance from the present while allowing ready recirculation. Nosutarujii products are not kitsch—not quite—by virtue of this mannered recirculation. They draw close to what American cultural critics have termed "camp." Rosalind Krauss, in reflecting on the possibilities of camp (as mediated through Andrew Ross's reflections) says this: "Camp gravitates toward those anachronistic spectacles provided by one or another strange holdover displaced, dinosaur-like, into a new technological world and serving there, alienated and powerless, as a symptom of the very evanescence of that newer, more powerful world, itself on the verge of being rendered obsolete by a next generation of media." [39] The referencing of 1930s products (as well as spectacles) in the late twentieth century foregrounds the inevitable obsolescence of all things commodified, while holding out the market promise of a second life as camp, or what I also like to think of as neo-kitsch. What emerges, then, to suture the difference between the life of kitsch and its revival is what I call "vintage Japan," within a full-blown recapitulation of the alienated desire of the commodity form. Just as the commodity body in capitalism is no longer tied to the producer, neither are product memories—yet the name "Japan" remains as the final holding place of all such unmoored phantasms, memories, and commodities.

Fredric Jameson in his justly celebrated writings on postmodernism has referred to the form of citational practice that no longer situates

---

39. Rosalind Krauss, "Nostalgie de la Boue," 117. Krauss is responding in this passage to Andrew Ross's discussion of the "camp effect"—the way it parodies the "thing on its way out"—in his book *No Respect: Intellectuals and Popular Culture.*

itself in relation to a stable referent as pastiche, which he sees as the dominant rhetorical style in late capitalism, a style which has eclipsed the parody that dominated modernism. He notes that pastiche flourishes in a milieu in which norms no longer exist to regulate parody, and it is highlighted in the so-called historicism of postmodern architecture, with its "random cannibalization of all the styles of the past, the play of random stylistic allusion, and in general what Henri Lefebvre has called the increasing primacy of the 'neo.'"[40] This "increasing primacy of the 'neo'" is precisely, then, what is implicated in the trend that marketers have named the "neo-Japonesque," in which elements of a revivified past operate as the amplified elements of the stylishly novel. The Japonesque, of course, already references the French appropriation of things Japanese in the realm of the aesthetic. In the realm of styled surfaces and commodity bodies, the neo-Japonesque counterpoints the distinctions that Exotic Japan rhetorically enfolds: the repetitively ever-new domestic (re)appropriation of what the French did to Japanese style, now retrofitted for hip Japanese delectation. Jameson has spoken of this kind of fascination with the past as the nostalgia mode or the retro mode:

> Nostalgia does not strike one as an altogether satisfactory word for such fascination (particularly when one thinks of the pain of a properly modernist nostalgia with a past beyond all but aesthetic retrieval), yet it directs our attention to what is a culturally far more generalized manifestation of the process in commercial art and taste, namely the so-called "nostalgia film" (or what the French call "la mode retro").
>
> These restructure the whole issue of pastiche and project it onto a collective and social level, where the desperate attempt to appropriate a missing past is now refracted through the iron law of fashion change and the emergent ideology of the "generation."[41]

The neo-Japonesque and the Exotic Japan mode operate on the level of pastiche as they citationally cannibalize images of Japan. Retro products and nostalgia advertisements in Japan today are not indicators of a "properly modernist nostalgia," with its associated intimation of loss and the desire to recover that loss. That sort of personalized, modernist nostalgia is clearly evident in the Discover Japan mode and

40. Fredric Jameson, "Postmodernism, or the Cultural Logic of Late Capitalism," 65–66.

41. Ibid., 66.

in the valorization of a rural, folkic past that has animated so many varied intellectual and political endeavors in modern Japan.

Although referential nostalgia may still dominate much of Japan's mass culture, the ascendant urban young and trendsetting copywriters and media workers have produced an aggressively evacuated nostalgia: nostalgia as style. A television commercial may juxtapose a fluorescent Mount Fuji to an art deco representation of it; a guidebook gives a photographic itinerary of bathhouse interiors; there are "catalogs" of Edo culture, as if one could order away for artifacts. There is, in short, an emphasis on mass culture and materiality that comes close to the fascinated dynamics of kitsch. Or rather, in keeping with the imperatives of neo-nostalgia, there is the emergence of neo-kitsch and the epiphany of vintage Japan.

In the rediscovery of everyday life in the facsimiled commodity forms of decades past, there is no Benjaminian romanticism of the fragment, of the object torn loose from its original enplacement. Still less is there a belief in the object's ability to call up a vanished past, although the dynamics of commodity desire still compel consumers to move from commodity lack to acquisition (thus, the commodity-as-fetish always and ever stands for a lack and compels desire). The very capacity to gain access to the image repertoire of Japanese modernity and to cite it is itself a mark of affluence. Yet whether in the older nostalgic mode of Discover Japan—which operated initially as a means to develop new possibilities for consumption—or the 1980s neo-Japonesque twist, "Japan" endures as the repository of value: essential, stylistic, monetary.

The question, however, remains: Is this Japan, then, the same as the previous object of nostalgic "(re)discovery"? The Japan of Ekizochikku Japan names a different topos from that of Jisukabā Japan, and it would therefore seem fitted for a different disciplinary endeavor: a neo-Japan for a neo-Japanology. It is, in fact, the possibility of a new Japanology and its implications that disclose how difficult it is to escape the gravitational pull of a referential Japan, the seductions of postmodern displacement notwithstanding. The difference between these Japans—despite the shift that neo-Japan and its associated neo-nostalgia implies—is resolved in the stabilizing narrative economy of the journey, back to an earlier modernist insistence on a vanishing "home" to which the journey would always return. However powerfully this modernist nostalgia of the 1990s differs from that, say, of the 1960s— or of the 1930s or 1910s—that mode still exists today as one of the dominant means of encompassing Japanese pasts, with a variety of political effects.

Re: New Japanology

Discover Japan did not occur in a vacuum. It cleverly refracted the intensity of a time when pollution scandals and urban overcrowding spurred reflection on the preindustrial Japanese past. Coincident with a movement backward in time via a spatial displacement from city to country, interest in folklore and folklore studies boomed in the late 1960s and early 1970s. This interest was reflected most tangibly in the renewed attention, both popular and scholarly, given to folklore studies' most renowned exponent, Yanagita Kunio (1875–1962). Attempts to reclaim the simplicity of origins through travel and the study of folkloric texts were of a piece: both held up an ideal of travel as ethnographic experience, of unmediated contact with native places and people in a pastoral mode and the possibility of entextualizing those encounters. Yanagita's voluminous works were best-sellers (often sold in sets of "collected works," or *zenshū*); new folklore societies and journals were formed throughout Japan as the ethnodocumentary impulse merged with the touristic one.[42] Yanagita's later interpreters and the historians of Japanese folklore studies are well aware of this explicit linkage: Discover Japan was a commercial, touristic metaphor for the recovery of a lost arcadia that had motivated Yanagita's early-twentieth-century project in the first place.

A collection of essays attempting to rethink the contours of Japanese knowledge caught my attention in the mid-1980s with its uncanny thematizing of this triad of travel, modernity's losses, and Japanese national-cultural identity. Still an emblematic textual revelation of "Japan" as pop topic and intellectual conundrum, it was published as part of the Fieldwork Series (Fuiirudo wāku shiriizu)—a reference, one assumes, both to the (field)work of ethnographic production and to the production of work in a variety of disciplinary "fields."[43] The volume I

42. One example of this overlap between travel, tourism, and ethnography was the magazine entitled *Aruku miru kiku* (Walk Look Listen), modeled not unambiguously on Yanagita Kunio's own ethnographic practice and his journal *Tabi to densetsu* (Travel and Tradition, or Travel and Legends).

43. Proposed Japanese titles included *Kazoku no jidai* (The Age of the Family), *Rondon poppu nau* (London Pop Now), and *Monogatari sabetsu tennōsei* (Narrative, Discrimination, and the Emperor System).

want to examine is entitled *Nyū Japanorojii*, with its title written in English—vertically, on the left side of the cover—as *New Japanology*, and, on the right, in katakana.[44] This declamation gave me pause, for Japanology is something to question; I always resist being primarily identified as a Japanologist (rather than an anthropologist, despite the problems inherent in that disciplinary identification) because of its orientalist associations and its constricted purview. Yet here was a book in Japanese for Japanese by a variety of young critics, folklorists, and historians proclaiming, in both English and Japanese, a new Japanology, in a reclamation of this reifying paradiscipline. *Nyū Japanorojii*, in its strangely nostalgic reference to western orientalist discourse, its complex relationship to the book as aesthetic artifact, and its further associations with the discipline of Japanese folklore studies and theories of travel, provoked me to think about the coalescence of issues which the text announced.

A look at the essays reveals that they can easily fall under the rubric of nativist ethnology: essays about mountain deities, "wild spirituality," the idea of the "cosmic tree" in Japanese mythology, a comparison of the Japanese notion of the "spirit of words" (*kotodama*) and Derridean *logos*, and the difference between the "folk" (*jōmin*) and the "masses" (*taishū*). The subtitle of the book announces that it is concerned with "Japanese thought—a key to unlock the present." Many of the classic themes of Japanese folklore studies—really what the authors mean by Japanology—are thus represented here. What is different are the poststructuralist-inspired analyses, and it is this difference that marks the collection as new Japanology. Yet Japan remains as the enigmatic object of the new folklorist's (Japanologist's?) desire, and new Japanology emerges as the new name for a refurbished folklorism.

In Japan, high theory has a mass audience; if American postmodernists believe that the distinction between mass and high culture has been effaced in the United States, Japan presents an even more complete elision of the difference (and a different history of that difference).[45] The editors of this book could expect a mass audience, and they enabled this mass interest by foregrounding some of Japan's young so-called new academics (the capitalist imperative remains, it seems, to make it new) in a *zadankai* (roundtable discussion), published as the lead article.[46]

44. Kosaka Shūhei, ed., *Nyū Japanorojii*.
45. See my "Critical Texts, Mass Artifacts."
46. Masao Miyoshi reflects on the ubiquity of the *taidan* (dialogue) and zadankai in *Off Center*, 216–31.

Again, titles reveal: "Ima, <Nihon> to wa." "What Is Japan Now?" one could translate it (although the English translation of the article's title printed in the book is "What Is 'the Japan' Now?"; the inclusion of the "the" in that [mis]translation deepens the objectification that Japan already bears in this text as the object of new Japanology). The editor's reference to the "Japanese thing"—the "Nihontekina mono" (in quotes in the original)—is an eerily direct echo of Slavoj Žižek's notion of the national thing.[47] Subtitles sometimes tell more: "The Universal Problems of Contemporary Thought Appear in the Beyond of Deep Structure," translates this one.[48] The appeal to deep structure locates its lineage in Japanese structural anthropology and its vigorous explorations of Japanese cosmologies, ritual life, theories of kingship, narrativity, and performance in the 1960s and 1970s.[49]

The visual surface of the book marks the book as a consumable, desirable commodity body of a piece with new Japanology itself. The front cover features a painting of a prewar girl in cropped hair and a *yukata* (informal kimono) printed with a distinctive hybrid pattern characteristic of the period. The picture looks as if it has been directly reproduced from a prewar publication, and in fact the credits state that the plate was taken from a popular magazine called *Shōjo kurabu* (Girls' Club), founded by Kodansha Publishing Company in 1923 (although the credits neglect to give the date). The cover, in short, is designed in precisely the retro style discussed above, redolent with new nosutaru-jii. The back cover depicts a traveling group of Japanese acrobats—the Royal Japan Troupe—in a print reproduced from an American playbill of the late nineteenth century, recapitulating the subject locations that exotic Japan demands (that is, the demand that Japanese look at Japan with the eyes of a foreigner).

It is telling, then, that the text begins with the editor's references to none other than the dialectic of Discover Japan and Exotic Japan:

> A little over ten years ago there was the national railways' Discover Japan campaign and the so-called "Japan boom." . . .
> Maybe it's a ten-year cycle or something, but now Exotic Japan

47. Žižek explores the dimensions of national identification—and the irreducible "kernel of enjoyment" necessary for that identification to take place—in "Eastern Europe's Republics of Gilead."

48. "Shinsō no kanata ni gendai shisō no fuhenteki mondai ga mieru," in Kosaka, Nyū Japanorojii, 18.

49. Well-known cultural anthropologist and performance theorist Yamaguchi Masao was most prominently associated with this mode of analysis. In English, see his "Kingship, Theatricality, and Marginal Reality in Japan."

ニュージャパノロジー

NEW JAPANOLOGY

〔フィールドワーク ■シリーズ■ I〕
〈日本思想〉………現代を解く鍵

編———— 小阪修平
発行———— 五月社

The book cover of *Nyū Japanrojii*

has appeared and once again I think we've entered into a "Japan boom" situation.[50]

This assertion of decade-long cycles clarifies a structure of repetition, the repeated inevitability that keeps recycling an obsessional interest in Japan (the explosive, mass-market metaphor of the boom makes clear the specifically obsessional nature of this interest). A 1984 Japan National Railway's poster exemplified this kind of repetitive mediation. It arrayed miniature reproductions of past Discover Japan posters around a Japanese housewife dreamily looking out from the center of the poster, as if evoking her younger, 1970s Discover Japan self. Some fifteen years after the advent of Discover Japan, then, this poster urged its now fully domesticated female audience not to (re)discover Japan itself, but rather to (re)discover Discover Japan. The identification with an absented Japan, a Japan open to potential discovery, had been replaced by an identification with a citation of that absence, an identification that repetitively moved toward rediscovering *not* the vanishing object itself, but the mass-mediated apparatus that claimed it could discover that object in the first place.

Returning to the roundtable, it is not surprising (it is, indeed, revealing) that the name of Yanagita Kunio should then immediately arise, for this rapid movement—from Japan as the contemporary object of touristic encompassment to Yanagita Kunio and his early-twentieth-century folklore studies—follows the itinerary that reflections on the Japanese thing often produce. Although the discussion ranges thereafter from new left politics, to an argumentative comparison of Barthes and Derrida, to Leibniz, Spinoza, Japanese religious cosmology, narrativity, and beyond, there is a recurrent return to the topos of Japan and its disciplinary demarcation in Yanagita's nativist ethnology.

Why the inevitability of citing Yanagita as originary author when the identity of Japan is at stake? It was Yanagita's work that first articulated modernity, travel, and ethnography with the belief in a perennial Japan that subsisted in the voices and practices of the "folk." In citing Yanagita, late-twentieth-century Japanese explicitly locate themselves in a lineage, sequentially reiterating his theoretical attempts to journey back to the national-cultural home. They work through a series of turns and returns in the pursuit, not unlike the rediscovery of Discover Japan urged by the 1984 poster, of an ever-receding object of desire: a rediscovery of the 1960s rediscovery of Yanagita's rediscovery of an authentic Japanese knowledge unmediated by western capitalist modernity.

50. Kosaka, *Nyū Japanorojii*, 19.

Triply displaced, then, and more: for the narrative knowledge waiting
to be discovered in the Meiji period—the tales and legends sometimes
called folklore—itself often thematized the problem of ghostly repetitions, repetitions I shall say more about in the next chapter.[51]

A return to the name of Yanagita is always in the works when the
question of Japanese ethnonational identity is raised, and the inevitability of that return indicates what could be called a transferential relationship. Marjorie Garber, writing about Shakespeare and authorship,
shows how the obligation in Euroamerican literary studies and theory
since the seventeenth century to come to terms with Shakespeare rests
on a deeply overdetermined relationship of transference (in the psychoanalytic context, transference refers most generally to the bond that
develops between the analyst and the analysand).[52] In a similar fashion, the compulsion in Japanese writings about the nation-culture to
gesture toward Yanagita's authorial name betrays the transference at
work between Japanese modernity and Yanagita as trope for the essentially native. Yanagita's authorial name operates not unlike the Lacanian name of the father, for Yanagita is routinely called the father of
Japanese folklore studies; indeed, his name operates as the veritable
synecdoche of all that the discipline authoritatively encompasses. The
canonical name, the paternal name, the authorial name: all coincide
with "Yanagita Kunio" as a critical transferential relay point for Japan's
modern national-cultural imaginary.

If Garber refers to the Shakespeare effect (following the insights of
Foucault in thinking about the notion of the effect), it is equally plausible to refer to the Yanagita effect in contemporary Japan.[53] Yet if a return to Yanagita is always mandated, what about the texts that produce
this authorial effect? That return is most signally embodied in the text
which became, retrospectively, Yanagita's first work of folklore studies:
the canonical founding work of Yanagita's discipline, *The Tales of Tōno*
(Tōno monogatari), published in 1910. Yet far from portraying the premodern paradisiacal communitas that beckoned to eighteenth-century
nativist scholars, the *Tales* speaks of murders, incest, disappearances,

51. And even more so, for Yanagita himself often referred to his folklore studies as
shinkokugaku, "new nativist studies," thus a recapitulation of the immense philological
and philosophical scholarship of the Tokugawa period concerned to locate an unsullied
space of native life and labor, against the intrusions of alien Chinese words and things.
H. D. Harootunian's study of kokugaku includes an epilogue on Yanagita and shinkokugaku. Harootunian, *Things Seen and Unseen.*
52. Marjorie Garber, *Shakespeare's Ghost Writers: Literature as Uncanny Causality.*
53. Foucault unfolds the necessity of starting with effects—rather than origins—in
his "Nietzsche, Genealogy, History."

famine, and—crucially—ghosts. The ghastliness of these tales and their repeated ghostliness participate in the same supplementation that the figure of travel produces. For the impossibility of returning to a selfsame national-cultural home is allegorized in these tales, which speak of the receding horizons of origins. In documenting the singular and abiding voices of the margins, of the peasant folk, Yanagita was constrained to write down narratives of duplicity and loss.

I have lingered on the contemporary surfaces of commodities, advertising slogans and touristic discourses, the visual rhetorics of posters, marketing manuals, and academic texts as public representations of a Japan open to a variety of nostalgic recuperations. Some of these forms have shifted from the 1960s to the 1990s. Some of them coexist, differing across generational, regional, or class lines. Neo-nostalgia has not completely overturned the palpable longings for the recovery of a lost past that many Japanese feel. Dominant ideologies in Japan still depend on a politics of nostalgia suitable for an advanced capitalist polity: a nostalgia for a Japan that is kept on the verge of vanishing, stable yet endangered (and thus open for commodifiable desire). Yet other strategies and appropriations of the past crosscut this national terrain, as hypertechnological development and modes of information nurture a younger generation not as easily contained within the bounds of the classic metanarrative of nostalgia. Any attempt to theorize Japan, it seems, still finds itself destined to detour through the narratives and representational densities of an earlier history, to the critical conjuncture of early-twentieth-century modernity. Yanagita Kunio's folklorism emerged from that conjuncture in the complex textual epiphany of *The Tales of Tōno*. The next chapter effects its own return to questions of representation, authority, and modernity in an effort at rethinking that impossible textual attempt to rediscover (yet) another Japan.

CHAPTER THREE

Ghastly Insufficiencies: *Tōno Monogatari* and the Origins of Nativist Ethnology

The most scandalous literary figure in twentieth-century Japan, Mishima Yukio, once wrote a short contribution for a weekly newspaper column in which writers and critics commented on prose masterpieces of their choice for the edification of the reading public. Mishima chose *Tōno monogatari* (The Tales of Tōno), which, as we know, had come to be recognized as the founding work of Japanese folklore studies as well as a literary classic.[1] He says this: *"The Tales of Tōno* speaks, coldly, of innumerable deaths. Taking those deaths as its place of origin, Japanese folklore studies is a discipline in which the smell of corpses drifts."[2] This chapter finds its own point of origin in Mishima's lurid assertion, unraveling its implications in an attempt to rethink the stakes of ethnographic representation within Japanese mo-

---

1. "Folklore studies" is the conventional translation for *minzokugaku*. I sometimes translate this term as "nativist ethnology" (H. D. Harootunian uses the translation "native ethnology," which I have also used in the past) because of its links with the nativist scholarship (kokugaku) of the Tokugawa period (1603–1868) and its claims as a discipline of indigenous Japanese knowledge and practices. There are multiple connections between the disciplines of folklore studies and anthropology in Japan, not the least of which is the homophonic congruence of the two terms: *minzokugaku* is also a standard term for "anthropology." It differs from the *minzokugaku* of folklore studies, however, in its graphic constitution (although both terms share the same Chinese character for "min" the characters used for "zoku" are different). I shall use both "folklore studies" and (Japanese) "nativist ethnology" to translate *minzokugaku* in this chapter. In addition, although the sole published English translation of *Tōno monogatari*, by Ronald Morse, renders the title as *The Legends of Tōno*, I have chosen to translate it as *The Tales of Tōno*, believing that "tale" is in fact much closer to the import of *monogatari* than "legend" is. The title—*The Tales of Tōno*—also forms a link between so-called tale literature of the Heian period and after and Yanagita's tales.

2. Mishima Yukio, "*Tōno monogatari*," 198.

dernity. What kind of discipline is founded on death and its aftereffect: the smell of corpses, a linked image both horrifically concrete and ungraspable? Indeed, Mishima's trope plays out in its very form the general contradiction of an ethnographic impulse that would want to document the punctual event, the unwritable (death), but must always displace that impulse through the vagaries of the figurative—what some would call the literary. *The Tales of Tōno* emerged in the early twentieth century both to embody and to allegorize that constitutive contradiction of modernity—that is, the difference between "science" and "literature"—with its literary rewritings of oral tales of ghosts and gruesome goings-on in the Japanese rural remote. At the specific origin of Japanese folklore studies as a discipline (*gakumon*), as a field of scholarship, is not simply death, but a text that speaks, figurally, of deaths. To anticipate my own end(s) here, literature and ethnography (in Japan, in modernity) are always in a ghostly complicity with one another. Even when one would most like to disavow that complicity (or conversely to insist on a sheer identity without distinction), the figure of the other returns to reinstitute the distinction, now made unstable and tenuous. And this complicity is unthinkable outside the interlinked struggles about literary authority, speech and writing, and the status of representable reality in twentieth-century Japan.

The textual birth of Japanese nativist ethnology is thus a strange one: a birth that is deathly, an appearance that is at the same time a disappearance. That doubleness is the necessary condition of folklore studies (and that necessity extends to a more generalized anthropology). "In the Beginning, a Death" reads a subheading in "The Beauty of the Dead: Nisard," Michel de Certeau's subtle reflections on the discursive birth of popular culture in nineteenth-century France and the internal exoticism it presumes.[3] For, as he shows, the disappearance of the object—whether newly imagined as the folk, the community, authentic voice, or tradition itself—is necessary for its ghostly reappearance in an authoritatively rendered text. The object does not exist outside its own disappearance. If its coming-to-be is never simply punctual, a sheer event, neither is its death. There is always a temporal structure of deferral, of loss and recovery, across which the fantasy of folklore, of ethnography, stretches; thus the spectral status of the ethnographic object. It is only in the difference between those moments that the object of the fantasy can be said to exist. Susan Stewart

---

3. Michel de Certeau, with Dominique Julia and Jacques Revel, "The Beauty of the Dead: Nisard," 119.

has spoken of those genres that fantastically detemporalize the difference between loss and recovery as "distressed":

> Thus distressed forms show us the gap between past and pres-
> ent as a structure of desire, a structure in which authority
> seeks legitimation by recontextualizing its object and thereby
> recontextualizing itself. If distressed forms involve a negation
> of the contingencies of their immediate history, they also in-
> volve an invention of a version of the past that could only arise
> from such contingencies. We see this structure of desire as the
> structure of nostalgia—that is, the desire for desire in which
> objects are the means of generation and not the ends.[4]

The generalization of that structure is, of course, inseparable from
the claims of modernity itself. That Mishima, some six months before
his own death, would choose to write about *The Tales of Tōno* is not
insignificant. For the scandal of Mishima lies not so much in his writing, however much his interlinking of eros and ultranationalism shocks
bourgeois sensibilities.[5] The scandal resides rather in his own spectacular death in November 1970, when Mishima—at the head of his own
little army—briefly took over the Self-Defense Forces Headquarters in
Tokyo and ritually disemboweled himself in front of a crowd of spectators. What Mishima opposed with his desperate, dangerously fascist,
finally suicidal attempts to recover the spiritual core of Japanese culture (exemplified by the fallen symbol of the Japanese emperor) was
modernity itself. In short, his was an attempt to regain the lost object
of modernity at the post-'60s moment when there was no question that
the Japanese economic miracle, the postwar civil society, and things
American were here (there) to stay. It seems, then, retrospectively fitting that Mishima would have been attracted to *The Tales of Tōno*. For
that text also demarcated a crisis of Japanese modernity in the early
twentieth century.

Civilization and Its Remainders

In 1910, the *Tales'* date of publication, Japan as a nation-state had existed only some forty years. To grasp the implications of that statement

4. Susan Stewart, "Notes on Distressed Genres," in her *Crimes of Writing: Problems in
the Containment of Representation,* 74.
5. Masao Miyoshi has written of the Japanese rejection of Mishima's literature, declaring that "Much of Mishima Yukio's dazzling performance now looks merely flamboyant,
or even kitschy. The list of his works is long, but the list of those that might as well

is to imagine the severity of the epistemological break that occurred with the Meiji Restoration of 1868 and the ending of Japan's 250-year virtual isolation and its elaborate system of "feudal" rule.[6] During that time (and during Japan's long history before the Tokugawa period) there had developed enormously complex worlds of philosophy, aesthetics, and sociality—worlds largely independent of concurrent developments in the West. Tokugawa Japan had many of the ideal-typical marks of the European early modern, including a wealthy merchant class, a professional literati (and a vast publishing industry), and heavily populated cities (including Edo, the pre-Meiji name for Tokyo, the largest city in the world in the eighteenth century). Yet its "forced opening" (as it is often called) by the United States in 1854 operated as perhaps the primary efficient cause in the decline of the Tokugawa order and the precipitate scramble for modern nationhood and its accoutrements. In the interests of state power and development, not only the technologies and institutions of western capitalism, but hundreds of years' worth of aesthetic theories, literary forms, and modes of representation were imported within an extraordinarily compressed span of time: not only railroads, but Descartes; not only finance capital, but Renaissance perspective; not only Prussian-style militarism, but Ibsen. Within the unequal relationship of power between Japan and the West transpired countless moments of intrusion and resistance, seduction and assimilation, but what the period following the Restoration meant in the largest terms was the construction of a modern nation-state at the same time that entire worlds of representation and thought were grafted onto existing indigenous ones, activating what one Japanese critic has called a veritable "overturning of the semiotic constellation" of pre-Meiji Japan.[7]

---

remain unread is nearly as long." Miyoshi, *Off Center,* 149. Mishima's short review of *The Tales of Tōno* remains a piece that bears reading.

6. The Meiji Restoration aimed to "restore" the emperor to his rightful place of authority after centuries of merely titular kingship under the military government of Japan, which held de facto power. For an analysis of the Meiji Restoration as the complex culmination of intellectual debates about authority and representation, see H. D. Harootunian, *Toward Restoration: The Growth of Political Consciousness in Tokugawa Japan.*

7. The concept is Karatani Kōjin's, developed in his *Nihon kindai bungaku no kigen*—translated as *The Origins of Modern Japanese Literature.* Karatani's book is an examination of the formation of modern Japanese literature, in which he emphasizes the discursive production of the category and institution of literature *(bungaku)* itself in the Meiji period. For Karatani, the written word shifts from its status as rhetorical instrument and assumes new significance in the Meiji period as a tool for reflecting reality through the innovations of the *genbunitchi* system, which sought to unify the spoken and written languages.

Tōno monogatari was written at a time when regional beliefs and practices were being threatened by the comprehensive state ideology of
"civilization and enlightenment" *(bunmei kaika)*; this ideology was
backed by fiercely ambitious policies and programs for inculcating
modern habits and ideas into the populace. The widespread importa-
tion of western knowledge during the Meiji period led to a questioning
and reassessment of native forms. The goal of parity with the West
inspired the single-minded incorporation of western structures and
institutions and a bureaucratization of power based on norms of objective rationality; the formation of national compulsory education and
conscription incorporated the newly emergent national citizenry *(ko-
kumin)* into ever-widening circles of standardized participation and co-
optation in establishing the body politic.[8] The building of railroads and
nationwide communication and transportation facilities, banking and
finance, and foreign trade—the infrastructure of the modern state—
advanced at a stunning pace, safely enclosed within civilization and
its associated enlightenment.

Modernizing rhetoric and policies were not uniformly received,
however, and new kinds of political associations and groups arose in
response to the state's attempts to regulate the interests of the polity.
The state became increasingly aware of the destabilizing social forces
that modernization could unleash, and came to temper its calls for
advancement with appeals to time-honored "tradition." In a nation
composed primarily of peasants (80 percent at the start of the Meiji
period), yet with capital and political power concentrated in the cities,
an increasingly valorized tradition *(dentō)* signified rural custom.[9]

Late Meiji Japan, particularly after the Russo-Japanese war (1904–
1905), witnessed a phenomenal increase in rural out-migration, largely
in response to straitened economic conditions after the war. In 1908,
nearly 60 percent of the population of Tokyo consisted of emigrants
from the country; this flow to the cities only increased over the next
ten years.[10] Migration to the cities, characterized as *tokai netsu* (city
fever) was a major factor in transforming village life, as social and
geographical mobility changed the character of farming household
structure. The development of the railroads, improved material conditions, heightened demands for education, and accompanying philosophies of striving and material success contributed to the continuing

8. For a sharp analysis of the process of rationalization at the state level, see Bernard
Silberman, "The Bureaucratic State in Japan: The Problem of Authority and Legitimacy."
9. Mikiso Hane, *Peasants, Rebels, and Outcastes: The Underside of Modern Japan,* 11.
10. Carol Gluck, *Japan's Modern Myths,* 159.

transformation of rural life. Along with the transformations came intensifying rhetoric from the central elite, praising the virtues of village custom, the beauty and purity of country life, and exhorting rural youth to stay put on their ancestral paddy lands in an elaboration of what Carol Gluck has called the "agrarian myth" of Meiji Japan. As Gluck states:

> Although the late Meiji ideologues did not regard cities, enterprise, education, and reading as social ills in themselves, they were nonetheless unprepared for the consequences of their diffusion, especially when these were associated with the breakdown of the agrarian order in the countryside and the emergence of new forms of social conflict in the cities and factories. Confronted with a modernity that threatened to shake the social foundations of the nation, the ideologues turned to the verities of the past—the village and the family, social harmony and communal custom—to cure civilization of its fevers so that society as they envisioned it might yet survive.[11]

The amplification of the agrarian myth and the concurrent decrying of urban values was accompanied by concrete policies and plans, debates and dialogues, about how to insure stability in an agricultural arcadia on the verge of destruction. The state constructed the notion of *jichi*, self-government through local, officially sanctioned organizations, as a means of social control in the regions. The Home Ministry developed its rural revitalization movement (*chihō kairyō undō*) from 1900 to 1918, a movement which sought to inculcate progressive practices in the countryside. The government reorganized localities into new administrative units, consolidated the vast number of local shrines via the Shrine Merger Act of 1908, encouraged conservative youth organizations, and extolled "traditional" agrarian lifeways all the more effusively the more its policies destroyed those lifeways.

It is important to recall that there was a trajectory to this process of extolling tradition. The two decades immediately following the Restoration of 1868 produced a dominant rhetoric more explicitly modernizing and renovationist in tone than traditionalist. In keeping with the reformist mood and the attempts to civilize and enlighten the masses in western ways, numerous "custom reform associations" arose. In this phase, concern with custom served essentially as the precondition for locating regressive aspects in need of reform and modernization. Yet as the more pragmatic and decisive nation-building years progressed,

11. Ibid., 177.

and the welter of contending and contentious groups advanced their own particular interests, the government began to revalorize rural customs as a means of stabilizing the nation. A preoccupation with custom developed as the pretext for definitively locating the traditional. Although works describing peasant beliefs and the customs of remote regions can be found in nativist scholarship (kokugaku) of the Tokugawa period, the earliest modern attempts to record folkloric data were the Ministry of Justice's surveys of customary precedents (minji kanrei ruishū) in 1877 and 1880, compiled prior to the first attempts to formulate a civil code. These bureaucratic, legalistic codifications of custom as the basis of law were not far removed from the interest in custom emerging in the private sphere. In 1884, the Ethnological Society (jinruigaku gakkai) was formed with ten members; in 1886 it changed its name to the Tokyo Ethnological Society and began publishing reports on manners and mores (fūzoku). Those of 1888, for example, detail regional variations in New Year's activities. The popular magazine Fūzoku gahō, published from 1889 to 1916, satisfied a larger public interest for descriptions and depictions of annual events and popular practices. The Tokyo Ethnological Society continued publishing reports, examining such topics as "taboo words" (imi kotoba), "five-man groups" (gonin gumi) as a basic unit of social organization, and Okinawan beliefs.[12]

Written at a moment (1909–1910) when it had become inescapably clear that western industrial capitalism would not only bring civilization and enlightenment but would efface much of an older Japanese world, The Tales of Tōno thematized this effacement in its descriptions of Tōno, an obscure region in northeastern Japan. Presented as an unmediated transcription of oral tales and lore told to its "author" (the father-to-be of the nascent discipline of folklore studies, Yanagita Kunio) by a local storyteller, the Tales enscripted the uncanny remainder of capitalist modernity, that which could not be contained within the nationalist, rationalist discourse of the maturing state system. The Tales took its place among numerous texts signifying the rediscovery of the rural countryside; in time, it would come to be one of the most famous of these late Meiji texts. The content of the "tales"—or, rather, the sequence of information that storyteller Sasaki Kizen gave to Yanagita—speaks of the same degradation and poverty that infused the ascendant form of the Meiji "naturalist novel" (shizenshugiteki shōsetsu);

---

12. I have taken the above from a chronology of Japanese folklore studies prepared by the National Museum of Japanese History and Folklore. Fukuda Ajio, "Nihon minzoku kenkyūshi nenpyō."

murder, incest, grotesque births, and famine are presented as commonplace. This revelation of rural misery was in itself later seen as exposing an immense, hidden underside of Meiji Japan, one completely at odds with the official discourse of civilization and enlightenment. Yet Tōno was a world not only of murders and incest, but of ghosts, mountain apparitions, deities, and monsters. Sasaki's stories revealed a universe of fear, of splits in appearance, of the irrational and fantastic. It was this aspect of the *Tales* that indicated the frightening seductions of an older world that had seemingly escaped the intrusions of the central state. The surviving numinous became the romantic object of those caught up in the disenchantment of the world.

So far we have a story that is not entirely unfamiliar. Anxieties about cultural transmission, valorizations of the unwritten, discoveries of the marginal, and textual constructions of the "folk" are the replicable constituents of modern cultural nationalisms throughout the world.[13] Japan is striking, however, for the lateness of its condensed absorption within the global problematic of national modernity and for the extremity of its difference from the Euroamerican context—a difference that was obsessively re-marked within the writings of Japanese nativist ethnology. For the discipline was concerned with preserving the traces of a folkic world not only as a representation of the unwritten essence of ethnic Japaneseness, but also as the indication of a non-West that could never be subsumed under the dominant signs of western modernity.[14]

The Distance between Speech and Writing

The difference between Japan and the West and the fear of Japan's subsumption was imagined, above all else, as a difference in language. With new forms of literary representation (primarily, realism and naturalism) and techniques of description came a particular anxiety about language and its powers. It is not as if objectifying, rationalist, even positivist, forms of discourse were unknown to pre-Meiji Japan. The intricacies of Confucian and Buddhist philosophy incorporated many of the problematics of representation that western science took to be uniquely its own. But these discourses had not been systematized into

13. See Katherine Trumpener's masterful work "The Voice of the Past: Anxieties of Cultural Transmission in Post-Enlightenment Europe."

14. The search to find a domain of pure ethnic Japaneseness merged with the nationalist project, culminating in the concerted effort to overcome the modern (kindai no chōkoku) in the 1930s and '40s.

the powerfully coherent practices, technologies, and apparatuses of western science, art, and literature. Both for state politics and for literature, the linkage of writing, speech, and external "reality" emerged as one of the core issues of the Meiji period, constituting what can be truly called a crisis in representation. This crisis appeared as a series of debates about the difference between speech and writing, truth and fiction, literature and its other in early-twentieth-century Japan. *The Tales of Tōno* enacted these differences within a hybrid text that would come to be read as a mysterious suturing of the fissures between forms of representation.

Meiji Japan's program of state-sponsored reform and standardization extended directly into the realm of language. Intense debates on the formation of a standard national language *(kokugo)* accompanied debates on the formation of the national polity. For the Japanese of pre-Meiji Japan spanned an awesome range of literary styles—many quite distant from the world of everyday speech—with a plethora of purely literary verb endings, formal conventions, Sinified compounds, and difficult Chinese characters. A hierarchy of delicate gradations separated different forms of literary Japanese: *kanbun,* written entirely in Chinese characters but read in Japanese word order; *sōrōbun,* the so-called epistolary style, with its mixed use of Chinese characters and the Japanese syllabary; *wabun,* a revival of classical Japanese style which used the syllabary as much as possible; and *wakankonkōbun,* primarily kanbun with an admixture of classical wabun style.[15] What might be thought of as the ideographic principle in Japanese writing determined that people speaking vastly different dialects could still read the same texts, because the Chinese characters used to write Japanese are graphic signs relatively independent of voicing: to those who were sufficiently literate their meaning was apparent to the eye.[16] This principle lent itself to the tendency, particularly apparent in the *kanbun* style, to create written worlds sharply distinct from everyday enunciations. Apart from certain forms of popular fiction, and sermons and tracts transcribed for the common listener, which faithfully reproduced colloquial dialogue, much literary writing, then, distanced itself

15. See Nanette Twine, "The Genbunitchi Movement: A Study of the Development of the Modern Colloquial Style in Japan," 4–43.

16. Of course Chinese characters—contrary to proposals by Derrida and others that they constitute a potentially nonlogocentric alternative to phonetic writing—*do* contain phonetic components that allow the reader to sound the character in many (if not all) instances. Nevertheless, ideographs allow the reader to read without voicing to a higher degree than phonetic writing normally does.

from the direct reproduction of everyday speech. One of the primary tasks of the new state was to codify the written language and align it more closely with the contours of the colloquial, an endeavor the Meiji ideologues grasped as essential for creating a unified national polity. In this the phonetic scripts of the West served as models of efficiency, ease, and transparency (one minister of education, Mori Arinori, even suggested replacing Japanese with English!).

But what was to serve as the standard colloquial language that the written language was to reflect? Hundreds of dialects existed throughout the country: spoken Japanese was fragmented and various and bore the marks of locale. The state sought to contain this diversity by establishing a standard spoken Japanese, then bringing written Japanese closer to this colloquial standard. In language as in everything else, the power of the center determined the result: the dominant dialect of Edo gradually became the standard spoken language in Japan.

Meiji writers and intellectuals, newly fascinated with European fiction, poetry, and thought, were also absorbed by this problematic. Their object was not, however, the creation of standard speech and colloquial writing as instruments for the formation of a unified polity; they instead were concerned with the representation of reality in fiction. At the heart of these debates, summarized by the expression *genbunitchi*, "the unification of spoken and written languages,"[17] lay the question of literary verisimilitude: How does one represent "reality" in prose fiction? The considerable difference between the spoken and written languages is the starting point for modern Japanese fiction.[18] Although Tokugawa-period writers had often reproduced dialogue faithfully, they still couched narrative passages in a formal written style. This split between dialogue and narrative was one of the first areas of debate among young Meiji writers influenced by western prose fiction. Many of these writers sought to increase verisimilitude in fiction not only by reproducing dialogue more faithfully, but by retaining the vernacular in narrative passages as well. By reproducing everyday speech accurately in literature, it was argued, greater realism could be attained in the novel. Thus, many of these writers became associated with what is now called Japanese naturalism (*shizenshugi*) in their efforts to transcribe reality directly through a technique they termed *shasei* or "sketching," a sketching from life. This visual metaphor sharply describes the attempt at an almost photographic repro-

---

17. See Twine, "The Genbunitchi Movement."
18. Masao Miyoshi, *Accomplices of Silence: The Modern Japanese Novel*, 3–37.

duction of external reality, including speech itself, within prose narratives.

The debates over genbunitchi started in the late 1880s and continued throughout the Meiji period. Yanagita Kunio, then a young bureaucrat in the Ministry of Agriculture and Commerce and a productive poet as well (and founder of the Ibsen Society of Japan), took an active part in these debates and was a friend of many of the leading luminaries of Meiji literary society: Kunikida Doppo, Shimazaki Tōson, Tayama Katai, Izumi Kyōka. Coming from a line of Shinto priests, Yanagita was involved with state agricultural policy, traveling to villages and talking to farmers about rural uplift. His rural background and continuing concern with nonurban Japan meshed with his literary preoccupations through a set of circumstances that brought the problematic of oral narratives to his attention.

In "'Sketching Technique' and the Essay" (Shasei to ronbun), an essay published in 1907, three years before the publication of *Tōno monogatari*, Yanagita came out in support of a colloquial literary style.[19] The essay is an examination of the premises of *shaseibun*, the "direct description" technique (again, modeled on "sketching") advocated by Masaoka Shiki. Yanagita states that previously he thought that literature was something constructed with difficult characters and crafted sentences, not something natural or easily achieved. But since the advent of the technique of direct description, literature is conceivable as something that "anyone can write," since it is written "just as one has seen and heard, without any artifice."

Direct description destroys the notion that literature, as a means to express thought, cannot attain its object unless it is difficult. To write essays, to write literature, merely cultivate your own sensibility, and write what you see, hear, think, and feel just as it is, Yanagita admonishes his readers. This admonition, clearly anticipates his famous prefatory remarks to *The Tales of Tōno*, where he would aver that he wrote down the tales "as they were related to me without adding a word or phrase."[20] Yanagita continues in his essay on "sketching technique":

19. Yanagita Kunio, "Shasei to ronbun." Extensive passages from this essay are analyzed in Iwamoto Yoshiteru, *Mō hitotsu no Tōno monogatari*, 105–6 (the title translates as *One More "Tales of Tōno"*). Iwamoto examines the contradictions surrounding the writing of *The Tales of Tōno*.

20. This is Ronald Morse's translation of the famous passage. Yanagita Kunio, *The Legends of Tōno*, 5.

Heretofore, if an essay [ronbun] were not written in literary style [bungotai], it did not seem like a real essay, and it was said that its power was diminished. But that is a narrow view caught up in convention. It is natural to assume that since writing is a method for expressing thought, the style of that writing should be as close as possible to thought. . . . Both speech and writing [gengo to bunshō] exist as means for expressing one's thoughts, *but at present writing is not as close to thought as speech is.* If speech is able to express eight thoughts out of ten, writing is only able to express six. . . . Just because colloquial style [genbunitchitai] is closer to speech than literary language is, I think it is able to express thought more intimately than literary language.[21]

In this essay we find a theory of language couched primarily in terms of expressing thoughts (shisō). Thoughts are placed on the same plane as externals, as realities to be expressed via language; embodied speech, placed in intimate proximity to thinking, naturally takes its place as the more desirable mode of expression. A writing that mimetically traces the contours of speech will thus accede as closely as possible to the transparent reflection of the object—whether conceptual, visual, or aural. And the writing that makes the closest approach to speech is the genbunitchi style.[22]

Yet something happened to Yanagita's theories of literature and representation between 1907 and 1909, a period in which he was begin-

21. Yanagita, "Shasei to ronbun," 31–32; emphasis added.
22. Speech here occupies (at least) two positions. One is externalized speech—speech-in-the-world, speech as natural object. People talk, one hears their voices; thus the imperative for writers to record speech as perfectly as possible, in the objective mode of the natural scientist. But speech also occupies a second position, one determined by what is *not* said. That is, speech is the sign of "thought," a vehicle for "expressing" thoughts that are silent. In this position speech indicates something other than itself, something more originary, that it carries forward. A relay is instituted, originating in thought, moving first to speech, then to written colloquial style, then to literary styles, which become, by degrees, more distant from speech. Because writing is viewed here as the graphic analog of speech, the dilemmas of "direct description" are more fraught when speech, as opposed to the visual, is the object. That is, it is assumed that a textual description of a scene in nature will of necessity be farther removed from that scene than is a faithful, "phonographic" textual transcription from the dialogue, for example, that it records: the former moves from the mode of the visual to that of language, whereas the latter moves only across forms of language, from the spoken to the written. But as the term *shasei* (direct description), with its provenance in art theory, indicates, similar debates took place about visual representation, where the continuum of arguments moved from the status of photography to western-style realism (effected by live "direct description") to the rediscovery of Japanese-style "impressionism."

ning to think more deeply about what he called the "invisible world."[23]
This shift marked a series of returns to the formal and figural powers
of a writing that no longer pretends to transcribe speech in all its transparency, a speech he now divested of its unique capacity to act as the
most intimate metaphor of inner thought. While it is not clear what
precisely prompted Yanagita's move to what has often been described
as an antinaturalist stance, his essays from this period suggest that
a growing familiarity with Japanese naturalist writings and his own
attempts to write in genbunitchi style convinced him of its impover-
ishment, as his 1909 essay "The Distance Between Speech and Writing"
(Genbun no kyori) reveals.[24] In this essay, Yanagita makes a full-blown
attempt to discredit the techniques of direct description; he now argues instead for the unabashed rhetoricity of texts. For Yanagita, this
rhetoricity consists in *not* giving all the facts, which paradoxically
gives the work more verisimilitude, more of an *appearance* of truth. He
upholds a form of withholding, a reticence within a rhetorical economy that by its constructed absences thus conveys the real all the more
sharply, rather than attempting an impossible transcription. Instead of
striving to record the brute fact itself, the work of literature should
"sound *as if* it were factual" *(jijitsu rashiku kikoeru).*[25]

Yanagita seeks to impress, to convey feelings, and to move the
reader, who has now emerged as the object of literary writing. He
insists on the paradoxical reversal of literary effects when writers attempt to imitate life too directly: the more one tries to imitate speech
and thus "reality," the more unnatural the result. Yet Yanagita goes
even further. Completely dismissing the claims of genbunitchi, he
states that on the contrary the spoken language should instead draw
closer to the written! No longer arguing that writing should draw
closer to oral discourse, Yanagita advocates an improvement, through
education, of spoken Japanese—an improvement that would then
bring spoken discourse closer to bungotai, or "literary style."[26] Litera-

23. Gerald Figal has discussed the intersection of the invisible world, the fantastic,
and questions of representation in his dissertation, "The Folk and the Fantastic in Japanese Modernity: Dialogues on Reason and the Imagination in Late Nineteenth and Early
Twentieth Century Japan."

24. Yanagita Kunio, "Genbun no kyori," 167–72.

25. Ibid., 169.

26. In this same essay, Yanagita asserts that spoken Japanese, unlike "western languages" with their clearly delineated progression of clauses and connecting articles, is
full of pauses, elisions, and repetitions. If one tries to write this confusion down, the
result is nothing but an incoherence that can hardly ascend to the literary. Therefore, it
is not possible to have a true *(shin)* genbunitchi at the present, he avers. To have a true

ture could only take its place as truly literary by keeping its distance from the chaos of Japanese speech, as well as from the pretensions of a photographic and phonographic reproduction of the world (he writes of Japanese naturalist writers as bad amateur photographers). The anticipation and containment of many of the concerns of grammatology—of the philosophical prerogatives of speech and its relationship to truth and the problem of writing as a subsidiary form of representation—are in striking evidence here, with an eventual reversal (the preeminence of writing over speech) that seems to double but of course historically differs in its discursive effects and location from Derrida's deconstructions proper. Nowhere does Yanagita question the distance between speech and writing that Derrida would put into undecidability. That Yanagita as the future founder of folklore studies would advocate not only a distancing from the (oral) object of nostalgia, but a disciplinary taming of vocal forms on the model of orderly writing reiterates the split in representation that the *Tales* would come to embody.

Near the end of this 1909 essay on the distance between speech and writing, Yanagita states, "I would like to try and write some sort of strong, solid book using literary style."[27] That book would not be a wholly fictional novel, but *The Tales of Tōno*, the one and only work of Yanagita's that is considered a masterpiece of prose literature, yet a work that Yanagita insisted was based on "present-day facts."[28] The book—the substitute for the novel he never wrote—would become, in time, the undisputed origin of the discipline of nativist ethnology, the science of the Japanese cultural unwritten.[29]

---

colloquial written language, *spoken* Japanese must move closer to the written (literary) language with its regularity and refinement. Education, starting with primary school, is the means to attain this remolding of spoken Japanese into a simulacrum of the (properly) written. What this passage also discloses is an example of the inexhaustible binarism situating the "Japanese" language in opposition to "western" ones—Japan versus the West. It is implied that in the West, because the spoken language is rational and coherent, truly objective, scientific, colloquial writing and literature is a possibility. This is an impossibility in Japan with the irrationalities of its spoken discourse, and thus literature should not aspire to reproduce the spoken as is, Yanagita insists. We can see the implications for a theory of Japanese cultural essentialism emerging from these reflections on speech and writing. Ibid., 170–172.

27. Ibid., 169.

28. Yanagita, *Tōno monogatari*, Yamato Shobō edition, 57.

29. Yanagita had already started his protoethnographic project between 1907 and 1909; the work of this period culminated in his self-published *Nochi no karikotoba no ki*, a collection of hunters' terminology from the mountains of the southern island of Kyūshū and his *Dialogues of the Stone Gods* (Ishigami mondō) published in 1909.

The Modern Uncanny

It was precisely during this period, starting in November 1908, that Yanagita began to listen to the stories of Sasaki Kizen in Tokyo. From his notebooks from 4 November, we find the following statement: "Sasaki is a person from Tōno in Iwate prefecture, and the mountain villages of that region are very interesting. I shall construct *Tōno monogatari* by writing down the stories of those villages just as they are." The entry for 5 November declares: "I shall write *Tōno monogatari*."[30] The very title of the collection—the rubric that would unify the real diversity of Sasaki's rumors, stories, and recollections under the name of narrative (monogatari)—had been fixed. The writing of the tales was not just a chance encounter with a rural storyteller (who was in fact a university student and an aspiring writer) and a casual, unmediated transcription of the facts, although Yanagita's preface to the *Tales* and other writings create that sense. It was instead a coherent, deliberate project that went through a series of mediations.

It is entirely clear that there is a theoretical trajectory that culminates in the writing of the text of the tales, and the question is why. Why does *The Tales of Tōno* provide the theoretical space Yanagita needed at that time? We know that Yanagita was deeply interested in what he called the "concealed" world—of ancestors, of the monstrous, of the unseen, of death. The concealed world indicates a discursive space articulated in peasant practice and by Tokugawa nativist thinkers; by the late Meiji period it doubly pointed to the marginalized obverse of Meiji civilization and enlightenment: the rural, the unwritten, the vanishing.[31] But was it sheerly Yanagita's interest in the concealed world—and his political concern to recover it—that attracted him to these tales that speak so obsessively of ghosts, deaths, and disappearances? That attraction would not account for the centrality of *these* stories in all their particularity. Nor would it fully account for their consolidation as the book that crystallized Yanagita's thoughts on representation and literature. I would argue that part of Yanagita's interest lay in that which resists representation—that which is left out of any attempt at naturalized direct description. Thinking about that which evades representation—voices, dialects, margins, ghosts,

30. Entries from Yanagita's diaries, cited by Kamata Hisako, "*Tōno monogatari* no shitazome."
31. See Harootunian, *Things Seen and Unseen*, on the discursive construction of the invisible and visible worlds in Tokugawa nativist thought.

deaths, monsters—was a way of thinking about literary writing: that writing which (for Yanagita) says more when it says less and thus writes what cannot be said.

Yet the *Tales* is not just a collection of fictional narratives. Yanagita takes great pains to distinguish his text from Tokugawa-period "ghost stories" *(kaidan)* or medieval "tale literature" *(setsuwa bungaku)*. The difference? These tales are "present-day facts."[32] Yanagita purports to be directly transmitting tales he has heard from the voice of another, who in many cases is describing his own experience or that of someone he knows or has heard of. The preface tells the tale, usurping as prefaces often do, the authority of the narrative remainder. Indeed, when contemporary critics cite *Tōno monogatari* as one of the masterpieces of modern Japanese literature, they usually linger on the preface as the most exquisite sample of prose in the entire text: the parasitic preface now significantly replaces the textual body. In that peerless preface Yanagita claims that "Kyōseki [Sasaki Kizen] is not a good storyteller" and that "I have been writing the stories down as they were told to me during his many evening visits since February 1909."[33] We know that Sasaki knew hundreds of tales and that he had been visiting Yanagita since at least November 1908. Japanese scholars have meticulously examined the various manuscripts of the text, and we thus know that Yanagita altered the tales enormously, rewriting and reworking them with great care.[34] Yet Yanagita also claims (in Ronald Morse's translation), "I have recorded the stories as they were related to me without adding a word or phrase."[35] This crucial line is, however, more complex in the original Japanese, implying that "I have written them down *as I have felt [kanjitaru mama]* without *neglecting [kagen sezu]* one word or phrase."[36] With the addition of feeling to the naturalist sensual relay of hearing and seeing—an addition that appeared in Yanagita's 1907 essay on direct description and writing—the author enables himself

32. Yanagita, *Legends of Tōno*, 8.

33. Ibid., 5. The original Japanese reads "mata ichiji ikku o mo kagen sezu kanjitaru mama o kakitari." Yanagita, *Tōno monogatari*, Yamato Shobō edition, 55.

34. See Oda Tomihime, "Shokōhon *Tōno monogatari* no mondai." Oda's article is a painstaking analysis of the various manuscripts, drafts, and proofs of the first edition of *Tōno monogatari*, an analysis that demonstrates how ornately crafted the finished text actually was.

35. Yanagita, *Legends of Tōno*, 5.

36. Iwamoto Yoshiteru interprets *kagen sezu* this way, although literally the phrase means "without adding or subtracting." If the nuance of "neglecting" is accepted, it points even more clearly to Yanagita's crafting of the text.

to assert an unmediated transmission from voice to writing in a preface that strangely announces the contradictions (if not untruths) of the conditions of its production.[37]

Under the guise of transparently recording someone else's tales Yanagita maintains the ruse of direct transcription and description, while his prose announces its distance from all worldly referents (exemplified by the voice itself). At the same time, the terseness and brevity of his literary writing mimics the simplicity of naturalistic writing; he writes as if he has abandoned all figuration. Yanagita had to repress a writing that was too close to voice in order to constitute the unwritten as the proper object of what would become nativist ethnology. Yet he dissimulated that repression by the appearance of a direct transcription, a dissimulation that allowed him to establish himself as the doubled amanuensis and author of the tales.

Yanagita is enabled in this doubled ruse by an expanded notion of fact (*jijitsu*, also translated as "truth" or "reality"), which by the 1909 essay had come to include an inner domain, a domain that in its complexity evokes an epistemological space akin to Freud's "psychical reality," whereby Freud renounced his insistence on the empirically real origins of (primal) fantasy in favor of the reality *effects* of fantasy. The empirical origin of fantasy was itself found to be ungraspable, sedimented within a structure of memory and retroactive desire not unlike the framework of nostalgia erected by distressed genres. It is not so much that the fact does not exist, nor is it the fact that only fantasy does. Rather, the two exist in an aporetic relationship to one another, ensuring that only across their difference can narratives of desire and loss find their way.[38]

What, then, constitutes these narratives of desire and loss? Yanagita's book (published at his own expense with only 350 copies) is a compendium of different sorts of narrative. Sequenced without comment or commentary, a description of the geography of Tōno lies next to a recounting of Tōno's feudal past as a castle town, which is juxtaposed to

37. The preface constitutes the most ethnographic moment of the text, including as it does Yanagita's description of his travels to Tōno (undertaken *after* he had heard the stories from Sasaki). A classic arrival scene is interspersed with a compelling description of a festival on the hillside, seen from a distance. The importance of distance—which is also central to Yanagita's theories of literature—in preserving the aura of the object recalls Walter Benjamin's writings on aura.

38. See Jean Laplanche and Jean-Bertrand Pontalis, "Fantasy and the Origins of Sexuality." Note also their discussion of "psychical reality" in Laplanche and Pontalis, *Language of Psycho-analysis*, 363, as well as Gerald Figal's discussion of Yanagita's analogue of "psychical reality" in his "The Folk and the Fantastic in Japanese Modernity."

a local legend about the origins of a bird's name, which comes before a recounting of a local ax murder, which precedes the report of a ghost sighting in the mountain, and so on. There are no titles to the tales, only numbers, in a serialization that indicates the possibility of infinite extension without resolution.[39] At the beginning of the text, however, is a table of themes (daimoku) that classify the tales: monkeys, bears, mountain gods, household gods, goddesses, apparitions, the destination of the dead, river sprites, folktales—some forty categories constructed along protoanthropological lines. Not, then, a collection like that of the Grimm brothers (although Yanagita is often compared to the Grimms), the tales rarely accede to the kind of narrative development and closure or moral finality of fairy tales. They instead strike the reader with their episodic, fragmented, even flattened qualities— qualities that Mishima spoke of as an "'unforeseen ghastliness,' like when someone starts to talk and then suddenly stops speaking."[40] What is that ghastliness of which Mishima speaks?

33. Should you go and spend a night in the mountains of Shiromi, you would see that late at night it becomes somewhat light. People who have gone to gather mushrooms in the autumn and stay overnight in the mountains have seen this strange phenomenon. The crash of a big tree falling or the voice of someone singing can sometimes be heard in the valley....

34. Along the mountainous area of Shiromi there is a spot called Hanare-mori (detached woods). One small area called the "chōja's grounds" has no one living there. There is a man who sometimes goes there to make charcoal. One night someone raised the straw mat that hung over the entrance to his hut and peeped in. It was a woman with long trailing hair. In this area it is not unusual to hear the screams of women late at night.

35. Mr. Sasaki's grandfather's younger brother went to the Shiromi mountains to gather mushrooms and spent the night there. He saw a woman run across in front of a large wooded area on the other side of the valley. It seemed as though she

39. That Yanagita was deeply invested in the process of collection itself is clear from his later mobilization of scores of disciples to gather data for his science and from the rivalry that later developed with Sasaki Kizen over the publication of additional folktales.

40. Mishima, "Tōno monogatari," 198.

were racing through the air. He heard her call out "just wait"
two times.[41]

In this sequence of three tales we can begin to grasp Mishima's "unforeseen ghastliness" (fusoku no kiki). Mishima, in the same paragraph,
had spoken of the preponderance of half-finished (shirikire tonbode),
fragmentary episodes in the Tales, that with their lack of completion
(kanketsu shinaide) can never give the reader a satisfactory explanation
(manzokuna setsumei).[42] He links, then, the unforeseen ghastliness of the
text with its fragmentation, its essential incompleteness, its insufficiency. (And is it a mere coincidence that a homonym of this fusoku—
"unforeseen"—translates as "insufficiency"?) Mishima puts the tales
and their abrupt ghastliness ("like when someone starts to talk and
then suddenly stops speaking") in the register of what we could call
uncanny lack. And within that register, we can begin to outline the
dimensions of these tales that articulate them within a certain psychical economy of the modern elaborated most clearly by Freud and then
Lacan. Freud's classic conception of the uncanny refers most broadly
to that class of objects or experiences—initially very familiar—that
return out of time and place to trouble the stable boundaries between
subject and object, interior and exterior: ghosts, automata, doubles,
animated objects, and all other species of the fantastic can fall into this
class. In Lacanian terms, the anxiety of the uncanny occurs when the
part of oneself that was repressed in order for one to be constituted as
a subject (what Lacan calls objet petit a, one's "self-being" before the
necessary split introduced by the mirror stage) returns in the guise of
a double (probably the most powerful instance of this return), a ghost,
or an untoward repetition. To constitute oneself as a subject which
can distinguish itself from an object requires an initial lack; the very
possibility of recognizing myself in a mirror, for example, implies that
I have already lost some essential, unmediated self-being. Many theorists of the uncanny or the fantastic (like Tzvetan Todorov) would argue that the uncanny lies in some uncertainty about what is real or
imaginary, self or other: it is an anxiety caused by an insufficiency of
knowledge not so different from the everyday anxiety that stems from
the constitutive lack of the subject. But Lacan and others argue differ-

41. Yanagita, Legends of Tōno, 31–32.
42. The sentence in Japanese goes like this: "Shikamo, kanketsu shinaide, shirikire
tonbode, nanra manzokuna setsumei mo ataerarenai danpenteki sōwa ga ōi kara, sore
wa mochiron katarite no sekinin de aru ga, sore ga kaette, iisashite futo kuchi o tsu-
gunda yōna fusoku no kiki o yobu." Mishima, "Tōno monogatari," 197–98.

ently. The uncanny effect does not arise from a simple lack of knowledge, for example; it instead erupts from an *excess* of what was supposed to be kept hidden and repressed (what Lacan would call the
"real," which comes about via lack). That is, there is an insufficiency
of "lack" and thus an excess of the "real" in his formulation: the repressed part of being that allows subjects to constitute themselves
("lack") has somehow reappeared in alienated form. Lack is now lacking, filled in, and it is the horror of being confronted with this excessive
and terrible certainty, a certainty based on lack, that accounts for the
anxiety of the uncanny.[43]

This story of the formation of the uncanny may seem to universalize;
but Freud was writing within a specific historical moment, although
he did not explicitly thematize it. That is, the Freudian uncanny (exemplified by his analysis of Hoffmann's tales, for example) emerges at a
distinct moment: that of modernity and industrial capitalism.[44] It is of
course not coincidental that Freud was theorizing the unconscious and
the notion of the uncanny at the same moment that Yanagita was reflecting on the invisible world, the question of the real and its relation
to language, and the specificity of the Japanese uncanny. It marks a
period when the uncanny becomes unplaceable, free-floating, part of
a new, larger national-cultural imaginary. And the modern uncanny
also arises as the double of the modern subject: the transcendental
subject as the very subject of the natural sciences (and by extension
literary naturalism) that Yanagita wanted both to retain and reject.

The ghostly and grisly nature of many of these tales has led Japanese
commentators (and there have been a great number of them) to note
how limited the inroads of "civilization and enlightenment" had been
in the Japanese outback. There is no doubt that Yanagita wanted to use
these tales as evidence, as it were, of a whole stratum of belief that
persisted despite the increasing sway of the modern rational, and that
this persistence had a connection with what was enduringly Japanese.
Yanagita and others later insisted that these stories pointed to a world

43. I am indebted to Mladen Dolar's explication of the modern uncanny (and the
distinction between Todorov's and Lacan's readings) in his "'I Shall Be with You on Your
Wedding-Night': Lacan and the Uncanny." Anxiety "is not produced by a lack or a loss
or an incertitude; it is not the anxiety of losing something (the firm support; one's bear-
ings, etc.). On the contrary, it is the anxiety of gaining something too much, of a too-
close presence of the object. What one loses with anxiety is precisely the loss—the loss
that made it possible to deal with a coherent reality . . . the lack lacks, and this brings
about the uncanny" (p. 13).

44. See the classic discussion of the uncanny in Sigmund Freud, "The 'Uncanny.'"

"before history," to an essential, timeless Japan resisting the incursions of western modernity.[45] But Yanagita equally considered the stories present-day facts (*genzai no jijitsu*), and it is the simultaneous insistence on timeless ahistoricity and factual contemporaneity that indicates precisely a structure of deferral and desire—of nostalgia—that shapes *Tōno monogatari*. The spectral status of an object that is both factually present and yet absent, that is dead but yet lives, describes, in a doubled fashion, the tales of *The Tales of Tōno*—tales that themselves speak, through the deferred writing of the memories of a storyteller, of things spectral. These present-day facts indicated not so much a resistance to the modern as the product of Japanese modernity, its uncanny counterpart. Of the 119 episodes recorded by Yanagita, 85 took place in the early Meiji period or happened to people who were actually living.[46] Fully 70 per cent are *Meiji* occurrences. Far from sheerly indicating a timeless Japan somehow preserved intact within the space of modernity, the tales became, through Yanagita's writing, modernity's uncanny other.

What Mishima finds insufficient, I think, is Yanagita's language. Nothing is finished, nothing is completed. These narratives are almost antinarratives; they are like stacks of lumber, Mishima says, one episode next to another, lacking the unifying gesture of the author—the authoritative subject who is supposed to know and complete the circuit of knowing for the reader. The information necessary to supply the lack is never given; instead, there is speech that is silenced, stories in abeyance that lead only to the next story. Thus, there is absolutely no logic of suspense in *The Tales of Tōno*. The reader does not wait to find out the resolution to a narrative conundrum, but rather to see if the terrible certainty of these "facts" could possibly be all there is.

What the privation of Yanagita's writing tries to convey are facts that exceed the expected—the darkness of night becomes light, screams occur where there should be none, women unexpectedly appear—all framed within a restricted rhetorical economy. The lack of explanation and of narrative suspense and resolution—written as if facts could speak for themselves—is at an extreme remove from the excessive, fantastic nature of the events narrativized. What is left out (and here one is certainly reminded of Yanagita's 1909 essay, where he insists that literary effects are increased by not telling all) evokes what goes be-

---

45. Kuwabara Takeo, "*Tōno monogatari* kara," 128. The original phrase is "rekishi izen no sekai."
46. Oda, "Shokōhon *Tōno monogatari* no mondai," 75.

yond representation. It is that disjunction alongside the events retold that is ghastly: there is no attempt to reinscribe the original lack that institutes the clear division between the real and the fantastic in the first place. If Yanagita had sustained the authorial role he displayed commenting on his collection in his preface, he would have placed it back into a normalized economy where lack plays its part, where the fantastic properly exists but can be accounted for. That normalization would describe the future trajectory of Japanese nativist ethnology, where its discursive construction as a bona fide discipline and the stabilization of its object as the "everyday folk" (jōmin) coincided with a diminution of its concern with the uncanny.[47]

Undecidable Authorities

Perhaps the most famous tale of the collection is number 22, one that Yanagita himself compared to Maeterlinck's "The Intruder":

> 22.   When the great grandmother of Mr. Sasaki died of old age the relatives assembled to put her into her coffin. . . . The daughter of the dead woman, who was insane and had been cut off from the family, was also in the group. Since it was the custom of the area to consider it taboo to let the fire die out during the period of mourning, the grandmother and the mother sat up alone on both sides of the large hearth. The mother put the charcoal basket beside her and from time to time added charcoal to the fire. Suddenly, hearing the sound of footsteps in the direction of the back door, she looked up and saw it was the old woman who had died. She recognized how the bottom of the old woman's kimono, which dragged because she bent down a lot, was pulled up as usual into a triangle and sewed in front. Other things were also the same, and she even recognized the striped kimono cloth. Just as she cried "Oh!" the old woman passed by the hearth where the two women sat and brushed the charcoal basket with the bottom of her kimono. The round basket wobbled as it went round and round. The mother who was a strong-nerved person, turned and watched where she went. Just as the old woman drew close to the parlor where the relatives were

47. Many commentators have noted how Yanagita shifted from his earlier concern with *yamabito* (mountain men), wanderers, and the fantastic in various forms, to a central concern with the "everyday folk" (jōmin) and what was common to all Japanese, particularly Japanese peasants. Figal has discussed this shift across a number of registers in his "From *tengu* to *senzo:* The Hidden World in the Writing of Yanagita Kunio."

asleep, the shrill voice of the mad woman screamed out, "Here comes granny!" The others were awakened by the voice and it is said they were all shocked.[48]

Mishima was a great admirer of this tale, particularly of the moment when the old woman brushes the charcoal basket and sends it spinning: "When the scuttle spins, all efforts to sustain reality [genjitsu] are over."[49] The charcoal basket becomes, in that punctual instance, the point of division between the revealed world and the concealed, a wobbly mediator between life and death. But rather than sheerly marking their division, that detail allows the troubling of the separation, for what is truly uncanny is not the transgression of a difference which then remains unproblematically in place after the occurrence, but the calling into question of the difference itself. Yanagita writes of the shock of the uncanny in a language that, in its restraint and narrative paucity, implies that there is no shock. That difference is once again left undecidable within the narrative economy of the tales.

The restrained writing by which Yanagita conveys the ghastliness of Tōno always maintains a distance from its immediate origins: the local storyteller and his voice, a voice couched in the dialect of the Tōno region. Although Yanagita makes no mention of dialect in the preface, a conversation that Yanagita had with Itō Keiichirō in 1953, discloses that dialect was indeed an issue. When Itō asked how he had come to know Sasaki, Yanagita responded:

> Mizuno Yōshū, who had written a novel, told me, "There's a really unusual person. He knows much about folktales and all sorts of things. I'll bring him to meet you." I wanted to meet him, so he introduced us. I think he had just left Waseda University. However, although we talked about various things, his dialect was really strong, and I just couldn't understand him ["iroiro hanasu ga, nantoshitemo namari ga hidokute kotoba ga tsūjinai"]. I gradually got to the point where I could understand him. . . . I was really amazed at the number of stories he knew. They caused a sort of abnormal state of mind [ijō shinri] to arise.[50]

Yanagita's reminiscence discloses what should be taken for granted: that a regional storyteller would speak in his or her region's dialect. There were a large number of dialects in premodern and Meiji Japan; many of these survive today but have gradually been supplanted by a

48. Yanagita, *Legends of Tōno*, 25–26.
49. Mishima Yukio, *Shōsetsu to wa nanika*, 133.
50. "Minzokugaku to Iwate: shinshun seidan."

standardized Japanese. Through a uniform national educational curriculum and the influence of the mass media, most people can now speak standard Japanese and almost everyone understands it.

Yanagita not only wrote down the unwritten and changed the vernacular to the literary, but also produced a *dialectal* vernacular as the standard literary. The dialect of Tōno was not just a variation on the Japanese that Yanagita spoke. It was an unintelligible deviation, a deviation Yanagita thus had to make intelligible—and this was a lengthy and painful process (as he indicates in this same interview), not a transparent and immediate transcription. Yanagita downplayed the importance of Sasaki in his preface to *The Tales of Tōno* by asserting that he was not a good storyteller ("Kyōseki-kun wa hanashi jōzu niwa arazaredomo").[51] What Yanagita meant by this assertion is not at all clear, for he stated in the later discussion with Itō that he was truly surprised at the number of stories Sasaki knew. Could it be that Yanagita meant that the storyteller was difficult to understand? Or, did he mean that his stories were episodic, fragmented, and therefore did not work as compelling narratives? Probably both Sasaki's dialect and the content of the tales themselves entered into Yanagita's cryptic devaluation of his informant. In any case, Sasaki's unskillful tales provided precisely the lack that Yanagita—as author and ethnographer—would supplement with his own literary skills. The spoken narratives of the "native"—both unintelligible and unskillful—provided the raw materials for Yanagita's elegant written Japanese and expressive skills.

But Yanagita's relationship with the storyteller did not end with the first publication of the *Tales*. Sasaki started publishing his own versions and variants of legends and lore from Tōno. For example, in April 1912, he published thirty-six stories under the title "Tōno zakki" in *Jinruigaku zasshi*; in 1918 and 1919 he published others in the journal *Kyōdo kenkyū*.[52] In 1931, he published a collection of *mukashi banashi*, bona fide folktales (as opposed to legends or hearsay), under the title *Kiki mimi zōshi*.[53] It seems that Yanagita had an ambivalent regard for Sasaki, although later scholars view him as a pioneer in the collection and transcription of folktales. For example, on the occasion of the reprinting of *Tōno monogatari* in 1935, Yanagita wrote a new set of "prefatory remarks" (Saihan oboegaki). In these remarks Yanagita asserts that he had asked Sasaki for more materials and Sasaki had obliged

51. Yanagita, *Tōno monogatari*, Yamato Shobō edition, 55.
52. "Sasaki Kizen zenchosaku mokuroku," in Sasaki, *Tōno no zashikiwarashi to oshirasama*, 5–6.
53. Ibid., 17.

with a large number of stories in manuscript form. Yet Yanagita complains that there were so many stories, in such a disorganized state, that he had a difficult time sorting them and correcting them for mistakes. While he was in the midst of these efforts, Sasaki published *Kiki mimi zōshi*. Yanagita now claimed that he had originally planned to include several of these folktales in a supplement (entitled "Tōno shūi") to the second edition of *Tōno monogatari*, but that Sasaki had scooped him. There is a tone of almost petulant disappointment in Yanagita's writing, as if the local storyteller had somehow stolen his own stories from Yanagita.[54]

Sasaki's life had a tragic denouement. Because of his time in Tokyo and his association with Yanagita, he was elected head of the village of Tsuchibuchi and also of a farmers' cooperative. The cooperative borrowed money which they could not pay back, and the responsibility was pushed onto Sasaki. He was forced to sell everything he owned, yet the money still was not adequate. He then wanted to move to Tokyo, appealing to Yanagita for help, but Yanagita strongly discouraged him. He spent the remaining years of his life futilely trying to pay back his debts by serializing novels and publishing folktales, dying in poverty and distress in 1933 at the age of forty-eight.[55] His struggle to attain recognition as a folklorist in his own right (a recognition that has been given him posthumously) conflicted with Yanagita's desires to maintain control over the tales, to retain ethnographic authority. Sasaki had to remain the native informant, the storyteller, for nativist ethnology to establish itself.

If the specificities of Sasaki as storyteller were repressed, even Tokyo-based everyday speech was passed over in favor of literary locutions. Only in moments of direct quotation (like "Here comes granny!" *[Obāsan ga kita!]* in tale number 22) do spoken voices intrude. Throughout, Yanagita's elegant, terse, "old-fashioned" literary constructions displace themselves from originary voices, voices that remain suspended through a writing that asserts yet obscures its own rhetoricity.

The origins of the tales almost always rest in the perceptual experience of one of Tōno's inhabitants; chains of hearsay culminate in narrative disclosures that, located within Sasaki's memory and his stories, speak the truth of Tōno. Tale number 22 defers the source of authority by saying "it is said," as do many other episodes. Yet the shifting of the ostensible narrator of the episodes continually leaves the authorial

54. Yanagita, "Saihan oboegaki" (Notes on the Second Edition), 59–60.
55. Iwamoto, *Mō hitotsu no Tōno monogatari*, 139–49.

position in question. For example, tale number 87 begins in the first person:

> **87.** I have forgotten the person's name, but he was the master of a wealthy family in the town of Tōno. He was seriously ill and on the brink of death, when one day he suddenly visited his family temple. The priest entertained him courteously and served tea. They chatted about things and then the priest, somewhat suspicious when the man was about to leave, sent his younger disciple to follow him. The man went out the gate and headed in the direction of home. Then he went around a corner in the town and disappeared. There were also other people who met him on that street and he greeted everyone as politely as ever.
>
> He died that night and, of course, was in no condition to be going out at that time. Later at the temple, the priest checked the spot where the tea cup was, to see if the tea had been drunk or not. He found that the tea had all been poured into the crack between the straw mats.[56]

Who has forgotten the name? If it is Yanagita, why has he inserted that question (particularly since Yanagita concealed the actual names of people that Sasaki told him, in good anthropological fashion)?[57] We assume that it is Sasaki, and that Yanagita has chosen to position his informant as the speaker/narrator. In this tale of a ghostly double who classically prefigures his own death, Sasaki stands in for the authorial voice of the folklorist. Indeed, Sasaki's attempts to become the double of the famed folklorist Yanagita is the stuff of Japanese intellectual drama.[58] In tale number 22, however, Yanagita is the speaker, as he opens by saying, "When the great grandmother of Mr. Sasaki died . . ."

By shifting the narrator's position, relaying the events within chains of deferred experience, and flattening the difference between speakers, Yanagita obscures the ultimate source of authorship, as the source becomes repeatedly displaced through hearsay. Yet the fact that most of the tales can be traced to an experiencing subject—one who inevitably has experienced something untoward—gives Yanagita's tales the aura of uncanny certainty. The displacement of narrators and the obvious (yet not too obvious) crafting of the tales marks them as literary; the naming and placing of origins and the insistence on tracing back

56. Yanagita, *Legends of Tōno*, 60.

57. Oda, "Shokōhon *Tōno monogatari* no mondai," 76.

58. The tragedy of their relationship is analyzed in Iwamoto, *Mō hitotsu no Tōno monogatari*, and also in a roundtable discussion among Nakazawa Shin'ichi, Kosaka Shūhei, and Kasai Kiyoshi, entitled "Ima 'Nihon' to wa," in Kosaka, *Nyū Japanorojii*, 18–76.

through remembered voices to improbable events claimed to be true, marks the text as (proto-) ethnographic. Yet that difference—to the extent that Yanagita was clearly aware of it—is allowed to remain in haunting undecidability. What is strange, then, is the way different orders of reality are juxtaposed and allowed to occupy the same textual and epistemological space; no hierarchy is imposed on these orders, no final demarcation is made between the factual and the fictional, the real and the fantastic. The fact that an experience is said to have occurred and the implausibility of the experience itself are placed on the same plane, enfolded within a larger notion of psychical reality.

An Originary Discipline

The Tales of Tōno is thus a peculiar hybrid, and it conformed to no law of genre in 1910. Although only 350 copies were printed, Yanagita's connections with the Japanese literary world ensured that prominent Meiji authors read and reviewed it. When it was first published, many readers did not know what to make of it: it seemed to fit most comfortably within the varied collections of "strange tales." Its status as literature (bungaku) was not even quite assured, and there was little or no conception of its status as a work of folklore.[59]

The novelist Tayama Katai—who is often credited with introducing the word "naturalism" into Japanese—stated:

> While Kunio maintains that I, a naturalist writer, cannot understand his feelings and am not really qualified to evaluate his work, I find the work infused with an extravagance of affected rusticity. I remain unmoved. His use of on-site observation to create the background in an essay is significant. The work's impressionistic and artistic qualities, however, derive more from the treatment of the data than the actual content.[60]

Another famous author and friend, Shimazaki Tōson (also an exponent of naturalism), wrote:

> That work [Tōno monogatari] consists in its entirety of a collection of legends [densetsu] from a remote region. As the author states in his preface, after having heard these stories and seen

59. Ōtō Tokihiko writes that most people just thought it was an unusual book with strange stories in it and were primarily attracted to it because of the beautiful writing. Ōtō, "Kaisetsu" (Commentary) to *Tōno monogatari*, Kadokawa bunko edition, 206.

60. Translated by Ronald Morse and cited in Morse, "Yanagita Kunio and the Modern Japanese Consciousness," 23–24.

their place of origin, he felt compelled to convey them to others, so fascinating where the realities contained therein. The concise and honest style of the stories—as well as the critical preface and thematic arrangement of the tales—immediately attracted me. The copy that Yanagita presented to me is here before me now, and I have just finished reading it. . . . After reading these kinds of story, I feel that I have come to know something, however faintly, about the wonder [kyōi] and terror [kyōfū] found within the midst of rural life [rūraru raifu]. These stories of mountain gods, goddesses, and strange men and women who live in the mountains—as well as stories of mysterious yet actual occurrences, like the tale that reminded Yanagita of Maeterlinck's "The Intruder"—have made me feel this way. . . .

Even though this work was written out of a scholarly interest in ethnic development [minzoku hattatsu], I still felt as if I could hear something like the distant, distant voices of the fields in this work. . . . I would like to know more about the place where these stories were born and passed down. The reason I would like to know more is due, I think, to the fact that the author of Tōno monogatari, more than being just a collector of strange tales or a scholar of ethnic psychology, is a traveler with acute powers of perception. As far as I know, there are few travelers like Yanagita, and there are even fewer travelers with Yanagita's powers of observation.[61]

Shimazaki astutely points out the "ethnic" dimension of Yanagita's tales, yet in 1910, there was no clear perception of folklore studies as a pursuit. Instead, the discipline of ethnology was in its early stages of formation, preceded by the founding of ethnological societies and journals. Shimazaki may have been one of the few critics to point out this dimension of Tōno monogatari, a dimension to which Yanagita himself does not clearly allude. Even so, the first person to recognize clearly the value of Tōno monogatari as folklore—not literature—was in fact a Chinese author and scholar of Japanese literature, Chou Tso-jēn (Shūsakujin in Japanese).[62] In 1933, twenty-three years after Yanagita had published the tales, Chou Tso-jēn "discovered" the text, praising its unequaled value for folklore studies.[63]

The preceding ten years had witnessed the establishment of nativist

61. Shimazaki Tōson, "Nochi no Shinkatamachi yori," 200–201.
62. Chou Tso-jēn (1885–1966) was a professor at Peking University and leader of the "new literature movement." He was also a translator and pioneer in the study of children's literature and tales. Kōjien, 2d ed., s.v. "Shūsakujin."
63. Ōtō, "Kaisetsu," 201.

ethnology as a discipline. In 1925, Yanagita founded the journal *Min-zoku*, which marked the beginning of all anthropological studies in Japan, according to the anthropologist Aruga Kizaemon.[64] Not until the 1930s, however, did nativist ethnology attain widespread credibility. *The Tales of Tōno* only became a recognized classic upon its republication in an expanded edition in 1935. Not coincidentally, 1935 marked in many ways the apogee of nativist ethnology as a discipline. It was the year of Yanagita's *kanreki* (sixtieth birthday celebration, always a landmark event in Japanese society); the journal *Minkan denshō* (Oral Tradition) was formed, and nativist ethnology as a discipline was finally established on a national scale.[65]

It is significant that the republication of the *Tales* coincided with the moment of nativist ethnology's disciplinary consolidation and the moment of high fascism and militarism in the Japanese empire. It is possible to see the entire trajectory of nativist ethnology, with its emphases on the unwritten, the marginal, and the impoverished, as a species of resistance to elite, documentary, modernist scholarship, and as such as providing an alternative to state-sponsored mainstream scholarship. Yet to the extent that it became constituted as the study of what was uniquely Japanese, that is, outside the corruptions of western modernity, Yanagita and his folklore studies (for there was no doubt it was his discipline) contributed to the chauvinism and cultural nationalism of the wartime period.[66]

It was with its expanded republication in 1935 that *The Tales of Tōno* emerged as the founding text of nativist ethnology. It finally achieved the complex acclaim that did not—could not—greet it on its initial publication. Only the passage of twenty-five years and the construction of a discipline allowed the retroactive recognition of the strange birth that the text commemorated. As Yanagita himself remarked in his comments to the second edition:

> In fact, when *Tōno monogatari* first came out, the public still had no knowledge of these matters, and it appears they judged the attitude of a "certain person" who was attempting to problematize them as that of a dilettante or curiosity seeker. But

64. Yoneyama Toshinao, "Yanagita and His Work," 41.
65. Kurata Hisako, "Nenpyō" (Chronology), 221.
66. Many critics have noted the critical dimension of Yanagita's work, and it is important to realize the utopian possibilities contained in his scholarship. See, for example, J. Victor Koschmann's penetrating essay "Folklore Studies and the Conservative Anti-Establishment in Modern Japan," in which he disentangles the immensely complex ideological weave of Yanagita's folklorism to reveal its simultaneously conservative and antiestablishment implications.

today, times have completely changed. These kinds of experience have now been repeated any number of times, and they
have come to be recognized as the important object of one field
of scholarly endeavor.[67]

The Tales of Tōno must be grasped as two publications across which
the birth of nativist ethnology took place. The import of the first appearance could not be known except as it occurred again. Only
through repetition could the text emerge as originary. The second edition contained a supplement to the first, a new collection of tales as-
sembled with the help of Sasaki Kizen: these were primarily bona fide
"folktales" and were *now* written in colloquial style. It is telling that
one of the most influential commentators on the Tales after its celebrated second birth complained about the supplement: "The tales of
the newly expanded second part are written in colloquial language,
but for me, the nostalgic flavor of the original edition's tales, left as
they are in straightforward literary style, is stronger."[68]

Nostalgia can only emerge across a temporal lag, and the nostalgic
flavor of a text is more potent the further it is from the ostensible source
and goal of desire. The Tales and its readings encode not only that
desire for a regressing world of orality (that in any case is more plea-
surably known through its deadly entextualization), but expose the
nostalgia of a discipline for its own origin: an origin, that in several
senses, remains dislocated from itself. To the extent that the Tales remains the obsessively re-marked "memorial marker of the birth of Japanese folklore studies" (Nihon minzokugaku no hasshō no kinentō) it becomes precisely that: a *memorial* marker, a monument to an absence,
to a loss that must be perpetually recovered through a discipline that
ensures the disappearance of its origins as it constructs them.

To return once more to Mishima, he reads the text as mysterious
(fushigina), not only because of the deaths it writes, but because it is
"data as it is, but at the same time it is literature—and that's what's
mysterious about this work."[69] The tales speak of ghastly matters that
can never properly become the objects of a discipline as such, because

67. Yanagita, "Saihan oboegaki," 60–61.
68. Kuwabara, "Tōno monogatari kara," 124.
69. Mishima, in working through the implications of Tōno monogatari's doubled status,
said that "to the extent that something is factual, it's the object of scholarship" ("fuakuto
de aru kagiri de wa, gakumon no taishō de aru"). Of course, part of Mishima's point is
that the strangeness of the tales, their very implausibility, attains the status of factuality
in Yanagita's rendering—the sheer factuality of language, if nothing else: "These data,
from one perspective, are nothing at all other than language" ("korera no genzairyō wa,
ichimen kara mireba, kotoba igai no nanimono demo nai"). Ibid., 198.

they cannot be situated in an objective relation to positive knowledge. Yet because literature intervenes as the sign of that discursive space where anything is possible, those deaths—already uncannily situated within the narratives—both thematize and exemplify an impossible knowledge, a knowledge enabled by the suspension of literature and science: nativist ethnology itself.[70]

Years later, Yanagita himself spoke of these matters:

> Hori Ichirō: How did you come to write *Tōno monogatari?*
> Yanagita: That was through Mizuno Yōshū, who died recently. He was a strange kind of poet, who had an interest in the village life of old. When we were talking about . . . our native places, the name of his friend Sasaki Kizen came up. Sasaki was, in fact, a naive, good person. He was stubborn about some things. He was a person who would oppose what we said—if we thought something was not so, he would believe it was, and would get angry. *It's probably correct to say that Tōno monogatari is mostly a literary work.*
> Hori: But *Tōno monogatari* has been very influential, hasn't it.
> Yanagita: That's true. *The special feature of that work is that there's absolutely no attempt at interpretation of or commenting upon its contents.* This seems to have appealed to European scholars. In England there was talk at one time of having it translated into English.
> Hori: That lack of interpretation was probably something that was different from the scholarly attitudes that had existed until then.
> Yanagita: I think that stance [taken in the writing of *Tōno monogatari*] was the same as the stance of the natural sciences or biological sciences.[71]

Yanagita first offers the opinion that the *Tales* is "mostly a literary work," then maintains that it involved no "interpretation" whatsoever, and finally states that its stance was scientific. One wonders at the serenity of his assertions, a serenity that has not been shared by a generation of Japanese critics struck by what they see as a founding con-

70. "What is heralded and refused under the name of literature cannot be identified with any other discourse. It will never be scientific, philosophical, conversational. But if it did not open onto all these discourses, if it did not open onto any of those discourses, it would not be literature either. There is no literature without a *suspended* relation to meaning and reference. . . . In its suspended condition literature can only exceed itself." Jacques Derrida, "'This Strange Institution Called Literature': An Interview with Jacques Derrida," 47–48.

71. Hori Ichirō and Yanagita Kunio, "Watashi no ayunde kita michi," 103–4; emphasis added.

tradiction in Yanagita's discipline. Yet without engaging the apparitions of *The Tales of Tōno* itself, no criticism can confront that discipline's
constitutive yet uncanny commingling of literature and science. Nativist ethnology, institutionally born out of the haunted undecidability of
literature and documentary ethnography, is devoted to preserving the
distinctiveness of the enduring Japanese customary, of cultural transmission itself. Yet the elaborate monstrosity of its textual origin—a
monstrosity that really consists of nothing more than the impossibility
of finally demarcating literature from science, the figural from the literal, the fantastic from the factual—returns to trouble contemporary
attempts to fix those demarcations. As a writing perpetually *between*
literature and documentary science, nativist ethnology must repeat the
uncanny gestures of its origin, insisting on a transmission without remainder from a beginning that can only ever be—finally—memorialized. And yet it is the memorialized status of *The Tales of Tōno* that has
led to its repeated reinscription in yet another set of tales. It is to the
site, then, of this originary reinscription that the next chapter moves.

CHAPTER FOUR

Narrative Returns, Uncanny Topographies

*T*he *Tales of Tōno* anticipated a newly imagined Japanese subject, a subject seemingly immersed in the immediacy of spoken language, subsisting outside the depredations of print culture and the technologies of modernity. Yet that subject only achieved discursive perdurability by means of the modern ghastliness of the writing that situated it. In its writing of the unwritten, the *Tales* has proved, in turn, to be utterly appropriate for its own succession of rewritings. As Iwamoto Yoshiteru's scrutiny of the original manuscripts has shown, the *Tales* is a veritable palimpsest, a layering of authors and authorial positions, narrative voices, and linguistic registers. If any and every text weaves a tissue of allusions, elusive voicings, and disappearing storytellers—that is, if it is inevitably and properly intertextual—then the *Tales* is a particularly resonant instance of that process in modern Japan. It has exercised, as a text and along with its canonical author, an ongoing fascination for Japanese, as its ghostliness has become the origin for a nativist ethnology devoted to securing Japanese national-cultural identities. And it has become an originary node for further interpretive exercises around the theme of Japaneseness itself. It is no wonder that Iwamoto's uncovering of the multiple versions of the *Tales* is entitled *Mō hitotsu Tōno monogatari* (One More "Tales of Tōno," or perhaps, Another "Tales of Tōno"). And there are any number of other *Tōno monogatari*, including one by the indefatigable writer Inoue Hisashi.[1] If one theme cuts through the literary productions of Inoue, it is

---

1. One of the best-known ethnographic studies of the area, co-authored by Katō Hidetoshi and Yoneyama Toshinao, is *Kitakami no bunka: shin Tōno monogatari* (The Culture of

the multiplicity and richness of language (which is always the Japanese language, crossed by dialects as it may be). Inoue's *Shinshaku: Tōno monogatari* (The "Tales of Tōno": A New Interpretation) gives itself over to a rewriting of (yet) another set of tales, to yet other positions in the sequence of deferred and delayed storytelling in which Yanagita was located. It does so by attempting to reinsert the lost enunciations of the oral everyday into the frame of Yanagita's tales. Inoue recognizes the erasure of the sonic specificity and nonstandard accents of the Tōno region in Yanagita's publication, and through parody, repetition, and reinterpretation *(shinshaku)* he works to situate those accents in the particularities of place: that place called Tōno. The narrator of Inoue's *Tales* visits a "native" storyteller in his hovel in the mountains near Tōno, a reversal of the situation of the original *Tales,* in which Sasaki told his stories in Yanagita's Tokyo house. Inoue relocates the place of narration, returning the scene of writing itself back to the local.[2]

His book (novel? ethnography? story?) opens by stating, "Yanagita Kunio started *The Tales of Tōno* like this," and quoting the famous opening lines of the preface, complete with Meiji-era locutions and formalities. Then: "Following Yanagita Kunio, I [he uses the informal masculine pronoun *boku* to refer to himself] think I'll also begin *Shinshaku: Tōno monogatari* with an opening preface like the following . . ."[3] This preface repeats Yanagita's lines, but with parodic inversions. Yanagita's disingenuous statement that "Kyoseki is not a good storyteller but he is honest and sincere, and I have recorded the stories as they were related to me without adding a word or phrase"—that crucial, telling line—is here transformed: "Old man Ibuse is a good storyteller, but there are a lot of places which reek of his tricks—and since I also tend to extravagance, there's not a reliable word or phrase."[4] The marks of good storytelling lead away from ethnographic truth, and the exaggerations of the ethnographer here playfully compound the unreliability always implied by the "good" teller of tales.

---

the Kitakami Region: A New "Tales of Tōno"). Again, Tōno can only be approached through a rediscovery and an ever-new reinscription of Yanagita's tales.

2. This is not unlike many recent attempts in anthropology to represent voices in specific relation to place. See, for example, the essays in *Cultural Anthropology* 3, no. 1 (1988), particularly Arjun Appadurai, "Introduction: Place and Voice in Anthropological Theory," and James Fernandez, "Andalusia on Our Minds: Two Contrasting Places in Spain as Seen in a Vernacular Poetic Duel of the Late Nineteenth Century."

3. Inoue Hisashi, *Shinshaku Tōno monogatari,* 8.

4. Ibid. In Japanese, "Ibuse rōjin wa hanashi jōzu da ga, zuibun inchiki kusai tokoro ga ari, boku mo mata tashō no kodai kuse ga aru node, ichiji ikku ate ni naranu koto bakari aru."

Tōno names a storied site which operates as a provocation for story-telling, and thence for written relays of reinterpretation. It names a place where voice and place, narrative and "tradition" *should* cohere, against all the disruptions of modernity. Yet, by virtue of that "should," Tōno stands for modernity's virtual disappointments. Those disap-pointments textually constitute *Tōno monogatari;* Tōno subsists as a national-cultural sign of modernity's losses, and a site for coming to terms with those losses. Tōno today is hard-pressed to live up to the textual mysteries embodied in the *Tales,* mysteries integral to its posi-tion as a marker for the marginalized (yet essential) residue of Ja-pan's modernity.

In this chapter I work across this relay of texts and stories, bringing together the concerns of chapter 2—national-cultural loss and the theme of the journey—and those of chapter 3, the originary fantasies circulating around Tōno: a further elaboration of the interpretive pro-cess begun by Yanagita, a returning "home" of the exegetical energies that first turned Tōno into a sign of the folkloric marginal, then gradu-ally into the canonical representative of Japanese "tradition."[5] The city of Tōno in the 1960s began actively reappropriating Yanagita's narra-tives, turning its romanticized history of darkness and primitivity into a civic asset. In these efforts, Tōno resembled other cities attempting to reclaim power from the center, to formulate local identities to counter those of the metropoles. Tōno's civic establishment depicted itself—through the *Tales*—not only as the undisputed home of nativist ethnology, but also the "homeland of folktales" *(minwa no furusato)* and even the "homeland of Japan" *(Nihon no furusato).* This reinscription of the imagery of origin and return—of "home"—by a site which repre-sented the ghostly aftereffects of modernity is the particular, and par-ticularly telling, process that I want to trace here.

Tōno's efforts coincided with the reevaluation of essential folk iden-tities that occurred in the wake of Japan's period of high economic growth from 1965 to 1975, a period which destroyed many of the ves-tiges of an older Japan (the parallel with the Meiji period, in which Yanagita wrote, is instructive). Along with rapid growth came an accel-erating destruction of both the environment and older lifeways, as the increasing concentration of power, people, and capital in the cities left many rural areas depopulated. Urban Japanese recognized this de-struction, as the tourist industry and mass media promised access to a vanishing (yet not vanished) Japan. All the long-codified elements of

---

5. I lived in Tōno at different times between 1983 and 1985.

landscape—castles, mountains, temples, views—took on added semiotic weight through their new importance as guarantees of a past that still cohered. Tōno had already become a singular locus of the "folk" after the republication of *Tōno monogatari* in the 1930s. It is not insignificant that this period also saw rising militarism and fascism; the establishment of elaborate politico-philosophical discourses aimed at "overcoming the modern" (*kindai no chōkoku*) and equally elaborate (and increasingly aggressive) efforts to reposition Japan at the apex of a pan-Asian empire. The 1970s were just distant enough from the intense modernist rejection of cultural essentialism that characterized the early postwar period to witness yet another resurgence of interest in the question of the Japanese folk (minzoku), folklore (minzokugaku), and place. Tōno emerged again as a site that could represent diffuse cultural longings, yet the scale of the 1970s resurgence (tied as it was to the mass media and an entire postwar history) far exceeded that of the prewar one.[6]

Urban, nationally disseminated interest in recovering rural origins was matched by local communities' reappraisals of their pasts. Some communities found in those pasts the cultural capital needed to boost both civic pride and outside investment.[7] Tōno as civic entity began to mobilize as the newly refurbished birthplace of Japanese nativist ethnology, experiencing a veritable boom as Japanese of all ages rediscovered *The Tales of Tōno* and started visiting the area in increasing numbers in the 1960s. Tōno thus found itself in a peculiar position during the period of the Discover Japan campaign; through the complex history of the reception of *Tōno monogatari*, it could both represent origins available for nostalgic recuperation *and* appeal to curiosity about the exotic, unknown, and strange aspects of yet another Japan. Not only could visitors surround themselves with archetypical views of mountain-ringed rice paddies, thatched roofs, waterwheels, packhorses, and decaying forest shrines. They could also encounter the quaintly nonstandard in Tōno's incomprehensible local dialect; fantasize about the dangerous world of Tōno's ghosts, mountain men, and *kappa* (a kind of water sprite, a staple of folktales throughout Japan);

6. David E. Whisnat has written a compelling history of the interlocked economic exploitation of Appalachian regions and the varied attempts by outsiders to salvage, recuperate, or reconstruct the "culture" of the people there. He focuses particularly on the period before World War II. Whisnat, *All That is Native and Fine: The Politics of Culture in an American Region*.

7. See, again, Kelly, "Japanese No-Noh," on the transformation of an "archaic" performance stream.

and be soothed by Tōno's warmth and rusticity, while yet retaining the uneasy knowledge of its dark past. Although many civic entities in Japan now promote themselves as official furusato of everything from pottery to airplanes, few have expanded this notion to incorporate the range of interpretations that Tōno has—a range that is possible because the associations that "Tōno" subsumes are so densely overdetermined. Tōno has become not only the (overdetermined) textual homeland of nativist ethnology and its practitioners, but a vanishing point of return for all Japanese.

The city responded to its new national prominence with a series of programs to boost community spirit, productivity, and tourist appeal, using Tōno monogatari as its urtext. These efforts culminated in the formulation of a comprehensive set of city plans, which publicly transformed Yanagita's dark Tōno, the epitome of the rural primitive, into "Tōnopia"—a "Tōno utopia"—a showcase of late-twentieth-century technology, a bright and productive "rural city" giving full measure to culture and human relations. These schemes, collectively known as the Tōnopia puran (Tōnopia plan), set out to construct a range of facilities— library, museum, civic center, solar-heated garbage disposal plant—to embody Tōno's utopian aspirations. The facilities (many of which were eventually completed) are notable for their high-technological sheen and architecture.

The plan's language is perhaps not so different from Japanese civic rhetoric in general, but the specifically utopian emphasis, in conjunction with Tōno's dystopic past, made the scheme seem bold. The plan not only outlined Tōno's productive development (including agriculture, forestry, and tourism), land use policy, neighborhood renewal, social welfare, cultural advancement, and folklore preservation. In a larger sense, it aimed to create a "museum-park city" (hakubutsukōen toshi) in which small neighborhood centers would double as museums, preserving the varied arts, crafts, artifacts, and narratives of the locale. The entire region would, in effect, become a museum, the logical endpoint of Yanagita's efforts to narrativize the frightening diversity of which Sasaki spoke. The plan formed yet another series of narratives written from the tales Yanagita heard from Sasaki, who in turn heard them narrated by Tōno's storytellers. The weight of Tōno monogatari as a literary artifact determined the contours of Tōno's imaginings of itself; no sort of civic image or self-presentation to outsiders was conceivable outside the parameters that Yanagita unwittingly defined. At the base of Tōno's reconfiguration as a utopia, however, is its presentation of itself as a nostalgic "hometown," not just for its residents, but for all Japanese. That the historically dark and impoverished Tono now identifies itself as a generic furusato is closely related to its transformation from a dystopia into a utopia, from the vanishing marginal into the centrally Japanese.

The Home Away from Home

Furusato, as the term is commonly used today, means one's hometown, one's native place—the place where one was born and raised, a place where one used to live and with which one is deeply familiar, or simply the place one identifies as home.[8] Other meanings refer to historic ruins, ancient sites of human habitation, old and dilapidated villages. The first entry in the authoritative encyclopedic dictionary, the *Kōjien,* defines *furusato* as "a place of ancient habitation," "historic ruins" (*koseki*), or an "ancient capital" (*kyūto*).[9] This latter range of meanings, more historical and public in scope than the more conventional meaning of an individual's "old homeplace," is crucial in understanding the notion, which invokes particular, personal memories as well as diffuse, publicly acknowledged traces of ancient sites.

The notion of the furusato has thus proved to be a labile and shifting one, open to conservative political uses as well as to sharply antiauthoritarian attempts to reimagine the democratic possibilities of community. Like the multiple appropriations of the maternal metaphor, it taps into a seemingly endless spring of longing for refuge and warmth (my association of this notion with the maternal one is far from gratuitous). Japanese scholars and critics have long been attuned to the politically fraught and semiotically complex appeal of the furusato ideal, and recent Euroamerican observers of Japan have also analyzed it in some detail. I do not wish merely to repeat their insights here, but rather to consider the additional complexities that arise when the very

8. Recent interpreters of Japan have translated *furusato* as "native place." The word can be written either in the indigenous Japanese syllabary or with Chinese characters. When written with characters, it can be read in either of two ways: either as *furusato,* the Japanese reading, or as *kokyō,* the Sino-Japanese reading. The second reading tends to be more formal and literary, while the first reading is more colloquial. Therefore, while "native place"—which incorporates the notion of origins and nativity—is a fine translation for *kokyō,* I think an appropriate colloquial American English translation of furusato would be "hometown" or "home" (even "old homeplace"). Jennifer Robertson has written of the uses of *kokyō* as opposed to those of *furusato*; she argues that the reading of *kokyō* as *furusato* has become particularly marked since the 1970s, with national, regional, and local promotions of "building furusato" (*furusato zukuri*). See the opening section of her *Native and Newcomer.*

9. *Kōjien,* s.v. "furusato."

site of return—the identitarian home itself—turns out to be doubled, deferred, and haunted.

Writing in 1978, some years before this problematic had impinged on the consciousness of most non-Japanese Japanologists, political theorist Kamishima Jirō stated that "those who are living continuously in the place where they were born don't usually call that place 'furusato'" ("umareta tochi ni zutto kurashite iru hito ga soko o 'furusato' to wa, futsū iwanai desu yo ne").[10] The furusato resides in the memory, but is linked to tangible reminders of the past; when the material, palpable reminders of one's childhood home no longer exist, then the furusato is in danger of vanishing. Since the majority of Japanese until the postwar period had rural roots, furusato strongly connoted the rural countryside while the urban landscape implied its loss. Kamishima states further that the notion crystallized in times of rural emigration to the cities; in Japan, then, the ideal only gained notable strength in the wake of late Meiji urbanization:

> The Meiji period witnessed the first generation of people who had left their homes for the city [shutsugōsha]. This generation had hometowns, but as it turned into the second, and then the third generation, their parents' or grandparents' furusato was no longer their own. These later generations therefore had to synthesize an image of the furusato through some kind of mediation. . . . In 1914, the Education Ministry published the song "Kokyō (Furusato)" in its official collection of school songs, and it came to be sung throughout the country. In its role of providing a synthesis of the furusato image, this song had a big influence on those people who had come to Tokyo from elsewhere, or people who moved around a lot—in short, those people who had no furusato.[11]

Through the loss of urban Japan's rural roots (a loss that has led to furusato literature and poetry since the Meiji period), however, the ideal of native place has expanded to become a more capacious metaphor, one both multiple and generic. And thus there is now a proliferation of national, generalized furusato, of what Kamishima calls substitute homelands (daiyō furusato).

Any number of sites in Japan—Ise, Nara, Kyoto, Tōno—claim with varying justifications to be the furusato of Japan (Nihon no furusato). Native places of particular objects, practices, performances, and festi-

10. Kamishima Jirō, "Intabyū: kokyō sōshitsu no genzai kara," 8.
11. Kamishima, "Intabyū," 9.

vals exist. Tōno is the self-proclaimed folktale and folklore furusato. There is even a furusato of the dead, the ultimate one: Mount Osore on the northernmost tip of Honshu, the subject of the following chapter.

Tōno became a special sign of the furusato in the 1960s and 1970s, perhaps the most photographed and studied site connected with the Yanagita renaissance. Its fame rested on two levels of narrative: on the folktales themselves, what the tales contained, and on the folktales as renarrativized objects of ethnographic longing. Precisely because of the eerie character of its tales, Tōno became a particularly haunting and complex example of a generalized ideal. Many of the tales of Sasaki were marked by extremes of violence, suffering, crime, and poverty. Yet these extremes have been vividly juxtaposed, in the case of Tōno as a contemporary furusato, with their opposites: Tōno as the warm, homey, authentic, natural, and beautiful. With the idea of Tōno as a furusato, then, there is a fusion of two horizons of desire. First, the desire to encounter the unexpected, the peripheral unknown, even (and even especially) the frightening—a desire that repeatedly reveals itself under the controlled and predictable conditions of everyday life in advanced consumer capitalism (in Japan as elsewhere); and second, a countervailing desire, pushed by an opposite longing, to return to a stable point of origin, to discover an authentically Japanese Japan that is disappearing yet still present, to encounter the always already *known* as coincident with one's (Japanese) self. The desire for the different and unknown—the hope that *kappa, zashiki warashi* (young children who appear and disappear mysteriously in the big farmhouses of Tōno), and mountain men might still exist—is framed within the boundaries of a return to pastoral hominess, security, and (not the least significant) identity. Tōno thus confronts Japanese and others with these questions: How do the terrifying and mysterious become objects of detached appreciation? How does the unhomelike become the homelike? How does the rejected become the longed-for? It is by provoking such questions that the imaginary Tōno opens up the generic furusato notion to further operations of difference.

Part of the answer lies, again, in the ambivalence of the ideal itself. Furusato is a modern notion. As Kamishima and others have shown, it attained force in the wake of large-scale changes in rural Japan, in particular, the exodus of people in search of work in the cities in the early twentieth century and, more recently, in the postwar period. Concern with the furusato indicates a fundamental alienation, a severance from "home." This essential alienation shows up even more clearly in various local and national movements in Japan to make one's place of residence a true "hometown" (summed up in the phrase *furusato zu-kuri*, or "making furusato").[12]

This home which is not-home, this contemporary notion of the furusato, comes compellingly close to what Freud called *das Unheimlich*, the "unhomelike," or as it is most commonly translated in English, the "uncanny." I have already discussed how the *Tales* themselves indicated Yanagita's emplotment of a certain modern uncanniness, which I have linked to what I term ghastly insufficiencies. Here I would like to linger further on the strikingly literal implications that the uncanny has for a refiguring of the modern notion of furusato.

Freud defines the uncanny as something terrifying which is at the same time familiar. He shows that the German term *unheimlich* seems to be clearly the opposite of *heimlich*, that which is "native" and "home-like": "We are tempted to conclude that what is 'uncanny' is frightening precisely because it is *not* known and familiar. . . . Something has to be added to what is novel and unfamiliar to make it uncanny"[13] (and what is added is the "return of the repressed" or, in Lacan's terms, the unsettling return of *objet petit a*, the "lack" constitutive of the subject, which should have remained repressed.) Yet through an extended examination of the etymological origins of both *heimlich* and *unheimlich*, Freud discovers that *heimlich*, in some usages, can mean *unheimlich*:

> In general we are reminded that the word *heimlich* is not unambiguous, but belongs to two sets of ideas, which without being contradictory are yet very different: on the one hand, it means that which is familiar and congenial, and on the other, that which is concealed and kept out of sight. . . . Schelling says something which throws quite a new light on the concept of the "uncanny," one which we had certainly not awaited. According to him everything is uncanny that ought to have remained hidden and secret, and yet comes to light.[14]

Freud demonstrates that the meaning of "homelike" developed into that which should be hidden from others (the "repressed," which Lacan speaks of as the "lack" that constitutes the subject). Through a detailed psychoanalytic anatomy of E. T. A. Hoffmann's "The Sand-

---

12. Again see Robertson, *Native and Newcomer.*
13. Freud, "The Uncanny," 21.
14. Ibid., 28.

man," he shows that the feeling of the uncanny in fiction is often produced by repetition and the figure of the double, which he traces back to infantile anxieties. This factor of involuntary repetition, what Freud calls the "repetition compulsion," is central to the notion of the uncanny as that class of the fearful which is simultaneously familiar and strange; it is an anxiety that comes from the "involuntary recurrence of the like." In sum, Freud states:

> This uncanny is in reality nothing new or foreign, but something familiar and old-established in the mind that has been estranged only by the process of repression. This reference to the factor of repression enables us, furthermore, to understand Schelling's definition of the uncanny as something which ought to have been kept concealed but which has nevertheless come to light.[15]

"Estranged only by the process of repression": does this not embody the historical weight of the furusato? The notion of the furusato was discursively established at that time in Japanese history when state-sponsored industrialization and processes of bureaucratic rationalism had repressed rural Japan in a myriad of tangible and everyday ways (see chapter 3). The countryside literally became regressive, opposed to the "progressive" powers of urban-based capitalism. Yet urban domination could not be sustained as such, but in time became open to the uncanny returns that such repression inevitably ensures. The rural homeland became a sign of infantile yearnings and was simultaneously valorized as the source of true Japanese virtue. The furusato is, then, properly uncanny, because it indicates a return of something estranged under the guise of the familiar. The concept of the furusato contains a split; there is no simple "home."[16] In this sense, then, it is also similar to the logic subsumed under the figure of travel (as opposed to the originating stability of "home," or *oikos*) that I traced in chapter 2.

Folklorists have emphasized an even more basic stratum of the furusato, one that predates modern Meiji nostalgia for the countryside (but was also part of that nostalgia). This is the idea that the furusato refers *not* to one's old village and one's family per se, but rather to the nearby mountains. In much of Japan, the spirits of one's ancestors were

---

15. Ibid., 47.
16. As James Boon commented on reading my analysis of Tōno as an uncanny homeland, "Home is the place there's no place like."

thought to return to the nearby mountains; these ancestral spirits then were transformed into *yama no kami*, or the "mountain deity," who seasonally descended to the village to become *ta no kami*, or "deity of the rice fields." [17] The mountain is a prototypical furusato, a place of return and security after death. Yet mountains are also sites of the terrifying and mysterious, of violent abductions and ghastly crimes. Thus mountains are at once familiar homes and strange territories, sites of death: sites of the ancestors' graves, sites of possible death for the living who venture into their recesses. It is not surprising, then, that many of the tales told by Sasaki take place in the mountains and involve encounters with ghosts. Those tales highlight the unfamiliar dead, the unpredictable, dangerous spirits of the mountains that became the object for Yanagita's prescient folkloric interest (and appropriate allegorical means for retheorizing the split between voice and writing, literature and science).

Yet the unfamiliar is made familiar—familial—by the originary scene of the tales' enunciation: these were tales first told around the *irori*, the domestic hearth. The tales, domesticated by their transmission from grandparents to grandchildren, locate and bound the mysterious, both spatially (the mountains, the village boundaries) and temporally (either by *mukashi mukashi*, "long, long ago," the formulaic opening of many tales, a deictic indicator erased from Yanagita's text, or by specific reference to a historical or legendary moment). Within the spoken transmissions of tales, chains of displacements defer the unknown. This chain, and the way in which it has become fixed in the classicized *Tōno monogatari*, has allowed Tōno to be endlessly reinterpreted, to be lifted out of its harsh historical context and transformed into a comforting sign of stability.

Tōno monogatari was received, by readers both of the initial, 1910 publication and of the 1935 edition, with shock and uneasiness, for the text uncovered that which should have remained hidden. Yanagita wrote that the tales would "make us who live in the lowlands shudder." [18] Yet nativist ethnology's later development regarded Tōno as its cherished birthplace. The contemporary revisioning of Tōno utilizes this double aspect to preserve a sense of the uncanny while remaining distant from it by generating a stable, museumized utopia.

17. See Hori Ichirō, "Mountains and the Their Importance for the Idea of the Other World," chapter 4 in his *Folk Religion in Japan: Continuity and Change*, 141–79. On the oscillation of yama no kami and ta no kami, see particularly pages 150–51.
18. Yanagita, *Legends of Tōno*, 5.

Museum'd Utopias

The city of Tōno did not initially promote itself as a sightseeing attraction; it was discovered as part of a renewed interest in folklore and the Discover Japan travel energies. *Tōno monogatari* presented Tōno as a name for the yet mysterious countryside, inhabited yet surrounded by the unknown. The mountains surrounding the Tōno basin became the setting for many of Sasaki's stories, for the mountains (as previously indicated) in fact did demarcate the boundaries of the unknown for settled agricultural villages. *The Tales of Tōno* not only functioned as a text that encoded the haunted remainders of the modern, but also included entries that lingered on historical and geographical actualities. We know, for example, that there were ten villages in the Tōno region, that Tōno as the central town of the basin was a thriving inland entrepôt connecting the seacoast with points farther west, that the main settlement of Tōno was once a castle town. But the *Tales* are not concerned to delineate the prosaic aspects of community organization or ordered, civic life. The mountains surrounding Tōno are the primary scenes of the various crimes and untoward occurrences Yanagita relayed, and the everyday facts of Tōno's history only counterpoint all the more vividly the disordered happenings in the villages and mountains.

Tōno had long been settled, and was surprisingly active given its remote location, as Yanagita himself pointed out. It was a planned castle town, established in the seventeenth century, and by the late eighteenth century it had gained importance as a market and post town. Packhorses loaded with fish and sea products made their way over the complex series of mountain passes that separate central Iwate prefecture from the ocean to the east; in Tōno, these products were exchanged for staples and produce, often brought in from Morioka, the major city in Iwate, to the west. Tōno also became an active site for horse trading, as much of northeastern Japan (known as Tōhoku) was famous for its "Nanbu horses"; Tōno's importance as a producer of horses lasted well into the Shōwa period. The area's characteristic house form (the L-shaped, thatch-roofed *magariya;* horses are stabled in the short leg of the L) and its most famous folktale, the story of a tragic interspecies love affair between a girl and a horse, both highlight the importance of horses in Tōno's history. The status of horse breeding as the main economic support increased, as the building of roads for stagecoaches that bypassed the mountains (1878) and the establishment of steamship service (1891) decreased the traffic over the Kitakami Mountains through Tōno: Tōno, no longer important as a post town, turned to the specialized breeding of stagecoach (and cavalry) horses for the national market.[19] The population declined dramatically (although it recovered somewhat later on), however, and this period saw the real beginnings of rural out-migration to the greener pastures of Hokkaidō and Japan's great urban centers.

"Tōno" became the name for an actual administrative unit, a *machi* or "town," under the Meiji state's reorganization of municipal divisions in 1889. The name had hitherto referred to a larger region, including the market center of town as well as the surrounding mountain villages, although it could indicate, informally, the main settlement "below the castle" *(jōka)*. The main settlement of Tōno, as an active trading center and small castle town, the outlying villages, and the mountains themselves existed in a hierarchy of remoteness and strangeness, which correlated to a rise in altitude. This division reproduced in miniature the division between larger urban centers and Tōno imagined as a totally isolated region. While it is undeniably true that the Tōno basin was far from any major urban center, within the economy of the Kitakami Mountain region (the "Tibet of Japan") Tōno was even considered a "little Kyoto," the Japanese appellation for a local center of high culture. This division between the local image of Tōno as castle and market town, as a small economic and cultural center, and the narrativized image, from the canonized national perspective, of Tōno as remote, frightening, and the site of ghosts and gruesome occurrences, must temper any analysis of Tōno as a signifier of the remote.

The old town of Tōno and the surrounding villages were incorporated into the new city *(shi)* of Tōno, formed in 1954 under the postwar municipal reorganization; the former villages (mura) were now renamed towns. Tōno's plans for further redesigning itself, initiated in the 1960s, were closely linked to Iwate prefecture's 1965 Kitakami Mountain Range Development Project, a project which envisioned the region as one of the "bread baskets of Japan" *(Nihon no shokuryō kyōkyū kichi)*. Local and prefectural government officials, including Tōno's, vigorously advanced this project, appealing to national agencies and ministries for financial assistance. In the midst of this prefectural activity, the national government's 1969 New Comprehensive National Development Plan appeared; it included large projects for the development of forestry, agriculture, and animal husbandry in Iwate

19. Kikuchi Teruo, *Tōno monogatari o yuku*, 72–75.

prefecture.[20] The plans thus overlapped, and Tōno's civic upsurge is only understandable within these larger contexts. Basic research was conducted from 1969 through 1971, but it was not until 1975 that actual development and construction began under the Kitakami plan.

The plans were initiated in the midst of Japan's period of high economic growth, with its enormous impact on rural areas. Although this was a time of rapid growth and rising standards of living for most, it also witnessed the exacerbation of urban crowding and congestion, skyrocketing land prices, and notorious pollution and environmental scandals. Communities throughout rural Japan became concerned with the question of continuing existence in the face of depopulation; thus the advent and rise of schemes and plans for attracting new business and new residents. Tōno was no exception. Its population peaked in 1956 at thirty-seven thousand; after 1965, the population decreased by as much as a thousand people a year.[21] Even more debilitating than this general decline in population, however, was the decline in the wage-earning population. Many of Tōno's workers moved to the cities or worked for part of the year outside the local communities (a practice known as *dekasegi*), leaving their families behind. It was in the midst of this economic growth and its reverse effect on many towns that Tōno created its utopian city plans.

The Tōnopia plan had its beginnings in 1965, as part of the campaign platform of a mayoral candidate—who went on to win the election and become a popular mayor—and was linked to the larger prefectural development plans. In 1968 twenty-four young city employees began drawing up the concrete specifics of the Tōnopia plan. Their formulation is striking for its highly idealistic rhetoric; it is in fact a discussion of what an ideal (*risō*) is. They expressly link the necessity for forging a new ideal Tōnopia with the "agitated waves of economic and social change" sweeping over Japan's agricultural regions; the planners assert that even in the midst of these changes, the residents of Tōno must recognize a new "role" for their land and must look toward the future in constructing an "eternal rural city" (*eien no den'en toshi*)[22] in which

20. Information for the history of Kitakami and Tōno regional development taken from Tōno-shi Kikaku Zaisei-ka, ed., *Tōno shisei sanjūnen no ayumi*, 68–76.

21. Ibid., 61.

22. The "rural city" would appear to be misnamed, since what is rural seems to preclude the existence of cities. *Den'en toshi* is sometimes translated as "garden city," derived from the garden city projects of England. But den'en toshi can also refer to "new towns" or planned communities on the outskirts of major cities. In Tōno's case, the planners are indicating a new concept of the city, one that is in harmony with nature, and which is really only a focal point for a constellation of smaller settlements which

"folktales still live and breathe" and there is a "coexistence of gods and humans" *(kami to ningen no kyōson)*.[23] The plan reformulates in futuristic, utopian terms the folkloric ideal of Japan, where gods and humans live together harmoniously, in a contemporary restatement of prewar ideology.

Projects such as Tōno's had parallels throughout Japan, in what was expressly seen as a movement towards recentering power in "regional society" *(chiiki shakai)*. Yet the projects that were initiated and elaborated at the municipal level were closely intertwined with prefectural and national plans, most specifically then-prime minister Tanaka Kakuei's much-heralded (and later denounced) scheme of "remodeling the Japanese archipelago" *(Nihon rettō kaizō)*, published as a best-selling book in 1972.[24] Critics saw that plan as nothing more than an exportation of urban ills to less populated areas, one that did nothing to redress the essential imbalance between the burgeoning major cities and the declining rural areas. Tanaka's plans, they maintained, did nothing to revitalize the rural regions as they were, but instead attempted to urbanize them. Land prices soared to record highs as real estate speculation flourished, yet the oil crisis of 1973 put a sudden stop to Tanaka's grand schemes.

The rhetoric of the Tōnopia plan in fact prefigures that of the later Third Comprehensive National Development Plan *(Sanzensō)*, which spoke of harmony with nature, balanced development, and a union of technocratic and spiritual qualities. This 1977 plan promoted the formation of "settlement regions" *(teijūken)* of two hundred thousand to three hundred thousand residents, "where a balance would be achieved among the natural environment, the human settlement, and production facilities."[25] These three aspects are precisely those of the Tōnopia plan's tripartite division, yet Tōno's rhetoric of local resistance to central intrusion was phrased, perhaps inevitably, in the terms of national development ideology.

The plan, both in its earliest form and in its current phase, seeks to create local pollution-free industries, preserve Tōno's natural resources, stimulate the agricultural and forestry sectors of the economy,

---

cluster around it. *Den'en toshi* could also be translated as a "regional city." Often when general terms such as "region" or "locale" are used in Japanese, it is automatically understood that they refer to what is outside the main metropolitan centers.

23. Tōno-shi Kikaku Zaisei-ka, *Tōno shisei*, 65.

24. For the English language edition of *Nihon rettō kaizōron*, see Tanaka Kakuei, *Building a New Japan: A Plan for Remodeling the Japanese Archipelago*.

25. *Kodansha Encyclopedia of Japan*, s.v. "urban planning."

encourage tourism and culture, and create a new type of rural city. The three pillars of its conception of Tōno's future have been described as follows:

1. A production and processing city of earth, light, water, and greenery: The Industrial Cycle
2. A culture-health city rich in humanity: The Human Cycle
3. A museum-park city of nature, history, and folklore: The Natural Cycle[26]

The plan thus uses the rhetoric of ecology and natural systems theory to plan an eternally recycling continuum of nature, humans, and society. The city's elaboration of the third part of this plan, published in 1975, reveals to what extent the city's image as created in *Tōno monogatari* was essential to its idealized reconstruction of itself. This phase of the project aimed to create a *"Shizen to rekishi to minzoku no hakubutsu-kōen toshi"*: a "museum-park city of nature, history, and folklore." *Hakubutsu* connotes a preserved natural historical specimen, and *hakubutsu-kan* is usually translated as "museum" in English. *Hakubutsukōen toshi* literally implies, then, a museumized park city. The city plans and publications thematize the entire Tōno basin into separate "country parks" *(kantorii pāku)*, which epitomize notable aspects of Tōno's heritage. These country parks ideally function both as community centers for local people and as tourist attractions for outsiders. For example, the village of Tsuchibuchi, the birthplace of storyteller Sasaki Kizen, was designated as Denshōen, "Folklore Park." Tsukumōshi was designated as a park to preserve and display artifacts relating to the raising of horses and cattle. Matsuzaki was to house an archaeological museum, Otomo a museum of mountain industries and mining, Kamigō a center for folk performing arts, and Aozasa a center for folk crafts. Each local unit had its own theme in the grand whole of the *Tōno bonchi minzoku kōen*, the "Tōno basin folklore park."

The creators of the plan thus envisioned the entire Tōno basin as a museum, with the former villages of the Tōno district thematized according to divisions found within nativist ethnology itself: folklore, crafts, performing arts, material culture. A plan in which the city of Tōno becomes a theme park is the last step in a process which started with Yanagita's desire to locate the vanishing point of a world on the wane. The planners explain the thinking behind the concept of a museum-park city:

26. Tōno-shi Kikaku Zaisei-ka, ed., *Tōno-shi sōgō keikaku*, 5.

The civilization and enlightenment movement of the Meiji period started almost entirely with systems imported from the
West, and coincided with a Westernization process. Modern
scholarly disciplines were also imported from overseas, but
folklore studies is notable among the few disciplines which
were created and which achieved independence within Japan.
Folklore studies became a scholarly system via *Tōno monogatari*. Tōno is the birthplace of Japanese folklore studies, even
now is the Mecca of folklore studies, and is the spiritual homeland of the Japanese.[27]

This passage repeats the trajectory outlined in the previous chapter:
from Western-style bureaucratic, state-sponsored development to the
response called "folklore studies," which located the essentially Japanese at representatively emblematic places (along with the insistence
that Japanese folklore studies is a pristinely indigenous discipline).
The report states that priceless folktales, crafts, performing arts, customs, and beliefs survive in the isolated valley region; these survivals
are simultaneously natural scientific and social scientific resources
which should be preserved—thus the construction of the region as a
museum-park city. Tōno is imagined as a preserved utopia, or rather
as a utopia constructed around preserving, displaying, and transmitting the elements associated with *The Tales of Tōno*. The plan assimilates
the dominant, metropolitan perspective of folklore studies, then reproduces it as a self-generated utopian conception. The plans further reca-
pitulate the viewpoint of nativist ethnology, which also sought to cata-
log artifacts and narratives, to locate them, to "produce place," in H. D.
Harootunian's words.[28] The "place" of Tōno is produced in these plans,
and the dark, dystopic qualities of Tōno's past—dystopic from a certain modern perspective—are refigured as precisely utopian, as the
basis of a "bright and prosperous" contemporary Tōno. If the rhetoric
of Japanese civic identity today generally contrasts the dark *(kurai)* atmosphere of the past with the bright *(akarui)* prospects of the future,
how much more is this contrast heightened in Tōno, the very epitome
of the dark and gloomy.[29] This rhetorical reversal—from dark to bright,
negative to positive, dystopic to utopian—can only be empowered, of

27. Tōno-shi, *Tōnopia puran III: shizen to rekishi to minzoku no hakubutsukōen toshi kensetsu
kōsō*, 6.
28. See H. D. Harootunian's "Disciplinizing Native Knowledge and Producing Place:
Yanagita Kunio, Origuchi Shinobu, Takata Yasuma."
29. A similar and profoundly unsettling discourse on brightness *(akarusa)* in Hiroshima today has recently been discussed by Lisa Yoneyama in "Hiroshima Narratives
and the Politics of Memory: A Study of Power, Knowledge and Identities."

course, through a containment of past terrors within the framework of nativist ethnology.

With bond issues passed in Tōno and assistance from the national government, a civic center and innovative municipal museum and library have been built, as well as spectacular public works facilities utilizing state-of-the-art high technology in folksy packaging. Tōno's Suikōen (Water Park) is the most striking example of this combination. A solar-operated water treatment and pumping plant, one of the most advanced in Japan, shares a park space with a Japanese inn (complete with solar-heated baths), a transplanted magariya farmhouse with restaurants and conference rooms, and another newly-built farmhouse that functions as a performance space. A garbage disposal plant, also solar-operated, contains an inn featuring, again, baths, in this case heated by the burning garbage (it is popularly called *gomi onsen*, "garbage hot springs," by the locals).

While echoing the ecological and holistic rhetoric of the 1970s, however, Tōno has depended to a large degree on national funding from various ministries and agencies in order to realize its development projects. The construction of its elaborate, multifacility civic center—including a museum, library, city hall, and sports center with indoor swimming pool—cost some 1.8 billion yen all told. This is an enormous sum for a city of only some thirty thousand residents, yet the national government paid almost half the total as *hojokin*, as "grants" or "subsidies."[30] Much of Tōno's success has come about because of the skill its planners and city officials have shown in making its case to prefectural and national agencies and ministries. Tōno's public facilities have been built with a patchwork of grants given by several different agencies; they constitute, as one author has suggested, a veritable Rubik's cube. The source of the various monies in fact determined the very architecture of the sprawling civic center. Because different agencies awarded grants for different facilities and functions, monies could not be combined within one facility. Therefore, each part of the civic center—the sports building, the library, the city hall, and so on—was built separately, and the parts then connected by a series of halls and corridors. Tōno's fragmented civic core reflects its heavy dependence on state funding for its material existence.[31]

Tōno has therefore become not just a symbol of folkloric mysteries,

30. Fukutomi Tōru, "Genchi no hōkoku: 'hojokin no tengoku' o yuku," 121–22. In 1994, one U.S. dollar was worth about one hundred yen. In the mid-1980s, the exchange rate hovered around two hundred fifty yen to the dollar.

31. Ibid., 122.

but a mecca for other communities aspiring to renovate their towns with the help of state funds. Mayors, planners, and development experts go to Tōno to gain access to its secrets.[32] Undoubtedly much of Tōno's success in procuring funds has stemmed from its well-planned and executed funding proposals, proposals which incorporate large-scale visionary changes with ecologically sound facilities to boost local production and visibility. The plans are impressive by almost any standards and intelligent in many respects, using the best of soft-energy and nonpolluting technology.

Tōno is in debt, however. The city passed a number of bond issues to fund its projects; it also borrowed money in the form of government low-interest loans. The early 1980s marked a retrenchment in Japanese government finances, with a planned reduction of one-fourth of its subsidies to locales such as Tōno. (Such subsidies have accounted for as much as one-third of the total national budget of Japan.) The national press cited Tōno as a city that had voraciously expended government funds in constructing its "culture city" (bunka toshi).[33] Many of the projects that were planned have not been realized; although the district centers have been built, the "themed" aspects have not come to fruition. The museum-park city still remains as an ideal, but the realization of Tōnopia has been forestalled. Citizens worry now about how the city can repay its debts, and there is continuing concern about stimulating local industries and stemming the flow of young people from the region. The latest development idea is for an international folklore center where scholars from around the world could study and conduct research, but my friends wondered both about the financing and the appeal of a center so far from any major city (and so cold in the winter).

Tōnoites are focusing more and more on tourism and the selling of local products as alternative sources of revenue to offset falling agricultural and forestry profits. Half-public, half-private structural arrangements align the Tourism and Commerce section (shōkō kankō ka) of the city government with wholly private groups of entrepreneurs, which carry out the business of buying and selling Tōno's guidebooks, kappa dolls, local delicacies, and other products. Various public corporations undertake specialized functions in publicizing, promoting, and selling

32. Tōno was the site for a 1981 national conference on the development of rural cities (den'en toshi), with the Tōnopia Plan and Tōno's "unique" characteristics providing the "ideal" model for other communities. The record of that conference has been published as Tōnopia puran: jiritsu toshi Tōno kara no hōkoku.

33. See Fukutomi, 118–27.

Tōno and its products: one, called Furusato Kōsha, manages Folklore Park (Denshōen) and promotes the selling of local agricultural products (grapes, apples, mushrooms) to subscribers who, for a fee, can have farm-fresh produce sent to their doors by mail.

The residents of Tōno expect tourism to increase, particularly now that the Tōhoku shinkansen (bullet train) has been extended through Iwate prefecture. They have created new events and activities: a folktale festival in February for the bitter cold of the off-season, demonstrations of traditional crafts, and silkworm cultivation. The renowned *kappa buchi* (kappa pool) described in the tales is one of the main points on the itinerary of tourists; the manager of Denshōen told me that plans were under way to renovate and enlarge the pool: "There's nothing to see there now—just a pond. We want to make it more mysterious, create an atmosphere where it will seem like a real kappa will jump out of the water—maybe even have a robot kappa." [34] Festivals, domestic rituals, and processions provide sightseers with something to see, while Tōno's most famous active storyteller (kataribe), Suzuki Satsu, has lured aficionados of folktales from all over the country. Yet the Tōno Civic Museum probably remains the major sightseeing attraction in the city.

Memorable Ruins

The Tōno Museum, a five-minute walk from the train station, replaces the dispersed locations of Tōno's mysteries with its own consolidated narrative structure. Designed by a Tokyo architectural firm (as was the civic center), it incorporates the perception of Tōno as a site where the transgenerational continuity of storytelling and practice is yet preserved. In fact the first exhibit one sees upon entering the museum is a replica of the domestic hearth (irori), the kernel of the household interior and the scene of storytelling. The museum brochure calls this space—a small alcove with a high, dark-timbered ceiling, burnished flooring, and a sunken hearth, selectively lit to maintain a certain darkness—the *denshō no ba*, the "place of oral tradition" (or of legends or folklore or all three, depending on the translation). Yet this space of narrative is uninhabited, both empty and silent, visible only through the penumbral reproduction of its material setting.

The storyteller's voice has been displaced from this site to yet an-

---

34. All English translations of informants' transcribed conversations are mine. The conversations with Mr. Abe and Mrs. Yamaguchi took place in August 1984.

other scene, the "storyteller's village" (kataribe no sato), which visitors reach by ascending from this darkened place to the second floor. Yet the village, like the replica hearth, is uninhabited: Tōno's "artless tales" (sobokuna monogatari) of magical foxes, kappa, mountain deities, and oshirasama (a deity associated throughout Tōhoku with silkworm cultivation), recorded by elders of the region, are recalled to sonic life by the touch of a button. Disembodied electronic voices echo through the room, a room that is also the setting for animated films of the tales, which repeat automatically throughout the day.

Establishing displaced spaces of narrative—of the narratives of Tōno monogatari—operates, then, as the initial framing device for the entire museum, as the theme of disembodied voices and bodies repeats throughout. It is via the fantastical world of The Tales of Tōno (Tōno monogatari no sekai, as this first exhibition area is called), through the attempt to evoke that world through doubly removed mimesis, that the civic imaginary of Tōno is approached. That is, it is the very phantasmatic status of these narratives that has guaranteed the status of Tōno as a place worthy of museumization in the first place. Without the accident of the ghostly tales themselves there would be no Tōno appropriate for museumization. It is thus strangely fitting that the museum literally reenacts the dilemma of the vanishing storyteller through vacated spaces of narration.

Yet there is a return to the prosaic stabilities of representation in other exhibits. Objects of daily use and belief are collected and displayed in the second large exhibition area, "Nature and Life in Tōno" (Tōno no shizen to kurashi). Agricultural tools, looms, and baskets abut specimens of alpine flora and fauna (the area's Mount Hayachine is well known to naturalists and meteorologists); yamabushi (mountain ascetic) paraphernalia, kagura masks (kagura is Japanese sacred dance drama, often performed at shrine rituals and closely related to Noh theater), and ema (votive tablets offered to shrines; they often depict horses) are displayed next to detailed distribution maps of local performance styles, folk beliefs, and domestic architecture. This setting is dedicated to the fidelity of representation and the preservation of artifactual authenticity. It describes a space of collection proper, of objects and specimens located at the midpoint between the natural history museum and the folklore museum.

Much of this space of display is thus organized around a discourse of everyday life, of tools now viewed as virtual relics. Michel de Certeau writes of "relics and pockets of the instrumental system" and of "populations of instruments [that] oscillate between the status of memorable ruins and an intense everyday activity."[35] This part of the museum organizes many of its objects around a rhetoric of everyday productivity outside contemporary commodity circuits. Yet it is a domain of superseded productivity, of productivity no longer productive of everyday life. The objects—hoes, baskets, looms—remain, however, productive of another order: memorability itself. They produce a partial—fragmentary, ruined—allegory of a lost relationship to subsistence, as their artifactualness remarks on the virtually dematerialized relationships of voice and image produced in the first exhibition site.[36]

Yet it is the third exhibition area, entitled "Tōno's Folklore Studies" (Tōno no minzokugaku), that purports to contain the dissonances set up between the disembodied voices of Tōno's tales and the useful objects of everyday life past. Viewing booths show a selection of videos: documentaries of a yearly domestic event (koshōgatsu, the so-called little New Year's) and various performances, as well as a taped lecture by the eminent folklorist Ikeda Yasaburō, one of the planning advisors for the Tōno Museum. Original manuscripts, letters, and notes of Yanagita, Sasaki, and a local anthropologist named Inō Kanoru, who attained fame with his cultural history of Taiwan, are displayed under glass, watched over by the enormous map that precisely traces Yanagita's itinerary on his first visit to Tōno. Tōno not only produced the "native" storyteller Sasaki, not only fatefully became the object of the Grimm of Japan, but also nurtured the emergence of an ethnologist of Japan's colonial other. The neutralities of the displayed juxtaposition—Sasaki,

35. Michel de Certeau, The Practice of Everyday Life, 146.

36. Some of the most provocative work in anthropology and cultural studies in recent years has focused on the museum as a site productive of social fantasies. The imperatives of collection displayed in museums repeat many of the dynamics of fetishism; the difference lies in the rule-bound, socially invested nature of public collection as opposed to the erotic, obsessive, and often socially transgressive nature of private fetishism. See for example the two excellent collections Objects and Others: Essays on Museums and Material Culture, edited by George W. Stocking, Jr., and Exhibiting Cultures: The Poetics and Politics of Museum Display, edited by Ivan Karp and Steven D. Lavine; see, in particular, James Boon's resonant tracing of the sad trope of the museum: "Why Museums Make Me Sad." I have been particularly instructed by James Clifford's afterword to the Stocking volume, "Objects and Selves—An Afterword"; see also the chapter "On Collecting Art and Culture" in his The Predicament of Culture: Twentieth-Century Ethnography, Literature, and Art. A powerful essay on museums—particularly art museums—is Theodor Adorno's "Valéry Proust Museum." I should mention Susan Stewart's examination of narratives of desire in her On Longing; one of her objects is the "collection." Walter Benjamin, of course, remains perhaps the most compelling theorist of the relationships triangulating capitalist modernity, nostalgia, and objects.

Yanagita, Inō—belie the historical densities that underlay their inclusions together in the Tōno Museum. The prominence of Inō and his placement alongside Yanagita in fact exposes an undertheorized linkage with Japanese state colonialism and the construction of an authentically indigenous Japanese folk. The formation of Japanese folklore studies is not thinkable outside the related project of Japan's colonialist ethnology, one that worked to draw the exclusionary boundaries of Japaneseness. Yanagita's position as a bureaucrat and his often-implicit cultural nationalism coordinated the terms of indigenous folklore studies as a counterpart to the external project of colonial anthropology.

Inō's birth as the ethnologist of tribal Taiwan is traced to Tōno as the birthplace of Japanese autoethnologizing. Indeed the museum's display placards declaim that "Tōno's folklore studies began with Inō Kanoru's publication in 1894 of an article entitled 'Oshirasama ni tsukite' ['Concerning Oshirasama'] in the journal of the Ethnology Association [Jinrui Gakkai]." Yet what a strange birth, for this nativity antedates— from what point of retrospection is not obvious—the canonical birth of Japanese folklore studies, the publication of Yanagita's *Tales*, by sixteen years. It is as if Inō's 1894 piece on oshirasama is being reclaimed as a specifically local event: the beginning of Tōno's folklore studies before "Tōno" became recognized as the representation of a national-cultural autoethnology.[37] Yet it is this *national* status—and the national birth of 1910—that is repeatedly invoked by folklorists and thus by Tōnoites hoping to locate themselves in relation to the desires of a larger Japan. That this tenuously local "prebirth" in 1894 became the start for an ethnology of what was *not* Tōno and thus *not* Japan (Inō's ethnology of tribal Taiwan)—and the potential object of a nationalist, colonialist project—speaks of the deep interconnections of Japanese folklorism and colonial anthropology.

The museum's tripartite logic of representation not only exhibits the material authenticity of Tōno's productivity through implements as relics, as "memorable ruins." It also attempts to restage, as it were, the scene of narration, now rendered doubly strange by the vacated place of narrative in the museum. The missing storyteller is reinstated in another scene, the "storytellers' village" upstairs, yet reinstated only

37. In 1924 the "native place research association" (*kyōdo kenkyūkai*) of Tōno was formed, with Inō Kanoru at its center and over fifty members. This period, the museum declares, could be called the "golden age of Tōno's history and folklore research" ("kono jiki ga Tōno no rekishi to minzokugaku kenkyū no saiseiki").

to be deferred yet again: the tellers of tales can only be theorized as missing bodies, absented voices. The explicit narrative of the production of Tōno's folklore studies in the third exhibition area then becomes the explanatory frame for the rest of the museum: Tōno as the birthplace of folklore studies as the discipline concerned with tales, ghosts, and peasant artifacts (and with obscured connections to Japanese colonialism).

What is remarkable about the Tōno Museum is that its own status as museum is part of what it must display. The place of Tōno as represented through Yanagita's fictions is fundamentally more productive of touristic interest than the objects, tools, and specimens that insistently remind viewers not to forget the material substratum of an actual Tōno. The museum must first of all articulate a displayed space of phantasm with hard realities, a split that reproduces the division Yanagita produced in *Tōno monogatari* itself: the split between literary phantasm and ethnographic science, between ghosts and bodies, between voice and writing. This split is rhetorically and spatially produced by the separation of the first two exhibition spaces but is then sutured by the metacommentary of the third.

The museum exhibits the fundamental forms and movements of Tōno's past; it adds an extra twist, however, with its exhibition of this past as an object of study. The museum both condenses this past *and* displays it as something that is already an object of folklore studies. In so doing it operates as a partial replacement, as a metonymic lure: with its stable repertoire of recorded voices, glass-encased artifacts, and animated narratives, it constitutes an appropriate utopian museum for the museumized utopia of the Tōnopia plans.

The plans are relentless in their mapping of Tōno, in their textual recreation of an entire landscape. Place names and districts are highlighted, excavated from obscurity. Circuits are completed—laid out for the bicyclist or the tourist, but always according to the narratives of Tōno. Tōnopia's planners used the concept of the furusato, both to create a sense of community involvement and to appeal to outsiders, city dwellers who may feel they have lost their own essential homes. The planners have in fact created the antithesis of a furusato: a utopia, which is nowhere, literally. By fusing the notion of the homeland— and particularly *this* homeland—with that of an ideal, utopic space, they have played out the nascent implications of the modern notion of the furusato. The furusato is nothing if not specific, even if that specificity resides in a fantasy of origins. Instead of producing place, the plans have produced no-place: Tōnopia. But the materiality of relics, rice fields, and stories yet told return to respecify the dislocations that the museum effects.

Textual Recursions

The intricate relay of texts that makes up the civic imaginary of Tōno simultaneously locates the city within a national fantasy of origins. That specific history led me to stay in Tōno for several months between 1983 and 1985, as I talked to residents and visitors in an attempt to understand the peculiar resonances the place has in modern Japan. How extraordinarily different from the darkness Sasaki described is the brightness and resilient boosterism of the museum city. That brightness, of course, reflects the relative prosperity of today. My conversations with older people of Tōno, who remember the poverty of the prewar era, uncovered a profound sense of change that fully acknowledged the benefits of the present; their reminiscences went beyond the utopian boosterism of the city's plans, however, in recognizing the problems accompanying technological and agricultural development. Interviews and conversations with people in Tōno revealed the attempt to locate civic identity within the national mapping that Yanagita first initiated, and it is to some of these narrative retracings that I want to return here. What many of these narratives replay is the lingering sense of mysteries not fully comprehended, even within the ardent representation of those mysteries as civic assets.

One of Tōno's most venerable inhabitants, Abe Yoichi, is popularly known as *kappabuchi no ojiisan,* the "old man of the kappa pond." He has lived near the pond his whole life, and for generations, he claims, his family has had a special relationship with animals, including kappa. Kappa are water sprites notorious for pulling animals and people into ponds; they are particularly apt to attack people who have mistreated or killed animals indiscriminately. Because Mr. Abe's family has long had a policy of not wantonly killing animals, they have enjoyed a long lineage (twenty-eight generations, he told me) and have never experienced any trouble with kappa. He retold the founding legend of this kappa pond: A kappa in the neighborhood kept pulling horses into the water. The neighborhood children banded together and decided to kill the kappa, using sickles and hoes. Suddenly their fathers (Mr. Abe's ancestors, it turned out) appeared and saved the kappa, extracting a promise that he would no longer kill their horses.

They then brought the kappa to this pond. This narrative is a variant of the classic *kappa komahiki* tale which is distributed throughout Japan, in which a kappa attempts to pull a horse into the water, and in the process is captured by humans who then extract a promise or a magical boon from the creature.[38]

Mr. Abe retold a story that is widely distributed throughout Japan, and is found as well in *Tōno monogatari*. Each year, dozens of folklore and literary pilgrims come to the pond as one point on an itinerary that retraces the sites mentioned in Yanagita's text, names filled with magical promise: Hayachine, Tsukumōshi, Rokkōshi, Sadato. They often speak to Mr. Abe, who talks of kappa not as something fantastic, but as something historically palpable, although he admitted to me that he had never seen one.

The kappa is a creature firmly entrenched in Japan's folkloric pantheon. It has long been the stuff of carvings, tales, rumors, and even political satire—for example, Akutagawa Ryūnosuke's famous work, entitled (not surprisingly) *Kappa*, published in 1927. The kappa of Tōno are so famous that they have even been featured in national weekly magazines. The women's magazine *Shūkan josei* ran a feature article headlined "Kappa Exist in This World!" that reported the eye-witness account of a kappa sighting by a Tōno housewife. Yet behind the contemporary image of the naughty kappa lie stories that attest to more dangerous origins. One such story sees kappa as representing aborted fetuses or newborn infants killed to control the population; these infants would be disposed of in streams or ponds. In this narrative, then, kappa are monstrous (and dangerous) transformations of infants, who trouble the human world by causing mysterious disappearances— much like their own mysterious "disappearances." Other tales and practices reveal kappa as other forms of human substitutes; in many cases, the kappa is regarded as a water deity, connected to agricultural fertility.

The Tales of Tōno includes stories of monstrous children born of human mothers and kappa fathers: "In a household beside the river in Matsuzaki village women have become pregnant with kappas' children for up to two generations. When they are born, these children are hacked to pieces, put into small wine casks, and buried in the ground. They are grotesque."[39] "Kappas' children" is here undoubtedly a supernatural euphemism for unwanted, possibly deformed, infants. Yet

38. *Nihon minzoku jiten*, s.v. "kappa" and "kappa komahiki."
39. Yanagita, *Legends of Tōno*, 41.

the image makers of Tōno reveal none of this chilling history in their promotions of kappa as icons of rusticity and folk naiveté. A large stone sculpture of a kappa adorns the landscaped traffic circle in front of Tōno's train station, alongside the omnipresent admonitions to avert traffic accidents—a fine irony, indeed, for a creature that causes accidental drownings.

There are at least five entries about kappa in *Tōno monogatari*, which also includes entries about elusive mountain dwellers, childlike beings who inhabit the inner recesses of old, established households (zashiki warashi), and the silkworm deity known as oshirasama, represented throughout northeastern Japan by enigmatic paired stick figures of a horse and a human being. The oshirasama tale is perhaps the most famous story in *Tōno monogatari*:

> Once upon a time there was a poor farmer. He had no wife but did have a beautiful daughter. He also had one horse. The daughter loved the horse, and at night she would go to the stable and sleep. Finally, she and the horse became husband and wife. One night the father learned of this, and the next day without saying anything to the daughter, he took the horse out and killed it by hanging it from a mulberry tree. That night the daughter asked her father why the horse was not anywhere around, and she learned of the act. Shocked, and filled with grief, she went to the spot beneath the mulberry tree and cried while clinging to the horse's head. The father abhorring the sight, took an axe and chopped off the horse's head from behind. Then all at once, the daughter, still clinging to the horse's head, flew off to the heavens. It was from this time on that Oshira-sama became a *kami*.[40]

Tōno's most famous tale is a story of forbidden sexuality, of interspecies incest and the ruin that results. From this tragic affair, however, comes a narrative that forms the basis for the worship of silkworm deities. Japanese folklorists have still not unraveled the threads that connect horses, sex, and silkworms, but the tale itself is retold and dramatized in numerous settings, including the Tōno Museum's films and electronic animations.

When I asked about oshirasama beliefs, Mr. Abe stated that long ago (mukashi) the deity was worshipped as a grain deity, as well as a deity of silkworm cultivation. Then it became much more directly related to silkworm cultivation. Now, however, when silkworm cultivation has almost completely disappeared from the Tōno region (it is still carried on at Denshōen, in order to teach it to local young people and

40. Ibid., 49–50.

to tourists), the deities' function has moved from silkworms to hu-mans: the deities are now worshipped for their protection of the family. In any case, he continued, people's thinking has changed dramatically. Previously people truly believed in the efficacy of the kami; now they do not. This decline in belief is linked most closely, he insisted, to the biggest change he has witnessed: the change to scientific knowledge; with the use of statistics and chemical fertilizers people now make more money than they used to. The fact is that people no longer have any need for oshirasama; there is no money in it. Even so, the style of many of the festivals and observances has not changed much; it is just that many of the people who perform them have died.

There was a strange sense here—one repeated in other conversa-tions—that the form, the style has continued, but that the human pro-tagonists of ritual forms have passed away. A permanence of form: something still survives, latently, but there is no one to perform it. The decline in practitioners was made clear when I asked about *itako*, medi-ums who are also healers. Mr. Abe told me that there used to be a number of itako in Tōno, but no longer. Usually the itako were pro-tected by ancestral spirits, and would beseech them for oracles. They would cure people's illnesses, often by locating the cause of illness in a neglect of ancestral rites; sickness was often evidence of the ancestors' displeasure. (The next chapter examines a site of itako practices at Mount Osore, at the very northern tip of the main island.)

Another interview, with an eighty-one-year-old woman, disclosed many of the same themes that occupied Mr. Abe. Mrs. Yamaguchi works at Denshōen supervising silkworm cultivation and teaching weaving. Memories of her childhood, around the time Yanagita visited Tōno, reveal crushing hardship. She was sent out to be a servant at the age of nine, and stayed until she was eighteen. At that time, a marriage was arranged for her, but she discovered that her prospective spouse had tuberculosis, and so she spent what little money she had buying her way out of the match. Her brothers and sisters had all died by then, and she was left with the responsibility of caring for her parents. She started learning weaving in her early twenties, was eventually married, but left her husband's household when she failed to have chil-dren. She returned to live with her mother and eventually adopted a son.

Mrs. Yamaguchi told me that she had never believed in the oshira-sama deities:

> It's said that if you worship oshirasama, you must continue to do so until you die, or it's no good. Once you start, you

shouldn't stop. So my mother said if you don't worship oshira-sama, it's better not to start. Oshirasama are connected to silk-worms, but I don't understand the meaning. I raised silk-worms a long time ago, but I didn't worship oshirasama. I worshipped other gods. I also don't let my grandchildren worship. It's all right for them to go and look at the oshirasama displayed here at Denshōen, but I won't let them worship them. There were houses in my village who worshipped, but those people all went bankrupt [kamakeshi]. No matter how much they worshipped, there were houses that went bankrupt.

The theme of florescence and decline punctuates many of the stories of Tōno, particularly stories about zashiki warashi and kappa. These creatures bring prosperity and good fortune with them when they decide to take up residence in a house, but they also take it with them when they leave. "People said there was a zashiki warashi in the big house of Manjurō in Nishinai, but the warashi left the house and it went bankrupt. There was also a kappa who hid himself under a boat by the stable, but when he disappeared the owners went bankrupt. I've heard many of those stories, but since I've never seen anything myself, I don't know."

Like Mr. Abe, Mrs. Yamaguchi remarked on the continuity of symbolic forms and practices but the absence of people to carry them on. *Mizuki dango*, the practice of hanging rice balls from twigs at "little New Year's," is one such practice, one that Mrs. Yamaguchi carried out until the mid-70s but which now is rarely enacted. The theme of decline was repeated when I asked her to comment on the difference between the festivals of today and those of her youth:

> Now, the people who perform them have dwindled . . . In the old days, people had very few pleasures, and dancing was one of the main joys you could have. Also, in terms of eating . . . we got up early and made boxed lunches and rice cakes. We would share our food with our neighbors and so would they. Before, we would make box lunches and so on and go to the festival. Now everybody eats in their houses, goes to the festival by car.

Practices are suspended, left at the point of vanishing. More than in most such Japanese communities, people in Tōno are constantly reminded of what should exist and continue to exist, because the very civic identity of Tōno is heavily overlaid by the national-cultural imaginary of Japan itself. Tōno exists in the public imagination—both locally and nationally—as a significant site where Japanese (and other moderns) hope to discover that the decline of "folk" practices has not advanced to the point of utter erasure. The preemptions of modernity have been contained in the official narratives of the city and there have been, as we have seen, any number of attempts to reconfigure modernity's disappointments by imaginative amalgamations of folkloric rhetoric with high-tech urban planning.

One of the most revelatory conversations I had about the place of Tōno occurred with the film director Murano Tetsutarō in Tōno. He had recently made a film of *Tōno monogatari*, based primarily on a reworking of the tale about oshirasama and the cross-species affair. For him, Tōno operated as a sign of an internal otherness still potent enough to inspire films and inspire expansive fantasies around the figures of loss. Murano's film did not try to reproduce the entire array of Yanagita's narratives. Instead, he focused on the oshirasama motif and located it alongside a tale of young love, set at the time of the Russo-Japanese War (1904–1905), the war that would definitively establish Japan as an emergent world power, with all the colonialist ambitions such power implies. But like Yanagita before him, Murano was adamant about his representation as a depiction of "present-day facts," impressing on me the amount of time he spent researching the film, how it was literally packed with ethnographic detail and careful folklorism:

> You know the opening scene of the film? It shows a pile of stones in the middle of a field. Those stones are offered as part of ancestor worship, but nobody knows that so they missed the reference. You know the Chiba house? There's a stone wall in front of that house to hold back the horses, but nobody knows that, so that's another missed point. When I first came to this area ten years ago, the forests were so deep that you had to turn on your headlights when you drove through them. There were many, many more magariya farmhouses. Most of them have been torn down now.
>
> In the Japanese heart [kokoro], there's veneration, whatever, of ancestors. Ones who have died recently are called *hotoke-sama* [sometimes translated as buddhas] and long-dead ancestors are *kamisama* [gods]. There's an alternation between the mountain and the sea that's linked to the natural cycle: the rain falls on the mountain, goes downstream to the ocean, evaporates again, and falls on the mountain. There's a movement between Buddhism and Shinto, too. Before *shinbutsu bunri* [the Meiji policy that forcibly tried to separate Buddhist practices from Shinto ones], Buddhism and Shinto were mixed together

in *shugendō* [mystical practices centering around sacred moun-
tains] and yamabushi [mountain ascetic] beliefs. The state's intervention in excluding Buddhism was very destructive.

Before shinbutsu bunri there were over three hundred tem-
ples on Dewa Sanzan [three famous sacred mountains—
Mount Haguro, Mount Gassan, and Mount Yudono—of
Yamagata prefecture, located in the northwestern part of the
Tōhoku region]. The Hayachine cult [Hayachine is one of the
most prominent mountains near Tōno and the focus of many
religious practices] was closely related to the worship of
Mount Haguro. There was a direct connection. Also from
Dewa Sanzan to Edo there were many routes, not marked with
stones: a trail of monuments. The priest at Gassan or Haguro
was in direct contact with the Shinto priest at Usa Hachiman
Shrine [Usa Hachiman is on the island of Kyūshū, far to the
south]. They would alternate back and forth. There was a linkage—a kind of sacred Japanese "silk road" between these
"power spots": Dewa Sanzan, Ise, Tōno/Hayachine. They also
connected up through Korea and China via the Silk Road. Korean monks originally brought most of this stuff over, to these
selected spots. And if you look at these spots, they're all very,
very similar: the topography, water, trees, everything. They're
connected power spots that form a network throughout Japan,
marked now by remaining stones. And this has everything to
do with esoteric Buddhism [mikkyō].

Tōno is fascinating precisely because of these same reasons.
It's the coldest place in Japan, and the city with the largest
area—a place of extremes. It was Yanagita Kunio's dream. A
place of *shisha*—of the dead.[41]

When I asked Murano about the difference, now, between this dream
and Tōno today he answered that the kokoro (heart) remains the
same—his movie was a dream showing the mysterious and profound
world of *Tōno monogatari*.

41. *Shisha* is literally translated as "dead people," but it more commonly evokes "ancestors." There is a rhetoric of traces that repetitively returns in many of the tales of
Tōno (Yanagita said that there seemed to be more stone markers in Tōno than elsewhere).
These markers become the evidence for the not quite complete purging of animistic
beliefs and mountain mysticism, and for the tenacity of ancestor beliefs articulated with
mountain worship. Many of the itineraries depicted in guidebooks or brochures circle
around stones—the markings of famine, deaths, and ancestors—and stones frequently
serve as incitements to memory: Tsuki-ishi (the "eternal stone"), *gohyaku rakan* (the five
hundred disciples of the Buddha, a recurrent motif throughout Japan, here carved into
a field of stones to commemorate a famine in the late eighteenth century), Haguro rock.

I made the film just in time, in the early '80s. Before the bullet train was opened. The hills around here have really been logged over, too. The bullet train means the end of Tōno—the end as dream, as image. Now it will be more and more of a movement of "preserving" things—that's no good.

Murano's fantasy (*yume*) about the fantasy of Tōno emerged in the quintessential phantasmatic medium—cinema—in a film about Yanagita's fantasies of Tōno. He felt that he had recorded something at its last remaining moment of viability, the moment just before it ceases to exist even in the register of dream, but only marks the modern impossibility of dream. That dream is the reality of Tōno, for him. Yet he was terrifically concerned about letting me know, letting his audience know, that he has been ethnographically faithful. In that sense, he retraces the fissure that Yanagita himself tried to close, the constitutive gap of ethnographic practice. And it is not inconsequential that Tōno, again, stands in for a place of deathliness that in the end is imaginatively constitutive of modern Japaneseness.[42]

Murano was in Tōno for the unlikeliest of convergences: Tōno was to become the sister city of Salerno, Italy, in a grand ceremony the next day (8 August 1984). Murano's film *Tōno monogatari* had moved the critics and audience at the Salerno International Film Festival the year before; the viewers, and particularly the mayor of Salerno, had been so impressed by Tōno that they created a move to make it Salerno's sister city.

So the next day there was a parade, in sweltering Japanese summer heat: a procession of sober-suited Tōno city officials, tanned Italian women in high heels, and a Tōno children's brass band—dressed in scout uniforms—playing "Santa Lucia," preceded by twirlers and a primary school glockenspiel and recorder ensemble. The procession to the civic center was followed by a three-hour signing ceremony in the civic auditorium. The entire occasion had been inspired by Murano's film, but the mayor he had impressed had been defeated in the last election, so to his chagrin the director was faced with an array of unknown Italians who had gathered to honor him and his fantasy of Tōno in the all-too-prosaic confines of the civic center. The party that night at the Suikōen (Water Park) peaked when the Italian men (clad in their summer kimono from the inn) started drunkenly dancing with *shishi*

---

42. Yoshimoto Takaaki considered *Tōno monogatari* an archive of evidence for the "collective fantasies" (*kyōdō gensō*) of modern Japanese. As such, Yoshimoto worked through the logic of dreams to comprehend the power of the *Tales*. See his *Kyōdō gensōron*.

odori (Tōno's distinctive masked "dance of the deer") performers in
full regalia, as the women—dressed in gold lamé sundresses and gold
heels—danced the fox-trot and rhumba with willing Tōnoites.
"They're lively," remarked the British translator accompanying the
group, "at least they're lively." Murano sat through it all, looking be-
mused. A representative from Japan's Foreign Ministry made a long
speech about Tōno and Salerno as museum cities (hakubutsu toshi).
The photographer from Tokyo sitting next to me laughed at the same
moment I did: "So the *things* are good, but the people aren't," he wryly
noted. As the gift exchanges went on, the representatives rhetorically
stressed the future of each city, the long traditions (Tōno as "Nihon no
furusato"), the development of tourism, the cultural resources. The
film music from *Tōno monogatari* kept repeating. The ludic mode of the
proceedings—recalled often over the coming days—was heightened
by the Mediterranean contrast to local sobriety. But the pathos of the
event was sharpened by the evident fascination the Salerno delegation
had for the dark mysteries they had glimpsed in the filmed version of
Tōno's tales, mysteries that cut across the differences that "Italy" and
"Japan" would seem to denote.

Such a festive event was indeed singular, indicative of Tōno's international status (although Murano grumbled about the secondary status of Salerno when compared to Rome or Milan). Yet Tōno as folkloric
origin primarily has to reproduce itself in the image of recurrent festivals and events, events that are timelessly tied to agricultural cycles
and repetitive moments—not in the punctual mode of sister city sign-
ings, for example. It is this recurrence—not unlike the narrative repetitions that occur whenever the place is invoked—that insists on an identity outside the intrusions of a hegemonizing modernity, whether
emanating from Salerno or Tokyo.

Reminders of the Archaic

Perhaps the most powerful moment of Yanagita's preface to *Tōno monogatari* is devoted to the moment of festival. Yet characteristically that
moment becomes the occasion for intense loneliness, for an encounter
with loss.

> At the Tenjin Shrine on the hill there was a festival with a lion
> dance. A light cloud of dust rose from the hill and bits of red
> could be seen against the green of the whole village. The dance
> in process, which they called a lion dance, was actually a

dance of the deer. Men wearing masks with deer horns attached to them danced along with five or six boys who were waving swords. The pitch of the flute was so high and the tone of the song so low that I could not understand what they were singing even though I was just off to the side. The sun sank lower and the wind began to blow; the voices of the drunkards calling out to others were lonely to hear.[43]

In Mishima's reflections on the *Tales*, he singled out this description of matsuri in order to invoke the twin qualities of lyricism (*jōjō*) and grief (*aishō*), which are best invoked by a poetics of absence and distance (and which are correlated to a certain kind of rhetorical privation). Yanagita first describes the festival from a remove; then, suddenly, his writing places him in proximity to the scene. Yet still there is something missing, a miscomprehension ("I could not understand what they were singing even though I was just off to the side"). In the end the reader is left with the lonely, unintelligible voices of drunkards at sunset.

The dance of the deer (shishi odori) is the most photographed performative image of Tōno, the one that calls up most readily the archaic festivity of rural community.[44] The role of the sword-wielding warriors who dance opposite the masked lion-deer is now most often played by junior high school girls; not enough boys are interested to form the all-male troupes demanded by convention. The junior high schools of Tōno are important places for the carrying on of traditionalized performance arts; as parents explained it to me, primary school children are too young and high school students too busy with exam preparations. The generational and gendered imperatives of carrying on the repetitive, emblematic events that underwrite civic identities are themselves open to displacement.

The deer dancers are a ubiquitous presence at civic events in Tōno (they made a striking appearance at the sister city ceremonies at Suikōen, for example) and at many shrine festivities as well. They are a primary folkloric component of Tōno's large city-wide matsuri each September, a festival for Hachiman, a deity found throughout Japan (known to older people as the Hachiman Matsuri). The festival has its origins in the seventeenth century, and its classic purpose has been to present entertainments for the pleasure of the kami and the local people in thanks for the harvest (many Hachiman festivals throughout

43. Yanagita, *Legends of Tōno*, 6.
44. For example, the English translation of *Tōno monogatari* features a photograph of the masked deer dancers on its cover.

Japan are held in September as harvest celebrations). In 1970, however, civic leaders enlarged the scope of the festival and expanded its reach as an area-wide event. They changed the name of the festival to the Tōno Matsuri and later went even further in naming it the Tōno Furusato Matsuri (Tōno Hometown Festival). By calling it a furusato matsuri the leaders tried to give the festival an appeal in keeping with the overall Tōnopia planning: the festival became a generic "hometown festival," both for Tōnoites and for tourists. The major attraction of the festival is the lengthy procession (now called a *pareido*) that winds from the Izu Shrine to the main staging ground of the Hachiman Shrine. Dozens of groups of dancers and musicians perform with the street as their stage in a display of Tōno's *minzoku geinō* (folk performing arts). Each neighborhood in the city sponsors several preservation societies (*hozonkai*); fifty-three groups participated in the 1983 festival.

Yet smaller-scale events more clearly invoke the linkages of repetition, loss, and festivity that Yanagita evoked in his preface's description of a shrine fete. Some of these events retain the older calendrical reckonings that most larger shrine festivals (and certainly the Tōno Furusato Matsuri) have long abandoned in favor of the Gregorian calendar. The region around Tōno is a repository of such practices, most of them well-documented and many of them no longer enacted. One, for example, called *umakko tsunagi* (horse tying ritual) occurs on the fifteenth day of the sixth month, according to the old lunar calendar. Straw figures of horses or woodblock-printed pictures of horses are placed along with offerings of rice cakes at crossroads, corners of rice fields, shrines, and borders. In Iwate prefecture the event features the placing of woodblock-printed images of horses (they resemble the images on *ema*, "votive tablets"). The process would seem to exemplify an agricultural event, but in fact umakko tsunagi has complex ties with the epitome of the elegant, urban festival—the Gion Matsuri of Kyoto, designed to pacify wrathful disease-carrying deities who, when placated, bring prosperity. Organized belief in these deities took the form of *goryō* cults. In the Gion beliefs the deity is known alternatively as the Yasaka deity; the "ox-headed emperor," Gozu-Tennō; or Susanō-no-mikoto, the violent god of the Japanese classics. Traveling ascetics disseminated this cult during the medieval period, and festivals and shrines of the Gion-Yasaka stream are found throughout Japan.[45] Ritual actions were performed to ward off disease in the midsummer, the

---

45. *Nihon minzoku jiten*, s.v. "Gion matsuri," "goryō," "somin shōrai," and "tennō matsuri."

Tōno's masked dance of the deer in
photographic progress

most dangerous time of the year for epidemics; in Tōno, the meaning
of the festival changed to indicate that children would grow as strong
as the horses depicted on the offered banners. Another explanation
states that the banners depict the swift horses that the local kami must
ride in order to make it in time for the festivities at the head shrines,
the Tsushima Shrine and the Yasaka Shrine, far away from the Tōhoku region.

Tōno also has its branch Yasaka Shrine, and umakko tsunagi occurs
there according to the western calendar, June 15. Yet there are still a
few moments in Tōno where older temporalities reemerge. I was included in an umakko tsunagi that occurred according to the old calendrical system, which in 1984 fell on July 12. A group of about twenty
neighbors and relatives had planned to gather at a mountaintop shrine
founded by wandering mountain ascetics from Mount Haguro (one of
the Dewa Sanzan, a classic locus of ascetic practices). The local supporters (kōchū) of this rustic shrine had decided that they would at
least gather to eat and to observe the day, but they had no plans for
actually performing the actions of umakko tsunagi itself. A well-
known photographer of Tōno associated with the city museum offered
to print the banners and bring them by, if someone from the group
would then place the offerings.[46]

The eighty-year-old grandmother of one of the organizing families
remembered the protocol. She made the arduous climb from the bottom with the rest of the women, as she became the ritual leader and
focus (the only one in the group who knew the correct order of the
event).[47] No one had made rice cakes (the canonically correct shrine
offering), so she put potato salad (the women had brought up water,
brooms, and rags in baskets on their backs, along with food) on each
banner, and led a small procession to the significant points around the
shrine: a stone marker dedicated to Batō Kannon (the horse-headed
Kannon, a permutation of one of Japan's most popular Buddhist-
derived deities, Kannon), a twisted pine tree, and lastly a cave where
beggars lived during the hard postwar period.

After the placing of the banners (repeated at least three times for

46. The photographer was Urata Hōichi, well known for his many distinguished images of the Tōno region.
47. What this discussion brackets, at the least, is the discursive emergence of the idea
of "ritual" itself as a disciplinary basic of anthropology. I am not entirely comfortable
with using "ritual" because of this particular history, but the Japanese terms used, such
as girei, are commonly translated as "ritual," "ceremony," or "rite." For a close anatomy
of the notion of ritual that traces its emergence in the specific historical-discursive context of Java—such that one could argue that a unified conception of "ritual" (upacara) did

the accompanying photographers) we gathered in the shrine building, which was practically empty except for some old festival banners, a tattered Japanese flag from World War II on the wall, and a spear that someone said had been used to drive away thieves. People drifted in slowly, walked immediately to the offering box at the back and threw money or rice into it. Then ensued the communal feast and sake drinking that seals most Japanese ritual activity.

The event was the only umakko tsunagi in Tōno to be held on the old calendrical date; even the Tsushima Shrine in the city had switched to the western calendar. Such kōchū-level events are increasingly rare, and the 1984 occasion took on the poignancy that such a lingering continuation of an older world invites. The participants themselves were well aware of this poignancy, as they talked about the changes in the Japanese spirit (postwar transformations and television were high on the list of causal agents), beliefs in kami, upkeep of shrine traditions, and the meaning of matsuri. They recognized that the children in the room would not observe this day when they reached adulthood fifteen years from now. They also realized that their meeting was a testament to the endurance of the small, cooperative community, what some call the kyōdōtai: "This is a *real* Japanese matsuri," I was told—meaning the small scale, intimate, and "simple" (soboku) activity that Yanagita and others found at the core of premodern Japanese religiosity.

In recognizing and noting this event as authentic, the participants clearly contrasted it to all the other matsuri in Japan that had lost these qualities. Even this most local and intimate of events became, then, representative: it signified something outside itself, as it came to stand generically for authentic Japanese folk rituals. The purposes of umakko tsunagi as explained in folklore texts or by the residents themselves receded into the background, peeling away from potential ritual efficacy, and instead the actions signified all that the ritual *used* to effect, performatively. The fact that the kōchū—urged on by the photographer affiliated with the museum—decided to hold this event one more time speaks for the value placed on sheer continuity. Indeed, that was perhaps the predominant inflection here: the significance of repetition itself, the value of preservation that tenaciously persists at such sublocal levels.

Another event that lingers as a reminder of the archaic in Tōno, yet

---

not even exist before the early twentieth century—see John Pemberton, *On the Subject of "Java."*

in quite a different register from umakko tsunagi, is *mushi okuri*, an event designed to expel harmful insects from the community. These bugs were identified with disease-carrying evil spirits, and a ritual to expel them from the village occurred after the midsummer weeding of the rice fields. Elderly men headed a procession with drums, banners, and bells and carried male and female straw effigies. The procession deposited the effigies at village boundaries, by rivers, or at crossroads; after that, the *buraku* (a small local residential grouping, the most common term used for this grouping in Tōno) held a communal feast. Variants of mushi okuri exist throughout Japan, but it has tended to become a clearly detachable performance piece as postwar pesticides eliminated the old antagonists of the ritual: the pesky bugs themselves.

In Tōno, pesticides had totally eliminated mushi okuri even as a performance event, but in July 1984 the Tōno city government resurrected it as a children's event renamed *kodomo mushi matsuri* (Children's Bug Festival); the host location was Denshōen. The flyer describing the day's activities summarized mushi matsuri this way:

> Farm families, who prayed for bountiful harvests, feared damage from harmful insects right along with wind and rain damage. Mushi matsuri was a collective event held to expel harmful insects. It was thought that an outbreak of disease-carrying or damaging insects was due to the workings of evil spirits, and these *akurei* were expelled or driven outside the village in the mushi matsuri.
>
> In the Tōno area, this event was performed at the time when insects are most prevalent: after weeding (first part of the sixth month) through the middle of the summer. The people who participated were generally the people of the buraku—at the least, fifteen people; at the most, forty. Straw male and female dolls were carried at the head of the procession, followed by musicians and banner carriers. The *idaina mono* [genitalia] were attached between the legs of the dolls, and this demonstrated the strength that would ward off evil spirits. The participants would sing, and while they sang they walked around the footpaths between the paddies. They would then send off the evil spirits to the village boundaries, rivers, or crossroads. After this, they returned to someone's house and had a feast.
>
> This event was popularly held until World War II; it completely faded away after the war because of the development of agricultural pesticides.[48]

48. The flyer gave a complete list of necessary ritual paraphernalia and the number of participants; it also printed the words of the song used during the procession.

The city explicitly resurrected this ritual as a Tōno-wide educational children's event, as something revived in order to transmit the old way to children (this educational, socializing function is one of the key roles set out for the local country parks). In this representation (which indeed stands for all the elusive power of vanished and vanishing practices), the middle generation, here identified with the Tōno city governmental and educational institutions, assumed management of the ritual process. This managing generation has a distanced relationship to the efficacy of mushi okuri—an agricultural event that, even more than many others, found its basis undermined by the scientific worldview and its practical chemical consequences. Older people who had participated in this event before the war constructed the *wara ningyō* (straw effigies), made the banners, and carried the dolls at the head of the procession. These elders, whose knowledge is no longer linked to ritual efficacy, now index the fact that such efficacy *used* to exist and are essential to re-creating the event. For the old folks, the procession and its preparations operated as a memorial event, something that induced nostalgic memories of the past (the elderly participants called it *natsukashii*, the Japanese correlate for "nostalgic"). For the children, mushi okuri was presented as instructional *asobi* (play).

Overseeing an event that is both a bittersweet memorial event and edifying play is the middle generation of adult teachers, museum workers, and city planners. The children and the old people assure this generation that they are, in fact, preserving and transmitting something construed as traditionally valuable; in many ways, then, the upper and lower generations are conflated (the actual participants in the performance of the event were elderly Tōnoites and children). Belief in the efficacy of eradicating pests by parading straw effigies through the rice fields, then expelling them at liminal points outside the village is a partial pretense held by the adults organizing the event: perhaps the old people believed it at some point and the children might believe their ritual explanations. To a significant extent, the children and old people act out the ritual for the sake of the organizing middle generation, as a form of assurance that things continue.

Mushi matsuri expels evil, so the explanations go. The straw dolls are human substitutes, scapegoat figures which absorb evil spirits (akurei) and are then driven out of the community. Attaching genitalia to the effigies was considered crucial in connecting the exorcism of evil bugs with fertile, life-giving powers. But in this *mane* ("imitation," or *imiteishon*, as one observer termed the event), these finer ritual points were lost. The genitalia were not attached to the dolls, and the effigies, instead of being expelled at a crossroads or riverbank, were

The origin and final resting
place for the straw effigies paraded
in Tōno's mushi matsuri

instead retained, returned to the starting point at Denshōen. The ritual process thus closed back on itself and came full circle, as the scapegoat figures were *preserved* rather than expelled, propped up in front of the stone markers at the point of origin for leisurely photo opportunities.

The event is an allegory, I think, of how such ritual processes are often constrained to operate under modern regimes of knowledge. Sacrificial logics do not operate. The moment of expulsion—of risk— is now foreclosed, as the tracing of a perfect circularity replaces the movement toward an outside. Rather than an opening toward alterity (however structurally determined that might be) a closed circuit takes its place. (Even in the Tōno Furusato Matsuri, a circular parade has replaced the earlier procession—*gyōretsu*—between the two sponsoring shrines.) The problem of excess—whether in exchange relations or in the calculus of purity and pollution—is not recognizable as such here.

However explicitly this particular event, with its civic sponsorship and educational intent, is parasitic on its older contexts and meanings, it is not merely recuperative or even imitative. In one sense, of course, it is. It is a mimesis of what mushi matsuri used to be; it is a performance of what the practices used to perform. But such events are not thereby rendered hollow. There was a certain dutifulness to the reenactment of mushi matsuri that was undeniably touching. And it is this very dutifulness that framed it as an enactment of the impossibilities of modernity. Not simply a nostalgic re-creation of practices past, it is instead—or rather, *also*—a dramatization of the once-more-removed situation of modern mimesis.

Continuity per se is acted out (and it is important to remember that the very notion of "tradition" really indicates, above all else, the imperatives of continuity). Some analysts of Japanese practices would argue that the doing of a ritual, in any case, is the key point; Japanese ritual practice is orthopractical: doing is believing, performativity is all. While I might agree with that argument where personal practices at shrines and temples are concerned—getting fortunes read, offering votive tablets for examination success, or buying protective amulets— such community-based performances as I have been describing have a different resonance. They designate a gap (a lack) that practice, the performance itself, does not—cannot—bridge. Indeed, the performances dramatize that very gap. "Ritual," rather than indicating those moments when ethos and worldview magically come together, or actualizing the "really real," in the contemporary Japanese case often points to a situation in which performance itself comes to the fore:

precisely the "*not* really real," if by the real we are to agree with the classic implications offered by Clifford Geertz.[49] If, however, the Lacanian idea of the real retains some force, then these performative acts sharply illustrate the dilemma of that which can only be called up through the evocation of absence (what could evoke the dilemma of the real more sharply than the missing genitalia of the effigies?). When that absence is breached, the uncanny emerges. These performances exemplify the modern desire to keep the uncanny at bay—to evoke the real without allowing its irruption into everyday life—within a community which has itself been fantasized as uncanny.

Many of Tōno's narratives and ritual events speak all too clearly of death and poverty, marginalized realities which now perform other poetic functions for the future of utopia. The sharply uncanny aspects of Tōno as a meta-furusato remain bounded by discourses of preservation and narratives of nostalgia, although the presence of those boundaries still recall the excessive traces of an all-too-haunted past. The next chapter looks more closely at other articulations of death, desire, and language in contemporary Japan, as it examines a site and a moment when national-cultural desire and personal loss coalesce in markedly intimate practices, practices devoted to recalling the dead.

49. The idea of religion as resting on the production of the "really real" through various forms of symbolic activity (primary among them "ritual") is developed in Clifford Geertz's essay "Religion as a Cultural System."

CHAPTER FIVE

Ghostly Epiphanies:
Recalling the Dead on Mount Osore

Few places present to contemporary Japanese as strange a reflection of the remainders of modernity as Mount Osore. Osorezan—the name could be translated as Mount Dread—is a mountain dominating the Shimokita peninsula, at the northernmost tip of Honshū, Japan's main island. This northern limit is one of the most remote regions of Japan. Dense forests cover over half the peninsula, and its wild coastline and mountainous terrain combine to give it a persistent aura of rugged inaccessibility, of being a last frontier. With its location as limit and boundary have come obscurity and poverty; a sense of secrets hidden, mysteries undiscovered, old practices still surviving lingers. Shimokita thus represents a limit to knowledge, knowledge of another Japan.[1]

Mount Osore is a singular, foreboding presence, covered with thick cypress forests, in what is sometimes romantically described as an unexplored region (*hikyō*). It rises out of the center of the peninsula, but precipitously reverses its slope at the summit. Almost coincident with this downslope comes something equally surprising: the unmistakable, overpowering odor of sulfur. This incongruous smell announces what lies ahead, at the bottom of the downslope. For the summit of Mount Osore is a crater, and the mountain itself a dormant volcano.

1. In 1903 the navy established a torpedo base at Ominato on the coast of the Shimokita peninsula, and in 1906 the harbor was declared vital to the national interest. Because of military secretiveness, Shimokita was excluded from much scholarly research until after World War II. There were, however, local histories, descriptions, and travel reports of some merit in the interim.

The first large-scale scholarly project concerning the Shimokita peninsula was carried

141

The crater is an expanse of volcanic rocks, steam vents, bubbling sulfurous pools, and hot springs extending to the shoreline of a deep blue, deadly still lake (the sulfur kills fish). Within this landscape, which resembles the site of an atomic explosion rendered uninhabitable by residual radioactivity, is a Buddhist temple complex; some of its buildings have stainless steel roofs to stave off the corrosive effects of sulfur. The complex resembles a frontier outpost; the buildings, guarding what is said to be one of the last remaining approaches to the "other world" in Japan, make no particular attempt to master or surpass their surroundings. The other two of the "three great holy places" (*sandai reijō*) in Japan with which Mount Osore is ranked (Mount Kōya and Mount Hiei) are topped with monumental, ancient, and enormous complexes: gates, pagodas, subtemples, massive statuary, graveyards. Osorezan's bleakness undercuts the basis for a focus on architectural grandeur. More than at many such famous Buddhist sites, the terrain itself overshadows its managing institution.

It is a terrain deathly enough to deserve its name, for the object of dread or terror (*osore*) at this place is death. In northeastern Japan, Mount Osore has long been the final destination of the spirits of the dead, the ultimate home where the dead continue to live a shadowy parallel "life." Yet more than just the home of the dead, the mountain is a place of practices for consoling, pacifying, and communicating with them, particularly during one delimited period of the summer. As such, Mount Osore has become a powerful site for the enactment of allegories of loss, a staging ground for practices that linger on the verge of vanishing. Blind female mediums (*itako*) become critical in these allegories of loss and recovery through their spirit recollections, *kuchiyose*, meaning "to call by mouth." Through their bodily voicings of the words of the dead—and through their other vocation of predicting the future—the itako enact scenarios of losses momentarily confronted, remembered, and mourned, allowing Japanese to confront both personal and historical pasts, often in ways that come to terms with Japanese modernity and its disappearances. Personal, visceral attempts to remember the particular dead strangely converge with the national-cultural reasons motivating many to come to Mount Osore: to see and experience a vanishing *Japanese* mode of encountering death. Even with that convergence, mourning at Mount Osore is often incomplete, haunted by yet other necessities and imperatives, influenced by

out in 1963–64 by a consortium of nine academic disciplines (termed the *kugakkai rengō*). Takamatsu Keikichi, *Shimokita hantō no minkan shinkō*, 11–14.

other interests and desires, inflected by unease. A range of visitors—metropolitan tourists, foreign anthropologists, local elderly, temple patrons, hip teenagers from Tokyo discovering (exotic) Japan, prefectural folklorists, NHK reporters—pluralizes any singular allegory that might unfold on its rugged terrain. Indeed, that terrain is already and expressly allegorical, inscribed with a profusion of sites that refer to heavens, hells, and liminal states within an old Buddhist cosmology. The very plurality of desires that motivate journeys to Mount Osore indicates the ways in which it draws together a tangled nexus of Japanese fantasies about death and its possible overcoming. Mount Osore exists alongside Tōno as an allegorical instance of Japanese remainders of modernity, yet it more explicitly foregrounds practices of death and recovery, not with remembered, narrativized tales of modernity's residues, but through fragmented revoicings of that which has passed on. The dead can literally be made to speak again on Mount Osore. And if the dead can speak again, both the archaic Japanese past and the past of individual seekers can be kept suspended on the threshold of vanishing (not gone, not quite).

Although Mount Osore now operates within a national, mass-mediated array of images and ideas about the folkic marginal, historically it was a specific, local topos of death. To many folklorists of Japan, this specific locating of death in nearby mountains forms an original stratum of Japanese folk beliefs. Mountains were often actual burial sites, abodes of dead spirits and of gods at one and the same time. The projection of death and its aftermath onto mountains, called *sanchūtakaikan* (belief in the 'other world' in the mountains), fused with postmedieval Buddhist conceptions which projected symbolic itineraries of pure lands (*jōdo*) and polluted hells (*jigoku*) onto mountains, creating a doubled structure of mountains as both literal and figurative domains of death. Mount Osore's strange topology and its remoteness augmented its image as an uncanny other world (*takai*) where the dead and the living exist simultaneously.[2]

From a local site of death specific to the people living near it, Mount Osore's notoriety expanded to become a generalized Japanese *reijō*

---

2. There is an enormous amount of research in Japanese folklore studies centered on the significance of mountains. For a brief description of sanchūtakaikan, see Sakurai Tokutarō, "Minkan shinkō to sangaku shūkyō." Sakurai initially makes a distinction between the other world as a strange or foreign land (*ikyō*) and the other world as the after-death state (*shigo takai*), but then says the two ideas have much in common, particularly when mountains become the loci of conceptions of the other world. Also see Hori Ichirō, *Folk Religion in Japan: Continuity and Change*, especially chapter 4, "Mountains and

(holy place, often precisely referring to such Buddhist-managed sacred mountains). By the mid-Tokugawa period (1603–1868), it had already emerged as a powerful site well known as far south as Osaka and Kyoto.[3] The proselytizing efforts of Entsūji, the Sōtō Zen temple that has claimed jurisdiction over the mountain since the sixteenth century, particularly recommended the miraculous efficacy of Enmei Jizō ("life-prolonging" Jizō), the main Buddhist deity enshrined there. Mount Osore's topography of death ensured its continuing fascination for a welter of sometimes contentious esoteric Buddhist priests, ascetic practitioners, worshipers, and travelers; it ensured as well an accompanying multiplicity of objects of worship, deities, shrines, and holy spots.[4] This multiplicity seemed to be unified only by virtue of the singular topos which supported it.

Within this cult of the mountain (*Osorezan shinkō*), however, the deity Jizō arose as the primary object of veneration. Not inappropriately, either: Mount Osore's sulfur, caldera, and hot springs had long weighted its image toward the infernal. Hell is indeed the perfect ground for the compassionate ministrations of Jizō, for this deity—perhaps the most

---

Their Importance for the Idea of the Other World," 141–79; and Komatsu Kazuhiko, "Yosute to sanchūtakai," in *Kamigami no seishinshi*, 177–98. Komatsu's essay was an early structuralist analysis (first published in 1972) of mountains as liminal other worlds.

Historically, mountains have been powerful locations of alterity in Japanese culture. They have represented the unknown, the inconceivable: sites of "terrible multiplicities." (Nakazawa Shin'ichi, personal communication). In both what is "terrible" (terror-inducing or awe-inspiring) and what is "multiple" (excessive, beyond language) mountains function as representations of what might be called a Japanese sublime. There is a vast discourse built up around mountains in Japan which fuses "death" and "mountains" as sublime unknowns, with attendant practices of framing, bounding, limiting, and troping this sublimity.

3. Sakurai Tokutarō, *Nihon no shamanizumu*, 1:150.

4. The history of Mount Osore before the sixteenth century is only sparsely documented. From the *Tōhoku taiheiki*, a military chronicle, it is evident that a mountain temple *(mine no tera)* of some sort was in existence before 1457, when it was destroyed, but little is known about religious practices centering around the mountain until the founding of the Sōtō Zen sect temple, Entsūji, in the early sixteenth century. The fortunes of the entire Shimokita region were tied up with those of the Nanbu clan, but there is a dearth of documents concerning the Nanbu clan and Mount Osore before the seventeenth century.

From the opening of Entsūji in the early sixteenth century until it consolidated its control in 1780, the management of Mount Osore was a source of contention. In particular, the period from 1670, when the esoteric Buddhist Tendai sect temple Rengeji was opened, until 1780, when it was closed and turned over to the Jōdo sect temple Jōnenji, was a time of marked struggle. Many local temples and ascetic practitioners sided with one sect or the other in the conflict. The Tendai sect even sent an emissary in 1698 from Hieizan, its mountain headquarters near Kyoto, to claim its rights over Mount Osore (a

ubiquitous, popular, and widely loved in Japanese religion   rescues
the dead from the torments of hell. Jizō is also perhaps the most muta-
ble of Japanese deities, subsuming an array of signifying possibilities
that exceed his classic role as savior of the damned. In Shimokita, local
religious associations centered around Jizō (Jizō-kō) in many of the villages ringing Mount Osore formed the backbone of belief in the mountain.[5] These associations, as well as individual households, relied
closely on the services of itako, who are hired at specific times to tell
fortunes, convey the predictions of kami, and to call down (kuchiyose)
spirits for their relatives.

Memorialization and Its Others

The feast day of Jizō, the twenty-fourth day of each month, is the occasion for a gathering of these religious associations. The biggest of these
feast days falls on the twenty-fourth day of the sixth month of the old
calendrical system, the so-called Jizō-bon. All of Jizō's feast days are
connected with death, but Jizō-bon is the one most explicitly regarded
as a day of return for the dead.[6]

Jizō-bon awakens the temple, which is usually as fitfully dormant as
the steaming crater on which it is built, into preparations for the biggest event of the year on the mountain, the Osorezan taisai (grand festival). Hundreds of Buddhist priests, workers, local faithful, curious
tourists, and hopeful bereaved from throughout Japan ascend the
mountain during the five-day "festival" (now fixed at July 20–24),
which is the main source of Mount Osore's fame. The temple on the
mountain, Entsūji, then holds an official range of rites aimed at memo-

---

touch ironic in view of Osorezan's current ranking alongside Hieizan as one of Japan's
three great holy places). It based its claims partially on the widespread belief that Enkaku Daishi, an early Tendai saint, "opened" the mountain for religious austerities (over
forty sacred mountains north of Iwate prefecture claim Enkaku Daishi as "opening"
them to Buddhism). A series of counterclaims followed, with the authorities of the
Nanbu domain (which controlled large areas of Iwate and Aomori prefectures, including Shimokita) recognizing Entsūji's control over the mountain at least by 1780. In the
process, Entsūji seems to have accommodated diverse esoteric shrines and practices,
with the result that the temple at Mount Osore is often taken to be a Shingon or Tendai
temple. From Kusunoki Masahiro, "Osorezan Shinkō."

5. For a description of Jizō beliefs, Jizō-kō, and itako see Nihon minzoku jiten, s.v. "Jizō-
kō," "Jizō shinkō," and "itako".

6. Hori, Folk Religion, 207–10.

rializing the dead (*kuyō*), rites which aim to pacify the dead by remembering them through offerings, prayers, and recitations of scripture.[7] By correctly remembering the dead through these practices, the living hope to console them as well as to keep them from troubling this world. Yet practices and beliefs which are not subsumed by official Buddhist methods for controlling the dead allow the living to contact the dead, potentially disrupting the authority of the temple.

Travelers, government inspectors, and other visitors to the far north would first mention the mountain's bizarre topography, and second its great summer event, when Mount Osore came alive with both festivity and practices surrounding death. Kōda Rohan, a significant Meiji-era author, described the scene he observed on a trip to Mount Osore in the 1880s:

> Lastly I arrived at the Jizō Hall, and what was this? A terrific hustle and bustle, and a confused clamor of voices; finely dyed big and small banners and flags, flapping in a strange wind, with "Usorizan Enmei Jizō-son" and words in the local dialect written in *manyōgana*; male and female worshipers walking around, left and right; old grandpas wearing *donza*; young women with their red leggings showing, calling out to their friends. . . . Young guys, drunk, with coin pouches dangling from their necks; children walking round munching on cheap sweets; old women gumming their mantras . . . everybody variously occupied with his own activities, in a scene of completely confused liveliness. . . . In the temple precincts, with the ground muddy from the warm water seeping up from below, the peddlers who come to the mountain at festival time had set up their stalls. Quite a few small toy and novelty craftsmen were there, stalls which sold all sorts of cheap goods and services: real bears' livers, peppermint water, clogs, martial arts demonstrations, moxabustion techniques "used by the

---

7. Kuyō is defined by *Kenkyūsha's New Japanese-English Dictionary* as a memorial service. Kuyō is a complex concept that refers to any Buddhist-influenced ritual performed in remembrance of living beings who have died, or objects which are broken or have outlived their usefulness. Thus there are *senzo kuyō* for the ancestral dead; *segaki kuyō* for *muenbotoke*, the dead who are "unconnected," who have no known living kin to memorialize them; *hari kuyō*, performed for old or broken needles. In Japan, kuyō can refer generally to any Buddhist matsuri. Kuyō is used almost interchangeably with another key term in Japanese Buddhism, *ekō*, translated by Buddhologists as "merit transference"—the idea that the living can store up merit and transfer it to others, in particular the dead—but defined popularly (and in the same Kenkyūsha dictionary as above) as a memorial service for the dead. For a discussion of memorialization and veneration of the dead, see Robert J. Smith, *Ancestor Worship in Contemporary Japan*.

saint Kōbō Daishi himself," and on and on, with the peddlers
calling out, hawking their wares to the worshipers. There were
some smiling young girls who had bought combs made of
cows' hooves; a big man, with his elaborately oiled old-
fashioned topknot pushed over to one side, was having "Kōbō
Daishi's moxabustion" applied to the exposed bald spot on the
top of his head.

I next went to the place on the mountain called Sainokawara.
From where they had come I don't know—but at the side of
the path there were a number of beggars lined up. One with a
scroll of Amida; one using a statue of Kannon Fudō as a deco-
ration; one wearing white pilgrim's garb.... From the other
direction I heard the groaning and moaning of uncanny voices
intoning sutras and mantras, and the shaking of bells. Suddenly, a sobbing voice pierced my ears. I ran toward the sound,
wondering what on earth was the matter. There, in front of a
statue of Jizō—what was she remembering?—was a woman
of some thirty-odd years, totally oblivious to the people
around her, sobbing with grief. Her companions, too—some
crying quietly, muffling their sobs; some screwing up their
eyes, holding back the tears.... There was an old woman
among them, who told them that instead of crying in vain, it
would be better if they would repeat the Nembutsu, and she
intoned it with all her might: Namada, Namada, Namada, Namada.... The first woman had probably lost a beloved child
recently; she had come to this inhospitable place, Sainokawara,
thinking back to the time of death and praying for the future
of her child—or so I imagined. Standing off to the side, looking on, I thought it was a pitiful sight; yet young men with
knowing faces passed by, deriding the worshipers and coldly
laughing at the crying women. Who can fathom the human
heart?[8]

The first thing that strikes Rohan is the clamor, the din of voices, persons, and sights at the festival scene. He describes the festival as a
confusion of voices, of simultaneous actions. There is a series of activities, seemingly unrelated except for the linkage provided by the field
of the temple fair. The festival is a scene of commerce, and the items
sold are as unrelated as the diversity of the people and sights there:
peppermint water, clogs, cows'-hoof combs. The cheap and everyday
are juxtaposed to the expensive and rare, toys to real bears' livers. Men
and women of both generations stride the temple grounds; gender and

8. Kōda Rohan, *Rohan zenshū* 10:95–96.

age commingle. Sights and sounds are exchanged in a commerce of signs: people call out, peddlers hawk their wares. And in Rohan's description, it is all coterminous, occurring in the space before the main temple that houses the mountain's "life-extending" deity, Jizō.

But now, even as the festive scene in front of the Jizō Hall continues, Rohan enters a different clamor of simultaneous voices and characters, occurring on a rocky, volcanic stretch that separates the temple complex proper from the lakefront called *gokuraku no hama* (shore of paradise): beggars, mantras, sobs, pilgrims, statues, groans, and crying women are juxtaposed as promiscuously as in the first scene. Mount Osore's festival of death, in this nineteenth-century traveler's account, is a site of disorderly, sensuous simultaneity where voices "pierce the ears" and lead the viewer onward. Rohan's evocation of the summer festival reveals a division of space and of practices at Mount Osore: a scene of commerce and festivity swirling around the temple's official center, and a scene of supplication and mourning on Sainokawara, the "dry riverbank" that is the boundary between this world and the other. Such scenes are presented as points in an itinerary, as places to be traversed, viewed, and again, heard.

Rohan's account of the Mount Osore temple fair provides a classic example of the carnivalesque plenitude and confusion that older Japanese remember from their childhood, and which contemporary events strive to recapture. A temple fair should be the site of commerce, festivity, and exchange. What struck Rohan as unusual, however, and what continues to strike contemporary travelers to Mount Osore is the simultaneous occurrence of mourning. Even though Buddhist temples form themselves around the managing of death, and temple fairs can also be occasions for orderly memorializing of the dead, it is not usual for people viscerally to grieve in close, confused juxtaposition to the space of festivity. Mount Osore was and is a divided territory where this juxtaposition could occur. In addition to official memorialization and its various practices—practices that aim to settle the dead person and to distance, in effect, the living from a too-close association with the dead—there are practices that supplement or even overturn, with a profusion of voices and ghostly epiphanies, memorialization and its writings. The mountain remains a divided space where death and its representations in memory and language cross each other.

Mount Osore is to Japanese today a doubled "other world," a place that is visited both to memorialize and thus safely distance loss (here described as "death"), and to communicate with that loss, particularly through spirit mediums. It has attained notoriety in the mass media both as an ancient repository of something basic to the Japanese spirit and as an uncanny repository of the dead. Mount Osore attains a powerful metaphorical edge because it is concurrently an image of the unrecoverability of tradition, of a vanishing cultural otherness—although paradigmatically Japanese—and of personal loss. It retains this edge in spite of, or perhaps because of, a current milieu that no longer generally sustains belief in other worlds, but rather brackets otherness and recuperates loss.

Practices at Mount Osore circulate around stabilizing the dead through memorialization and the momentary unbinding of that stability through grief and remembrance, through mourning. Cross-cutting these two modalities are persistent rumors and stories of ghosts and the contemporary production of excess in the form of offerings.⁹ Memorialization and mourning involve distinct ensembles of practices, narratives, and uses of language: memorialization practices tend to be enfolded more explicitly within what could be called, following Michel de Certeau, a "scriptural" economy (and their articulation with official Buddhist scripture is only the most obvious one here), while the recallings of the dead by the blind mediums and the voicings of grief they inspire are peripheral (literally, as we shall see) to this economy. Yet the clarity of this distinction cannot be sustained, despite the temple's overt attempts to contain the interventions of the mediums. The promiscuous repeating of ghost rumors, too, troubles the distinctions between the scriptural and the oral, memorialization and mourning, and official and nonofficial practices of the dead.¹⁰

In conventional Buddhist thought in Japan, a distinction is made between the "newly" dead and the "settled" dead. The newly dead are those that have died, usually, within the last forty-nine days and thus are not yet settled. There are many other kinds of unsettled dead,

9. I visited Mount Osore in the summer of 1984. This chapter is based on my research there as well as later archival research. While there I conversed with and interviewed pilgrims, visitors, tourists, and local residents. The narratives I recount here come from those encounters and conversations.

10. See Bakhtin, *The Dialogic Imagination.* On the difference between speech and writing, see the works of Jacques Derrida, but particularly *Of Grammatology.* Derrida's work is a deconstruction proper of the valorization of voice over writing in Western discourse, as he necessarily undoes the very distinction between voice and writing. For a very different sort of analysis, one that analyzes the technological dimensions of speech and writing in a pre-Derridean mode, see Walter Ong, *Orality and Literacy.* Michel de Certeau's collection of essays, *The Practice of Everyday Life* is concerned with the relationship of language, spatial practices, and power, as he develops the implications of a modern, capitalist "scriptural economy" and its implications for the place of orality as the "remainder" of that system.

but in all cases, memorial services are intended to settle them. That is the primary goal of many Buddhist rites (*segakie*, for example) and the domestic household rites connected with so-called ancestor worship.[11] Memorialization is really the remembering of the dead in order to settle them. When correct memorialization occurs, the unsettled newly dead (*shirei*) can become settled "ancestral dead" (*sorei*), and as ancestors (*senzo*) can benefit and protect the living. Those that are not remembered—or who have not been remembered adequately—remain unsettled and are thus on the loose, dangerous: if the living forget or neglect the dead, then the dead can haunt them as ghosts. Ghosts indicate that the structure of remembering through memorialization is not completely efficacious, that the line between life and death that remembering the dead institutes is not secure.

Memorial practices thus allow the living to work through grief, to idealize the dead, and to substitute images of the person as really "dead" for the memory of the person as he or she was in life. Through memorialization, memory becomes once-removed from all the images that surround the thought of the person and evoke grief.[12] By "remembering" the dead, by carrying out practices that ensure they will settle into buddahood and become beneficial ancestors, the living are able to relinquish mourning. Properly memorialized, the dead also become sources of blessings in this world (*gense riyaku*) and offer protection for their memorializers. Memorializing the dead is intimately connected with the fear of misfortune (provoked by the unsettled dead)

---

11. See Richard Huntington and Peter Metcalf, *Celebrations of Death: The Anthropology of Mortuary Ritual*, for an overview of mortuary practices and approaches to death in several western and nonwestern societies. The most comprehensive English-language work on Japanese ancestor worship, memorial practices, and spirit beliefs is Robert J. Smith's *Ancestor Worship in Contemporary Japan*.

12. Freud explores this process of working through memories in his 1917 essay "Mourning and Melancholia," in which he states that the survivor must recall and work through all the memories of the loved person, confirming the reality of loss and withdrawing all attachments to those memories. Only after this lengthy and painful process is completed can the dead person be remembered without grief; only then can the dead's memory be set aside.

In Japan this process is helped along by the idealization of the dead that occurs through memorialization and accession to ancestral status. In another society, Java, there seems to be an almost complete lack of mourning as Freud describes it: the dead person is almost instantly idealized. James T. Siegel describes the interworkings of language, memory, and sensory experience in interpreting this Javanese absence of mourning in his brilliant "Images and Odors in Javanese Practices Surrounding Death." A strongly contrasting essay that describes the interweaving of grief, memory, and rage in Ilongot culture is Renato Rosaldo's "Grief and a Headhunter's Rage: On the Cultural Force of Emotions."

and the hope for blessings (afforded by the settled dead). Both depend on the failure or efficacy of the living's remembrance.

Mount Osore is constructed as one vast memorialization apparatus, through which the dead can be properly remembered. Buying memorial tablets, giving offerings, performing rituals to console *muenbotoke*, the "unconnected dead"—all these constitute an official round of memorial practices. They fall within the purview of the temple's ritual specialists and often culminate in marked, designated allegorical inscriptions of space through which worshipers walk and follow along performing acts of *kuyō* (Buddhist memorialization). One of the most significant of these practices is the offering of stones or commodities.

Boundaries of Excess: Markings, Offerings, Garbage

People from the surrounding areas who come regularly follow a fixed round of practices at Mount Osore. They might take a bath in one of the rustic bathhouses built above the hot springs, dance *bon odori* (a group dance performed at the annual festival of the dead) at night, or consult a spirit medium on the condition of a dead relative; but the first and foremost practice for many is to memorialize the dead through a combination of approved practices.

To memorialize often simply means to buy a *tōba* (in this case, a wooden memorial stupa), or in the local dialect, to "buy a Buddha" *(hotoge o kau)*, using the euphemism (*hotoke* in standard Japanese) that can refer to a corpse, a dead person's spirit, or an enlightened being. Local people who buy tōba at Mount Osore's summer festival are those who, for one reason or another (often because of money) could not have the regular memorial services performed by their family temple *(danka no tera)* below. Instead, they will buy a Buddha at Mount Osore. There is a local superstition that one should have only a single memorial service performed per year; if you do it twice, then "you might have to do it a third time," which means that somebody will die. In other words, if you have already had a memorial service performed at the family temple, then you should avoid buying a tōba at Mount Osore.

Hotoke o kau vividly signifies the process of substitution of a tōba for the dead person's body. Memorializing the dead is a way of replacing the memory of the dead person by substituting a marker (or memorial) for the image of the dead. The practice of buying a hotoke

starts to unravel the connection between death, memory, and signification.

Buying a tōba is one of the main objectives of visiting Mount Osore,
one that is deeply connected with the Sōtō-sect temple's management
of death and ancestor worship. After paying a specified amount (the
tōba come in different sizes), the buyer receives a receipt and a blank
wooden plaque; he or she then usually waits again for a priest to
"write" the tōba. Tōba are always written; in this practice the stupa
itself is inseparable from the inscription. Only the inscription can acti-
vate the efficacy of the tōba in consoling and settling the dead. This
priestly function of writing has not been eclipsed at contemporary Japanese temples; a formalized writing insures that memorialization—
correct and beneficial remembering of the dead—will occur.

The priest writes "Osorezan Jizō," the month and date of birth of
the person being memorialized, and "Senzo daidai kuyōtō" (perpetual
memorial stupa for the ancestors) or a similar phrase, and then at least
the family name of the dead person. The person receives the tōba, then
walks outside to the adjoining *sotobakūyōdō* (chapel for offering the memorial stupas). People usually hand their tōba to one of the workers
in the chapel, light incense, bow, and then wait. During the five days
of the festival I witnessed, rarely was an actual priest on hand; usually
tape-recorded sutras took the place of the priest's voice. When a priest
was there, he read the names on the stupas in succession, and intoned
sutras. Then workers gathered up the plaques and distributed them to
waiting relatives, who set them up on the open ground next to the
chapel, called the *tōbajō.*

At the tōbajō were several large wooden plaques, each with a different family name on it. The stacking of the tōba at Mount Osore seemed
to be random, with a profusion of wooden tōba leaning against one
another and the permanent wooden plaques. After setting up the tōba,
the families put out offerings and lit incense. They then often sat or
reclined on mats, made small fires, talked, laughed, ate, and drank.
The tobajō had the appearance of a picnic ground.

Tōba are conventionally clustered around graves and are put up at
different points in the memorial cycle. Ordinarily, too, graves have
some relationship to the cremated remains *(ikotsu)* of the dead (the
ashes are placed in compartments beneath the tombstones). Yet at
Mount Osore—the home of the dead—there is no large graveyard.
This partial separation from material remains (which retain a powerful
metonymic tie with the dead person) allows an abstracted notion of
"death" to be detached from its associations with the dead's physical

Surrounded by memorial tablets,
worshipers rest in front
of their offerings

remains. Mount Osore is at one and the same time a place of palpable death, as the home of spirits, and a site that works precisely to distance death.[13]

There is, however, an ossuary (*hōkotsutō*), a place where priests deposit the ashes (or part of the ashes) of the dead. This ossuary is separate from the place for offering the tōba, and thus is not immediately associated with the memorial stupa. It is as if Mount Osore, as a generalized place for the dead, could not quite do without bits of physical remains as reminders of specific deaths. In local lore, a dead person will trouble one's dreams and ask to be "taken" to Mount Osore; there is also the belief that the remains or part of the remains (often expressed as *shikotsu*, the teeth or jawbone) must be offered to the hōkotsutō within one year of a person's death. Yet all the remains are commingled in this ossuary; there are no separate compartments for different families' ashes—no insistence on segregating a particular person's ashes in a particular, named resting place—and no graveyard covers the mountain. Despite its one ossuary, which takes its place as yet another stupalike prominence to be regarded as a site for offerings, Mount Osore effectively severs the connections between death, physical remains, and permanent family gravesites. Instead, it becomes a generalized site of death, a metagraveyard in which all the dead can be memorialized without reference to specific graves.

The tōbajō functions as a substitute graveyard, with its forest of memorial markers recalling the density of monuments in many actual graveyards in Japan. Each tōba (again, also called *hotoge* in the local dialect) substitutes for a particular dead person; all together, the profusion of tōba—all written by priestly authorities—reassures the worshiper that within this defined area death is ordered and put in its place, marked off and indicated by the tōba themselves. This distancing of the dead provides a comfort and reassurance that seems to foreclose any actual mourning here. More than any other open space I observed at Mount Osore, the tōbajō was familiar, relaxed; here a festive air prevailed.

The tōbajō is not a place for the expression of grief partly, I think, because it is a place where death has been clearly and sufficiently demarcated. The specific act of buying a memorial tōba brings the dead person more securely within the domain of controlled, orderly ances-

---

13. Although many reijō memorialize the dead with monuments and stupas, it is somewhat unusual to have a reijō of this size without a noticeable graveyard on the premises. It is unusual enough that many folklore scholars and visitors to the mountain have commented on the fact.

torhood. People relax here because they have done all that is necessary: having remembered the dead person and marked that remembrance with a memorial stupa, they are in no danger of being surprised by an untoward encounter with the dead. Such an encounter would indicate a failure of memorialization to detach and fix the memory of the dead person. The activities at the tōbajō substitute a fixed (one could almost say "dead") memory of the dead person, signified by the personalized tōba, for a living, grief-stricken recalling.

Memorialization occurs in a controlled fashion at the tōbajō; the stupa, individually and in their multiplicity, signify that correct remembering is taking place. Yet on the wide stretch of rocky terrain separating the main temple hall (and the tōbajō) from the lake's green "other shore" (a site that denotes paradise in the mountain's allegorical scenario), an itinerary and a round of offerings develop another relationship with signification and the remembering of the dead.

The tōbajō occupies a small area before the hall which houses the primary image of the deity Jizō. People pray and make offerings to this image, seeking both his protection for the dead and this-worldly benefits, solicited through varieties of magical prayers and incantations called kitō. There is thus a doubled structure at Mount Osore of kuyō and kitō, memorialization and incantation, doubled because the worldly benefits that incantations might secure can only accrue if the dead are properly memorialized.

All around the portico that surrounds the hall, and extending as far as the eye can see over the rocky expanse of Buddhist hells and heavens, are small stone statues of Jizō, almost hidden by the heaps of offerings placed in front of them: pinwheels, straw sandals, flowers, food, and money, as well as objects associated with particular dead persons—cigarettes, beer, toys, comic books, and clothes. Other than these offerings, the most common things to place are stones. People make the rounds of this expanse, going through the "valley of hells" (jigoku no tani) and stopping at each prominence, named site, or statue of Jizō to place offerings—and stones. The stones themselves turn into "stone stupas" (shakutō), to which people then offer more stones, as the piles of stone offerings become almost indistinguishable from the natural rock formations. Each offering leads to more offerings; a pebble casually placed on the ground leads to a whole collection of pebbles, one-yen coins, and candy. There is thus a logic of sheer accumulation and repetition. The point is not to make one, efficacious offering, but to make a multitude of offerings at each point that someone else has designated. On the middle day of the festival, lines of people followed this route through the afterlife, each dropping money, food, and flowers almost indiscriminately at the same points as had the person in front of them. The offerings formed enormous mounds, sometimes completely covering the Jizō that were the original objects of the offerings.

An allegorical scenario underwrites this round of offerings—in particular, the offerings of stones. This rocky stretch where people pile up offerings is, again, called Sainokawara, the dry riverbed in Japanese folklore that separates this world (kono yo) from the other world (ano yo). In the commonly known Japanese narrative of Sainokawara, dead children pile up stones on this dry riverbed to make memorial stupas (ekō no tō), but at night demons (oni) from hell come and knock over their accumulated labors.[14] In this scenario, dead children are engaged in a Sisyphean labor, a cycle of meaningless accumulation and disaccumulation in a liminal wasteland, a place which is neither heaven nor hell, but is nevertheless a place for the dead. Into this infernal round Jizō intervenes. He walks over the riverbed at night and gathers the sobbing children under his sleeves, saving them from their torments.

What are the qualities of Jizō that enable him to intervene? Jizō's image and powers have a labyrinthine history. In Japanese folklore, the name Jizō has referred to the container for the bones of the dead, the stupas that mark graves, and the piles of pebbles that can be considered both as offerings at boundaries and as memorial stupas for the dead.[15] His connection with Sainokawara, the place named for the dis-

14. According to some interpretations, Sainokawara is the name for the distinction between this world and the other world. One etymology of the name suggests that it comes from the place called Saiin (western temple) that marked the western border of medieval Kyoto. Rivers or dry riverbeds often constituted the outskirts of settlements; thus Saiin no kawara indicated the "dry riverbed on the western outskirts" of Kyoto. "Saiin" metamorphosed into the word sai, which means "difference" in Japanese; dry riverbeds, mountain passes, and crossroads were places that marked the "difference" between this world and the other, between settlements and unsettled lands (these areas were often actual burial places as well). The notion of Sainokawara is distributed throughout Japan. Haga Noboru, Sōgi no rekishi, 117–18.

The general notion of Sainokawara first made its appearance in the otogizōshi (fairy tales) of the Muromachi period, and in the seventeenth century, hymns to Jizō began to appear, describing the scene of Sainokawara, with its suffering children and tormenting demons. These hymns were called Saiin kawara Jizō wasan. Many of these wasan were products of the eighteenth century. Hayami Tasuku, Jizō shinkō, 152–56.

15. Jizō was part of esoteric Buddhist (Shingon) belief. He was originally not worshipped on riverbeds, but secretly in temples deep within the mountains. From the Heian period on, Jizō and the fearsome judge of dead souls, Enma, were conflated; from this conflation arose the idea that believing in Jizō would save one from the tortures of hell. Jizō came to be responsible for rebirth as well. Because of his great compassion he would descend from his inner mountain abode to burial or funeral sites (where it was

tinction between the worlds of the living and the dead, is similarly complex. In Japanese rural society, village boundaries took on symbolic importance as dividing lines between this world and the other. Evil came from the other world and stone deities were erected at village boundaries to block (sai or sae) its entry. Representations of this sainokami (guardian deity, deity of the crossroads) were often phallic; stone images called dōsojin, placed at crossroads and mountain passes, were thus appropriately phallic, or else depicted an embracing male and female couple. Sainokami came to be conflated with dōsojin, and in time Jizō—originally conceived of as a savior of the dead in China— also merged with these phallic and fertile deities of boundaries and crossings.

Jizō became a deity standing guard between worlds, especially as the savior of dead children. In folktales he often functions as a migawari, as a literal substitute for one's body, a scapegoat who takes on human sufferings. Jizō has the ability to intercede in hell; he is a mediator who can cross the line between life and death, which he himself institutes by his presence. On closer examination, it is clear that Jizō stands for signification itself. This savior of the dead marks a boundary between presence and absence; as a signifier he is the mark of a separation, of a difference. Like the tōba or grave markers which sometimes bear his name, the presence of Jizō substitutes for the absence of death. Giving stones to Jizō or to any phallic prominences is thus similar to setting up memorial stupas. These acts institute a division between presence and absence within the round of memorialization, and the markers become substitutes for the untoward memory of the dead person.[16]

---

thought the dead would be reincarnated). These burial sites were (as stated in footnote 14) often riverbeds, seacoasts, or other wastelands (arachi) outside settlement boundaries.

This connection of Jizō with death and desolate sites of burial merged with other Buddhist-derived ritual activities, such as building stone stupas on dry riverbeds in order to console dead souls or to protect from disease—a practice popular since the mid-Heian period. Tanaka Hisao, "Jizō shinkō to minzoku."

16. Putting down stones in front of Jizō, or building stone stupas, is a matter of marking boundaries. Each time someone puts down a pebble, he or she is delineating a new boundary between the other world and this world: the stretch of Sainokawara and the various hells become a whole territory of boundaries. The convergence of stone stupas, stone gods (ishigami), fertility deities and deities of crossroads (dōsojin, also called sainokami), and as we have seen, Jizō (as a deity of death, fertility, and boundaries) traces out an interconnected history of Japanese thinking about the relationship of death, otherness, and signification. Dōsojin/Jizō were even used to mark out property boundaries on the medieval regional manors (shōen). At Mount Osore they operate similarly to the

By accumulating stones the living participate in the labor of the dead. Each stone they pile up means one less stone for the dead children to accumulate; the living somehow aid this process of accumulation, one which, according to the narrative of Sainokawara, is doomed to fail. In this narrative and the practices it induces, the offerings of the living can never be adequate to the labor of the dead, despite the comforts of Jizō.

Visitors to Mount Osore know about Sainokawara and the demons of hell, and the practice of giving stones to Jizō is widespread throughout Japan. What is striking about the scene at Sainokawara is that the dead children are building none other than memorial stupa for the living. They who are dead (yet not fully dead because they have not settled into the after-death state), repeat a labor of setting up markers between this world and that. In effect, they are memorializing the living. The words of one of the hymns to Jizō say that "the first stone is for my father, the second for my mother, the third for my home . . ." The dead are engaged in a reverse memorialization, one that mirrors and inverts the actions of the living. The dead children's memorialization of the living comes about because their memorialization by the living is not sufficient. If the living could complete their memorialization, they would be saved; if the living's remembrance of the dead were perfect, and the ministrations of Jizō as miraculous as described, then the scene at Sainokawara would not be repeated endlessly. Jizō supplements the structure of inadequacy mirrored in the actions of the children; he represents both sexual fertility (revealed by his status as a phallic deity and deity of childbirth) and signification, as he draws the boundaries between the other world and this one, between absence and presence. His power to stop the Sisyphean labor of the dead nonetheless depends on the actions of the living, who must continue, repeatedly, to care for and remember the dead. The narrative of Sainokawara shows that the labor of memorialization is unlimited, as Sisyphean as that of the dead children.

Greek *xoana*, "statuettes whose invention is attributed to the clever Daedalus: they are crafty like Daedalus and mark out limits only by moving themselves (and the limits). . . . Boundaries are transportable limits and transportations of limits; they are . . . *metaphorai*." Michel de Certeau, *The Practice of Everyday Life*, 129. Dōsojin/stone stupas/Jizō find a correspondence as well with Hermes, "etymologically 'he of the *stone heap*,' [who] was associated with *boundary stones*. The herm, a head and a phallus on a pillar, later replaced the stone heap. . . . Hermes was a phallic god and a god of fertility." Vincent Crapanzano, "Hermes' Dilemma: The Masking of Subversion in Ethnographic Description," 52, referring to Norman O. Brown, *Hermes the Thief: The Evolution of a Myth*; emphasis added.

The mimesis by the living of the actions of the dead children—using stones to build structures of memorialization—has changed in recent years to include offerings of food, flowers, and money, in addition to clothes, straw sandals, and toys (typical offerings to Jizō throughout Japan). One of the old caretakers at the mountain put it this way:

> To perform simple memorial services is good; to pile up stones in front of a Jizō or a stone lantern for the sake of our dead children is good. But now people offer candy and all sorts of food. And on top of that they put money. They go from point to point and put down rocks and cakes and money. But bees and wasps breed on the food, and they sting people—it's bad. It's unclean. And when it rains, the smell gets worse and worse.
>
> It changes from a holy place where buddhas are, to an ugly, unsanitary mountain with the odor of a horrible gas that seems to come from hell. I want people to stop putting food outside at the Jizō and stone stupas. They should just offer it to the buddhas inside the temple buildings.[17]

The "odor of a terrible gas that seems to come from hell" is the precise description of the infernal smell of sulfur, yet here the caretaker is describing the "unclean" smell of decaying food. A reporter writing in a Nagasaki newspaper says something similar, that the mixture of the odors of cheap sweets and sulfur "made him sick" and was surely appropriate for a "contemporary hell."[18] Another odor pervades Mount Osore today, however, as a direct result of the worshipers abandoning their old practice of offering only stones: the smell of burning garbage. Near the lake is an inner Jizōdō, or Jizō Hall. Its interior is impenetrably filled with clouds of incense smoke, and surrounded by piles of offerings. Yet in front of it, past a small rise, is a huge garbage pit filled with those perishable offerings that the caretaker deplored. The offerings are burned regularly during the festival.

The odor of sulfur has deathly connotations for many Japanese. The incense which pervades the area is associated with death, too, but with memorialized, safe death. Young tourists from Tokyo told me that the smell of incense quiets (*yasumeru*) their hearts. Incense is closely associated with Buddhist memorial rituals, and thus with the system that takes care of death. Interposing itself between the two olfactory representations of death are new odors, ones that have emerged within recent memory. The odors of cheap sweets and burning garbage

---

17. Quoted in Mori Yūo, *Reijō Osorezan monogatari*, 10.
18. "Ima mo senshisha o yobu hitobito," *Nagasaki shinbun*, 6 January 1986.

Smoke rises from offerings
burned on Mount Osore, as
Jizō looks on in the background

strangely intrude as signs of the contemporary milieu, of capitalist practices of consumption and expenditure. Not content to offer only stones—signs of accumulation with no monetary value—worshipers now supplement these signs with modern excess that quickly turns into garbage.

A woman walking alongside me as we made the itinerary of hells railed at what she perceived as the wastefulness of the offerings:

> Look at all this money, this food! Why doesn't the temple have people give it to the poor or something? Osorezan's mountain of garbage! [*Oyama no gomi no yama.*] If I saw all this money just lying on the ground anywhere else, I would pick it up, but somehow it doesn't feel right to pick it up here—even though I don't believe. There's something disgusting about it [*kimochi-warui*].

The woman felt that the association of these offerings with death is what makes them taboo for the living—even though she "doesn't believe." Yet many people did not view this excess of wilted flowers and decaying food as wasteful (*mottainai*). Young women I met from Osaka seemed puzzled at the notion of "waste" here. The dead are pitiful (*kawaisō*) and hungry, they said; they must be given food. They were surprised when I told them that Christians, for example, in the United States usually give only flowers, not food, to the dead. Giving food offerings at all the places on the route seemed to them a necessary part of memorializing and consoling the dead. Yet unlike the caretaker of Mount Osore and older worshipers from the area, they knew of no distinction between former and current customs surrounding offerings. It is not as if food offerings or offerings of objects were never given in the past, but such offerings were not left out in the open: they were eaten, reused, or put inside the Jizō hall.[19]

Older people, more familiar with such things, regarded offerings as perfectly good to eat, indeed magically good. One of the workers, hauling off food in huge plastic sacks, said, when I asked him about the offerings, "It's really too bad, but we burn it all. Would you like

19. Offerings to the Jizō in the Jizō hall of Sainokawara were particularly valued. People put on straw sandals offered there and wore them as they walked around the mountain as protection from snake bites. Old women also used them in the baths at Mount Osore, hitting their backs or shoulders with them: the sandals were said to take away any stiffness or pain. Wearing the hand towels offered to Jizō averted disasters. Worshipers also took away remnants of candles and incense offered at Mount Osore, and sprinkled them over their fields to drive away harmful insects. Taking sand or rocks away from Mount Osore, however, was a sure way to invite disaster. Takamatsu Keikichi, *Shimokita hantō no minkan shinkō*, 266–67.

some?" Later I came across an older woman from Tanabu, the city below the mountain, who was setting up an array of offerings at the edge of the lake, a place where many people put offerings and build stone stupas. She had rice, sake, yogurt drinks, incense, flowers, and cigarettes for her husband, who had died six years earlier. (In most cases, people open the beer or sake and light cigarettes when they are offered.) She asked if I wanted any food and told me it was all right to accept it *(Itadaite mo ii desu yo)*. She said she was going to have some, as she explained the sequence of practices: first you set it out, next you bow, and then it becomes a talisman (*gofu*). Offerings to the dead become talismanic and should be eaten, yet many of the visitors at Mount Osore were unaware of this fact. Since part of the reason for memorializing dead people is to insure this-worldly safety and security, one might expect eating talismanic food offered to the dead to be a popular pastime at Mount Osore; yet the contrary idea, that it is somehow dangerous, even disgusting, indicates that food offerings placed in the open are perceived as something left over, as unassimilable to "life" and therefore better left to be burned as "garbage."

As the caretaker attested earlier, older practices at Sainokawara consisted mainly in offering stones, not perishables. The accumulation of stones—intractable, imperishable, and abundant at Mount Osore—placed the offerer in a mimetic relation to the dead in the narrative of Sainokawara. An offering of food represented a surplus, something left over from the exigencies of daily life that could thus be offered as nourishment to the dead. This offering in itself turned the food into talismanic, magical food, that when eaten by the living would do more than simply nourish, but would provide (again) surplus good fortune. Circulating food offerings, emblems of positive excess, back to the living thus activated a direct relationship between the living and the dead.

This nutritive circuit has generally been abandoned on the mountain. Food given at the established sites for such offerings—the main hall and the inner Jizō hall—is now capitalist excess, garbage that must be burned throughout the festival. And the prevalence of throwing food and money (if one can literally throw money away, then surely there is an "excess") onto the ground or at stone stupa without any possibility of their becoming talismanic, further reveals a shift in the nature of belief in memorialization and the efficacy of offerings. The shift from magical excess to waste (garbage) is consonant with the contemporary memorializer's desire to hurry through the itinerary. Sheer repetition, for many of the visitors, overrides the necessity of lingering too long at this dolorous site of dead children and their labors; there is no real desire to implicate oneself in an exchange relationship with the dead at this site. The narrative at Sainokawara remains, providing the condition against which worshipers constitute themselves as safely alive and as givers in a one-way trajectory of offerings to those who are dead.

In Kōda Rohan's late-nineteenth-century account of the festival at Mount Osore, the strand of Sainokawara was described as a place for mourning and the assembly of ascetics and beggars. The grief of the narrative of Sainokawara evoked the sorrow and fear of the living who had lost children. Yet now this section of the mountain has become an itinerary where offerings and practices distance worshipers from sorrow, where one can participate in practices that distinguish one from the narrative of Sainokawara. The narrative is maintained, the practices repeated. Yet as the caretaker revealed, the products of these practices in the form of garbage concretely exceed the control of the temple.

Access to mourning—to an embodied recalling of the dead instead of a bracketed "remembering"—is set aside, left for the intercessions of the itako, or for one part of Sainokawara behind the main worship hall and nearest the hills in the back. Encounters with the mediums— attempts to speak with the dead, to hear their voices—become the real occasions for mourning at Mount Osore. But within this doubled structure of reassuring memorialization on the one hand and cathartic recalling of the dead on the other, a third term intervenes: that of fear of the dead, specifically the fear of meeting with the unsettled dead. The circulation of ghost stories and tales of uncanny occurrences at the mountain attests to the prevalence of this fear.

Ghosts in the Machine

A mention of Mount Osore to contemporary Japanese elicits predictable adjectives: *bukimi* (weird), *fushigi* (mysterious), *kimiwarui* (creepy). Stories told about Mount Osore are correspondingly unearthly, as befits a place which links conceptions of otherworldliness with fear (again, *osore*). When Japanese refer to Mount Osore as *bukimi*, they are referring to a general aura of death, but they are often specifically thinking of untoward meetings with the dead. There are both desirable and undesirable meetings; an undesirable encounter is always with a ghost, someone who should be absent but is uncannily present.

Although all memorial practices at Mount Osore are aimed at ensur-

ing the passage from unsettled, dangerous new death to stable, beneficial, settled death, the stories of ghosts (*yūrei*) at the mountain indicate that these practices are not always effective. There are gaps in the
edifice of memorialization, and through these gaps the unsettled dead
appear: a ghost is a sign that memorialization is not fully adequate.

Stories emanating from Mount Osore speak of doubling, of echoes,
and of disappearances. The lone caretaker of the mountain during the
long winter months related his experiences with yūrei:

> I'm not the only one—seven or eight people I know have seen
> ghosts on the mountain. A lot of times it first sounds like
> someone talking. Among these, there are some voices that are
> bright and cheerful—lively—but you can't understand what
> they're saying. But if they're loud, you can at least hear them.
> The voices aren't limited to nighttime. Where you hear them
> and what time you hear them varies.
>
> Voices that are talking don't really get to me that much, but
> the crying voices are really eerie. Those voices remain in my
> ears.
>
> Sometimes I hear songs. Country drinking songs, drivers'
> songs, and so on. I've heard them, oh, any number of times.[20]

The caretaker tells of voices without a clear source; one can hear the
voices, but can't quite understand their meaning. The voices that remain in the ears are the crying voices—voices that express sorrow, yes,
but voices that are also not connected with speech, not tied to spoken
meanings, even incomprehensible meanings. The most unnerving
voices are those that present the crying voice severed from its dependence on speech. The time and place of the voices are unpredictable
(again, the impossibility of predicting an encounter with a ghost is
much of what is fearful about such an encounter). The caretaker's visual descriptions of ghosts trace a similar logic of uncertainty:

> In plays and movies ghosts wear white clothes, and you can't
> see their feet. They come out with their hands hanging down
> and with ghastly pale faces. But the ones I've seen—first of
> all, the color isn't fixed. There are times when their color is
> black, and times when they suddenly appear with a glaring,
> harsh color.
>
> The ones I've seen appear in a flash. Just when I look again
> in surprise, thinking that nobody should be there, they split
> apart from the top and the bottom, and turn into something

20. Quoted in Mori, *Reijō Osorezan monogatari*, 11.

that looks like a ball and disappears. Even if I take a deep breath, look again, and screw up my courage and wait, they don't come back. Without fail, the ones I've seen turn into balls and zoom away. . . .

They never show themselves for more than twenty or thirty seconds—never as much as a minute. There was a person who came here for the baths, and said that she had seen the face of her father's brother, who was supposed to be at home. . . . That's scary, and if you talk about it nobody will come up here to Osorezan. I told her not to say anything about it, even if she did see something.

People say that ghosts don't exist, that it's just a lie that ghosts appear. But I've seen them many times. The ghosts look really strange around the eyes and mouth. They never stand and look directly at you; they always appear at the side. Sometimes they appear on the right and sometimes on the left. When you suddenly notice a ghost and look, it will lower its face and look in the opposite direction. It avoids your eyes.[21]

The caretaker's Mount Osore ghosts never appear directly: one can never look a ghost in the eyes.[22] They suddenly appear, and just as suddenly disappear. Their shape changes; their color is indeterminate. They do not linger, and they just as surely do not come back once they have gone away.

In the visual and auditory phenomena here described, there is no dialogue, no communication with the dead spirits; instead the voices reveal a spectral communication only among themselves, a communication whose meaning cannot be understood by the living. They constitute a discursive world which haunts this world with its exemption from meaning. What the figure or the voice of the ghost spectrally embodies, then, is the recalcitrance of representation itself, the impossibility of stabilizing meaning. If Mount Osore is a discursive apparatus for delimiting the boundaries of representation—for fixing the terms for presence and absence that "life" and "death" trope—then ghosts uncover the instability of those boundaries: ghosts are haunting precisely because they reveal an inability to control representation.

Yet not only reports of ghost sightings or hearings reveal the instability of representation. A woman from the old "downtown" (shitamachi) section of Tokyo who was staying in the same hostel as I was told

21. Ibid., 10–13.
22. Robert Smith brought to my attention the fact that Japanese ghosts never look the living in the eye: they are too *hazukashii* (ashamed) at being ghosts.

me, while pointing to a large statue of Jizō on a rise to the left of the temple approach:

> That Jizō extends life. My friend told me that when she took a
> picture of that statue—when the film was developed, it didn't
> show up. Everything else, including the people around it and
> the background did, but not that Jizō. There are a lot of stories
> like that.

This story thematizes the magical ability to resist being represented by a deity that in many ways is the principle of representation itself, that operates as a substitute, scapegoat, and sexual symbol in Japanese folk religion, while functioning as a Buddhist deity that mediates between the world of the living and the world of the dead. How does one represent representation itself? What this small story and others handed down about Mount Osore indicate is that many Japanese perceive something about the contemporary scene at Mount Osore that resists recording. Photographers and people with tape recorders, omnipresent at any event in Japan and particularly at any so-called folk performance, were here curiously surreptitious. The feeling of being a voyeur usually does not stop the activity of recording in Japan, but at Mount Osore it took on a transgressive feeling. People were furtive about using their cameras, especially in the areas that were not on the main approach. Those areas to the side were the sites where the itako, the peddlers, and a few elderly ascetics sat; they were also the places where people tended to express their mourning overtly. What reminds the photographer of what is most extreme, what is most closely connected to a now-scandalous past or to the tragedy of death, calls into question the inviolability of the photographic voyeur, even as it resists its own status as a fully representable object.

In descriptions of ghostly apparitions and auditions at Mount Osore—and in tales told about ghosts—there is often a gap, a discrepancy between the aural and the visual. One hears a sound, looks to see, and no one is there. It is not just that one hears voices, but that one hears voices emanating from places where no one is supposed to be, and where on inspection no one is: voices without a visual source. Or, if an apparition appears, it is wordless, only peripherally apprehended. Ghosts appear where no one should be, at times when no one is expected: a transgression of expectation. This undercutting of expectation about reality shows itself as a split between a phenomenon and its origin, the voices of ghosts displacing the visual origins of sound. This rift between an auditory phenomenon and its visual source appears as well in the spirit recallings of the blind mediums.

Ghosts inhabit that uncertain territory between the seen and the heard, the differential gap between the two. That gap is also an aporia in the structure of remembering the dead as dead: a ghost appears as a sign of forgetting and as a fissure in the structure of perceptions that constitutes life. Ghosts reveal an irruption of the other world that is beyond the control of the living, beyond the reach of memory or the predictability of the senses. They indicate a point where the control of the dead is called into question, and thus are a matter of great concern to the temple authorities.

"The temple's told me not to spread it around that ghosts and spirits and other such things appear at Mount Osore, but after all, these things are real." The temple's admonition to the caretaker echoes his own earlier warning to the visitor who saw the face of an absent relative in the baths: it's frightening, so don't say anything about it, even if you did see something. There is an attempt to deny the existence of ghosts by discouraging rumors about them.

Yet talking about ghosts, repeating rumors of them, is a preoccupation at Mount Osore. The possibility of encountering a ghost holds an undeniable attraction for contemporary tourists and visitors from afar. The possibility, yes; but that possibility is kept within the narrative bounds of ghostly reportage. Repeating ghost stories tames the fear of ghosts; as long as one can talk about ghosts, the fear that an encounter would bring is deferred. It frames the fear of ghosts while at the same time reserving the possibility of encounter. Ghost stories and the Buddhist memorial services and practices thus domesticate death in a strangely parallel, but inverted, fashion. Both are concerned with taking care of the return of the dead. Yet the system of memorialization, which creates a boundary between life and death, produces what it claims to manage: ghosts. Ghost stories reproduce a fear of the dangerous dead, which in turn call for a memorial system to deal with them. Like an orthodoxy and its heresies, each is constituted by the other.

Yet, again like an orthodoxy and its heresies, there is a difference in power and authority. The temple, and the metanarrative of Buddhist efficacy in dealing with death that underlies its function, are authoritative. Temple authorities can discourage the belief—and the telling of stories that attest to at least a lingering desire to have a belief—in ghosts. The temple wants to deny the activity of ghosts and the telling of stories about them, testifying to an uneasiness with its failure to account for the unsettled dead, which in a very real sense it creates, as the exterior of its own discursive system. Yet without the refractory remainder that ghosts provide, the power of the memorialization system could not function. Ghostly narratives supplement Mount Osore's institutional structure; at the same time they are an alterity necessary for the exercise of the power of that structure. They allow the temple system to succeed by failing.

Telling ghost stories generates a narrative practice complementary to the formal Buddhist-derived metanarratives: the stories domesticate the fear of ghosts by narrativizing them. In this sense they take care of the excess that memorialization cannot subsume. Yet as they create a complicity among visitors to the mountain, they also create an alternative way of talking about death. In all the stories I heard, the apparition or audition happened to individuals, separately. Seeing or hearing a ghost is personal and not subject to verification by a group. There is instead a desire to repeat what one has heard about ghosts: a logic of hearsay that brings tales of ghosts close to gossip and rumor. A plural, heterogeneous narrative practice ensues based on the repeated tellings of encounters with ghosts. Stories of strange occurrences at Mount Osore are often prefaced by "My friend told me . . ." or "My grandmother said she saw . . ." Stories are told secondhand, their experiential origins displaced in a fashion that parallels the shifting origins of the ghosts themselves. It is enough to be linked to someone who has said that he or she has seen a ghost and to retain the possibility—both dreaded and desired—that one too might experience the numinous.

Buddhist narratives of redemption and the procedures and rationales for rites for the dead lie in the public domain. Enscripted and formalized, they set the outer limits of Mount Osore's Buddhist control of the dead. The repeated telling of reports of ghosts forms a reserve of private, minute experiences not subject to formal verification. Ghost stories circulate, rarely promising or describing an actual communication with a specific dead one. Hearing a sound without a source or seeing a specter (again, rarely are the two conjoined) is an unsettling reminder of a failure in memorialization.

Even though encounters with the dead are limited to those few who claim them, narratives of these encounters vicariously extend the possibility. In Shimokita, relatives of a person who had just died or who was in the last stages of death would climb to the top of the roof and call out the person's name in an effort to lure the spirit back to earth. This practice is termed *tamayobai*, "calling the spirit"; if the person failed to revive, then he or she was said to have "gone to Osorezan"

(Osorezan e itte shimau).[23] The mountainous areas behind Sainokawara were thought to be the particular sites where the dead went; the bereaved would go there to call out the name of the dead. In one story, a woman was so distraught about the loss of her child that she wandered into the mountains behind the temple site, following the echoes of her own voice repeating the name of the dead child. Many accounts exist of attempts to call a person back from death, or to initiate, by an enunciation of the name of the dead, another encounter. Tamayobai reveals an intense attachment to the dead person and an attempt to rebind the dissolution of spirit and body, to reunite the fragmented person by calling the name. The naming of the dead can recall them back to corporeal life, or alternatively, to a presence that corresponds to the desires of the bereaved for an encounter.

Dividing the Voice

If ghost stories augment Mount Osore's national image as a site of lingering mysteries by telling of the problematic presence of the properly absent, and if calling the dead by name was once seen as powerful enough to recall them to life, then the itako go a step further with their promise of actual communication with the dead. Kuchiyose, the calling down of spirits by mediums, not only promises a dialogue with the specific dead, but also becomes a source of knowledge about the future. Encounters with itako are occasions both for hearing and talking to the dead (which also involves mourning the dead) and for receiving predictions and recommendations from them. There is a double trajectory of wishfulness: towards the past, when the dead one was alive, and towards the future which the dead have the power to foresee and to protect *(mamoru)*.

The blind mediums have become the preeminent attraction at

---

23. There are various forms of *tamayobai*. Some are performed in the hope of resurrecting the dead or keeping somebody who is about to die from dying; some to invite the dead spirit (which is thought to separate from the body at death and go, temporarily, to the local graveyard, temple, or sacred mountain) to return to the corpse so it can receive the various rituals for the dead; and some with the more general aim of calling out for the dead in order to effect a reencounter. See Sakurai Tokutarō, *Nihon no shamanizumu*, 2:382–96. An itako from Shimokita describes a scene in which the relatives of an old woman who was clearly in her last hour pulled her hair and screamed her name repeatedly in order to keep her from dying. The itako, Nishimura Rie, arrived at that moment and performed a great purification ritual for three and a half hours. The next day the old woman had completely recovered. Takamatsu, *Shimokita hantō no minkan shinkō*, 44–45.

Mount Osore, and their calling down of the dead is regarded as something intrinsic to the mountain. Several people told me at the site that "this is how the Japanese used to call down the dead," or that the mediums have performed kuchiyose there since ancient times. But the historical linkage of the mountain and kuchiyose is, on examination, a forged one. The gathering of the itako at Mount Osore is a relatively recent phenomenon, one that has become significant only in the postwar period.[24] While the number of blind mediums who ply their trade in the villages of Shimokita is decreasing (there were only six left in the early 1970s), this does not directly affect the group gathering (*itako machi*) on the mountain.[25] That is because most of the itako at the festival are not from Shimokita. They come instead from other regions of northeastern Japan to participate in the festival. The itako from the surrounding areas have long had an ambivalent relationship to the Jizō cult groups and initially were not part of the festival. Now there are one or two Shimokita itako who "climb the mountain," and who also perform kuchiyose for tourists at the hot springs hotels around the mountain during the off-season. Yet the great majority of the itako associated with the festival are from other parts of Aomori prefecture (Tsugaru and Hachinohe).

24. The early history of the mediums' relationship to Mount Osore is obscure. Mori states that the itako did not climb Mount Osore to ply their trade until after the Meiji state, in the interest of "civilization and enlightenment," started discouraging the activities of mountain ascetics, mediums, fortune tellers, and other suspicious practitioners of occult arts; the government viewed them as remnants of irrationality who were leading the populace astray. The itako could no longer carry out their business in the towns as before and were thus forced out into the countryside and mountains, where they performed kuchiyose at isolated shrines to Jizō. He concludes that itako started climbing Mount Osore sometime between the late Meiji and early Taishō periods (between the 1890s and 1915 or so). He affirms, however, that the large-scale appearance of itako at Mount Osore is a product of the postwar period, a development he attributes to the liberalization of religion after the war and the improvement of the road that leads to the summit. See Mori, *Reijō Osorezan monogatari*, 54.

Sakurai speculates that a few wandering itako may have started working at Mount Osore during the mid-eighteenth century, but states that in all reports and descriptions of the mountain from the eighteenth century on, there is no mention at all of itako. For example, Sugae Masumi (1754–1829), a late-Tokugawa-period traveler and protofolklorist, journeyed throughout the Tohoku region, climbed Mount Osore three different times, and left descriptions of the mountain, but wrote not a word about itako. There are several good descriptions of Mount Osore from the Meiji period as well (including Kōda Rohan's), none of which touches on the itako. Sakurai later states that the history of any sort of group gathering goes back to no earlier than 1924, and cites an old priest as saying that only two or three itako performed kuchiyose at Mount Osore before the war. See Sakurai, *Nihon no shamanizumu*, 1:157, 160; 2:69, 495.

25. Anthropologist Ellen Schattschneider has reported a revival of itako in Iwate prefecture and other areas of Tōhoku since the 1980s.

A notice at the entrance to the temple proclaimed: "Osorezan is not the itako mountain and this is not an itako festival. We only lend the itako space at the time of the festival." The temple disclaims any official sponsorship of the itako and has asserted various controls over the gathering. The itako formerly set up their places throughout the temple grounds; through negotiations with representatives of the itako, the temple has, since the early 1960s, confined them to the area directly around the main Jizō hall.[26] By 1984 this area had been reduced even further, to only one side of the hall, the side facing away from Sainokawara and the itineraries. It is said that the area around the main hall is the most efficacious for trance (*mottomo reikan ga utsuri-yasui*) and that is why the itako gather there; yet considerations of management seem to have played a larger part in putting the mediums to the side of the hall than a belief in its inherent spiritual power.

The temple management sees the itako as nuisances (*yakkaimono*, a term which also connotes something parasitic). The itako cause traffic jams, media glare, and vulgar crowds to appear on the mountain, and they disrupt the more sober, orderly rites and processions of the event. One reason the temple disavows any connection with the mediums is that people complain to the temple when the itako's predictions are off the mark (*yogen ga ataranai*); another is the fact that kuchiyose conjoins a vocal calling of the dead with money. That is why the itako have been segregated from the allegorical space of the itineraries, and why, at the same time, they sit alongside fortune-tellers, charm sellers, palm readers, and herbalists who hawk their services above the low-pitched, constant din of the medium's chants and rustle of rosaries.[27]

There were about fifteen itako in 1984. Unlike earlier festivals, at which, according to photographs, the itako spread mats on the ground and conducted their callings of the dead in the open air (surrounded by crowds and sometimes protected from the sun by assistants holding parasols), the itako now individually occupied identical army-fatigue green nylon tents arrayed in two facing rows. The itako (and the others) worked continuously throughout the five days of the festival, late into the night. At one end of the tents was an herbalist, keeping up the nonstop persuasive patter for which peddlers and salesmen in Japan are noted. At the other end was an equally garrulous young man

26. Sakurai, *Nihon no shamanizumu*, 1:151.
27. The itako straightforwardly consider their occult practices as business, using the most general Japanese term for business of any kind—*shōbai*—to describe their livelihood, which consists of calling down dead spirits and deities, predictions, and divinations of sundry kinds. Takamatsu, *Shimokita hantō no minkan shinkō*, 23–89.

dressed in Buddhist black, imitating the demeanor of a priest and sell-ing magical rings. Both were reminiscent of carnival barkers in the insistence of their voices and the extravagance of their claims. The rows of identical tents, with lines of people waiting for audiences with the blind mediums hidden inside, indeed resembled carnival sideshow attractions (known to Japanese as *misemono goya*, "show tents"). By linking the mediums in their tents with the "quacks and peddlers" outside, the organizers were stating that they belonged in the same place: that the medium's disclosures of the dead and predictions of the future were of the same order as the amulet seller's or herbalist's assurances and vice versa. A conjoining of voice and commerce was kept out of the precincts of proper death and its inscribed places and prescribed routings of piety.

This marginalization reflects the itako's historical position as well. Plural etymologies of the name *itako* (a word disliked by Shimokita mediums for its subsidiary connotations of "beggar" or "vagabond") lead not to any certain historical origin, but to a series of possibilities. One etymology derives itako from *eta no ko*, a "child of the *eta*," one name for the so-called outcaste groups in Japan. The word *eta* itself is replete with different readings, but most of them point to an associa-tion with death and defilement. Wanderers and refugees from the nu-merous famines and disorders that plagued premodern Japan (as well as artisans and craftspeople from the continent) are said to have formed groups which survived by performing both polluted tasks (handling corpses, tanning leather) and theatrico-ritual ones. Some groups and individuals wandered as traveling artistes *(tabi geinin)*, peddlers, prostitutes, religious specialists, or craftspeople; these people were often viewed ambivalently, as welcome strangers or as little more than beggars, by the villages they visited. Others settled on land outside already established communities or on the fringes of temple lands, performing designated duties for the residents. There is thus a strong interconnection in Japanese history between outcaste sta-tus, charismatic religious power, and the performing arts. The itako of northeastern Japan trace their uncertain history to the so-called *aruki miko*, or itinerant mediums, who themselves were often of outcaste status.[28]

Another possible origin traces the word itako to the writing of the dead person's posthumous Buddhist name *(kaimyō)* on a slat *(ita)*,

---

28. See Yamaguchi Masao, "Kingship, Theatricality, and Marginal Reality in Japan," and Moriya Takeshi, "Geinō o enzuru hitotachi."

which the itako would use for Buddhist memorial services (ekō or kuyō). Thus the medium's local name is traced to what in Buddhist institutional contexts is a priestly function. That this etymology would point to an assumption by the itako (who are blind) of the properly priestly function of inscribing the wooden stupa is all the more striking when we consider that the itako function as mouthpieces of the dead, and that their powers are based on an oral recalling of the departed. This orality and its tendency to get out of control is what the authorities distrust about the mediums—the impossible promise of oral communications with the dead, enacted for money for hordes of bereaved visitors.

In 1984, the place was palpably alive with voices: the hawking of the pitchmen, the continuous chanting emanating from the dark interiors of the tents, the questions of the bereaved, the whispers of those waiting. Muffled sobs also punctuated the air, because this site of voices—scandalous, persuasive—has become the main scene of mourning at Mount Osore. The dead may be said to be everywhere at Mount Osore, but they are most explicitly mourned in the itakos' tents, where they are viscerally and vocally recalled. The customers take their turns one by one in the tents. Many bring offerings to the itako, such as fresh fruit, candy, or packaged crackers; they put them down in front of the itako as they kneel facing her. There is a prescribed set of questions that the itako asks the customer. Without fail, the itako must know the day of death (the *meinichi*), the sex, and the age of the person to be contacted. She also often asks the relationship of the dead to the living questioner and how the person died; she does not ask the name of the dead person. This knowledge allows her to search for and locate the dead one and to describe his or her present condition accordingly. She then begins an incantation in which she calls up the dead person from the other world.

Compared to the kuchiyose that are held at private homes in the area, the ritual preliminaries are much abbreviated at Mount Osore. Some itako explain this reduction by saying that since the dead are already present at Mount Osore, there is no necessity for the elaborate altar, profuse offerings, and lengthy incantations usually required to call down the dead persons in question.[29] Others say that the ritual is abbreviated in order to accommodate as many customers as possible

29. Takamatsu, *Shimokita hantō no minkan shinkō*, 132. What is necessary to induce the dead spirit to descend in standard kuchiyose is a *yorishiro*, a long, thin object through which the spirit or deity descends and then temporarily dwells in. In the Shimokita region this yorishiro is called a *yamatage* and consists of a branch from a peach tree

during the five-day festival. At the beginning of the incantation, the itako states that she is calling a hotoke who died on such and such a date and invokes myriads of kami to descend and watch over the ku- chiyose. At an unspecified point in the incantation, the person of the speaker shifts to the hotoke, who then addresses the patron directly. This moment also marks a shift from an almost incomprehensible in- cantatory style to one that is more conversational.

The dead characteristically start by thanking their living interlocu- tors for calling them back to this world. They sometimes say that they "never dreamed" they would be able to meet the living again. They state that they are now satisfied *(manzoku)* and can hold their heads up and face the other dead ones. The hotoke then recount the condi- tions of the after-death state. The portrayal and revelation of the dead's experiences are consistent with their status and age at death. Although there are conventionally a number of distinctions itako make between new and old spirits, at Mount Osore the purity of the distinctions is not always maintained.[30] The overriding tone of this recounting of the after-death state is one of sorrow and regret, of unsatisfied desire.

There is then a shift towards recollections of life. These recollections

---

festooned with red and white cut paper placed in the middle of a small wooden tub filled with rice.

This normally essential ritual apparatus is not used at Mount Osore, nor are other aspects of the ritual used. In particular, the *saimon,* the long initial and closing incanta- tions, are dramatically shortened at Mount Osore. Sakurai states that this ritual abbrevia- tion gives the impression of a neglectful or lazy attitude on the part of the itako, who don't really "give it their all" and go into trance at the festival because of the demands of the occasion. He thus maintains the possibility of authentic trance for the itako at other times. Sakurai, *Nihon no shamanizumu,* 1:132–33.

30. Sakurai states that at the newly formed itako machi, kuchiyose of *shinbotoke* (the newly dead, also called *niibotoke* in some regions) cannot be performed. The itako say that the dead person will not speak until one hundred days after death. Even if the dead person appears, he or she will not say anything. Thus, only kuchiyose for the settled dead *(furubotoke)* will work. His partial explanation for this is as follows. In *shinkuchi* (the kuchiyose for the newly dead), the person who has recently died is called and speaks in turn to each of his or her survivors. It is thus a group calling, and the dead person speaks to the survivors following the status order of the people who offered incense at the funeral. But in calling people who have been dead more than one hundred days (the length of time varies according to region), *one* supplicant requests the calling of one or more dead people and asks questions in relation to only him or herself. There is usually an order to the dead called in this pattern also (although sometimes it is random): sometimes it parallels the nearness of kinship to the supplicant; sometimes the calling starts from the oldest spirit (measured by the date of death). Only individuals request kuchiyose at Mount Osore; therefore, the itako can legitimately perform furu- kuchi in the absence of a larger legitimating kinship group. Sakurai, *Nihon no shamani- zumu,* 1:132–33.

focus on the experiences the dead person shared with the living inter-locutor. After recollections of life comes a recital of wishes and unful-filled desires and of ways to fulfill them. The customer can interrupt to ask questions: Is there anything you want? Do you ever get to see Papa? Is your cancer completely cured? Sometimes the dead answer directly; sometimes the itako comes in to answer or to clarify the ques-tion. The dead one then gives a few general cautions and admonitions for the future (some on the order of "Be careful not to catch cold" or "Work hard"), as well as specific predictions: Don't go out of the house on August 25; watch out for fires on December 11. They say farewell, and then there is a return to the voice of the itako speaking in her own persona as she chants the *hotokeokuri*, the ritual send-off of the dead back to the other world. At Mount Osore this whole process may take only five minutes, ten or fifteen at the most. The fee for one kuchiyose, for each "mouth" (*kuchi*) opened, was fifteen hundred yen in 1984, which the customer would give the itako at the end.[31]

The kuchiyose, then, follows an order, and this order is repeated at each calling. Unlike sightings of ghosts, there is no surprise here. It is a repeatable, conventionalized, predictable, yet *specific* encounter with the dead. The itako's voice does not change; there is no perceptible shift in her voice when the dead speak through her. If she is calling down a man, for example, there is no change in the pitch of her voice, although the use of status language changes accordingly. There is no explicit attempt to "sound" like the dead person. Why is it then that so many of the questioners—both those from the area and those from far away—are overwhelmed with grief?

Trance Effects: Mourning and Predictions

To folklorists and anthropologists of Japanese religion, kuchiyose at Mount Osore calls into question the authenticity of trance. Most agree that itako exhibit no trace of "real" trance: they are merely performing a series of patterned roles for their customers:

31. In 1973, the fee was two hundred yen; in 1974, seven hundred yen; and in 1975, one thousand yen. There is an agreed-upon price that all the itako charge at Mount Osore during the festival, and which also holds in the hotoke kuchiyose in the villages of Shimokita. The elderly women of the region used kuchiyose primarily for memorializ-ing the dead. In the past they could afford to call many dead relatives any number of times at one sitting. Now this function of repeated memorialization is unthinkable be-cause of the expense. Takamatsu, *Shimokita hantō no minkan shinkō*, 85.

Clearly the itako were simply reciting the most suitable among a repertory of fixed chants learnt by heart in the course of their training as purporting to come from the dead. Their performance belonged to the category of *geinō* or folk drama, and at the same time functioned as a *kuyō* or requiem comfort for the dead.

On their audiences, however, the effect of these hackneyed effusions was pathetically touching. Round each itako was to be seen a little group of sobbing women, old and young, their faces screwed up with emotion. . . . Here and there I noticed women sitting in rapt attention, as though at the theatre, and eagerly begging with proffered coins for "One more!" as soon as the itako's chanting stopped.[32]

Carmen Blacker, the author of this description, puts these "hackneyed effusions" within a framework of theatrical or performative conventions: "That such utterances should still strike the sobbing audiences as convincing communications from the dead argues for a suspension of disbelief of the same order as that which sees the invisible world behind the sacred drama, the ritual mask or the recital of a myth."[33] What Blacker is questioning here is how the stereotypical could be believable, and therefore moving. In her analysis, one could legitimately cry only if one really believed that he or she was hearing the voice of the dead; otherwise, tears could only be the result of theatrical illusion. But because the itako's words are repetitive, they cannot be believable, that is, they cannot be mistaken for authentic, spontaneous communications from the dead obtained in trance.

Blacker argues that "what passes for a trance among them is seen on shrewd inspection to be mere imitation."[34] She contrasts authentic trance with the imitative (i.e., false) performance of trance which is kuchiyose. Thus Blacker supports the description by Japanese folklorists of the itako as *gisei shaman* (fake shamans). Later she implies that the itako do not even imitate trance: "They exhibited none of the usual symptoms of stertorous breathing and convulsively shaking hands."[35] Hori Ichirō explains why the itako are not shamans: they do not go into trance or ecstasy *(ekusutashii)* and their kuchiyose is monotonous, songlike, performatized.[36] Blacker also states that kuchiyose is only

32. Carmen Blacker, *The Catalpa Bow*, 160–61.
33. Ibid., 163.
34. Ibid., 140.
35. Ibid., 160.
36. Hori Ichirō, *Nihon no shamanizumu*, 185–86. Hori also gives other characteristics of the itako which disqualify them as bona fide shamans.

a dilapidated trace of what used to be an authentically transgressive rupture. Kuchiyose claims to be transgressive, to broach a rupture between life and death, but it is not even that: it is a spurious transgressive.

Descriptions of trance in Japanese anthropology are not only concerned to maintain the integrity and authenticity of something called "shamanic trance"; they are also concerned to say that this trance state has something to do with authentic communications from the dead. The convulsive hands and gasps of the shaman are said to indicate trance, as if a real sphere of extraordinary knowledge were signaled by the convulsed body. These descriptions imply that the message emanating from a gasping mouth has more truth value than the itako's performatized recitation, that the convulsed hands of the shaman become the last guarantee of authenticity, a guarantee that the itako do not give.[37]

The convulsive sobbing of the listeners, however, remains as the anomalous guarantee of kuchiyose's effects. Despite being depicted as merely a spurious reenactment of genuine trance, kuchiyose produces effects (for example, sobbing) which only a real communication with the dead should produce. It produces effects it has no right to produce,

37. I do not question a typology of outward symptoms that would indicate or contraindicate a particular state as "trance." Clearly by the typologies that Mircea Eliade and others have constructed, the itako are not in trance and cannot even be said to pretend to be. What I am questioning is an analysis that regards symptoms of trance as somehow naturally expressing a communication with the dead, that believes that trance is any less performative than any other mode of approaching the dead. What seems to be at stake in these discussions of trance, genuine and spurious, is false belief: if a shamanic trance is extreme, if it exhibits those convulsive or extraordinary characteristics that go beyond everyday experience, then trickery should not, could not, be involved. There is a notion of purity here, of authenticity that disregards Mauss's discoveries concerning the conventional power of magic and belief. Lévi-Strauss retells the remarkable story of a Kwakiutl Indian, a skeptic, who stumbled into the shamanic profession by an urge to learn the tricks of the trade. And so he did, as his "narrative recounts the details of his first lessons, a curious mixture of pantomime, prestidigitation, and empirical knowledge, including the art of simulating fainting and nervous fits, the learning of sacred songs. . . ." Yet this fake shaman had great success as a healer, and what Lévi-Strauss elicits from the facts of this narrative is the power of a socially based complex of beliefs in determining "reality," even a reality as resistant to manipulation as illness. What Lévi-Strauss has uncovered is the role of trickery, of duping, in any system of conventions that calls for belief; he thus discounts the possibility of any preperformative trance. Lévi-Strauss strangely denies the power of this insight later in the same essay, however, by reverting to an explanation that now sees shamanic trance as reproducing an initial series of revelations "in all their vividness, originality, and violence." To this representation he assigns the psychoanalytic term "abreaction," and calls the shaman a "professional abreactor." He thus both asserts and denies the constitutive possibility of trickery in producing effects like healing. Claude Lévi-Strauss, "The Sorcerer and His Magic."

but those effects—specifically, expressions of grief—go beyond any suspension of belief: the genuine effects of a spurious spectacle. Only by examining the position of language in kuchiyose can we understand these effects, revealed both by people from the locale who use kuchiyose as a regular means of approaching the dead, and outsiders who come to Mount Osore for a one-shot attempt.

Much of kuchiyose consists of what might be called ritual language: formalized, archaic, formulaic. These utterances are repeated at each kuchiyose. They, in fact, set up the encounter with the dead; they predict it. The patterns—the *kata*—of the performance are prescribed, yet this prescriptive patterning does not indicate that the itako is unbelievable. On the contrary, it indicates the itako's words as magical. The formalization, unintelligibility, repetition, and ornamentation of the itako's words are exactly what Marcel Mauss designated as the hallmarks of magical discourse. In such language, the conventionality of language comes to the fore. The words are meaningless; they refer not in the least to the desired effect of the ritual or performance. Their unintelligibility and formalization mark them as exotic, as coming from without—and thus as socially determined. In Mauss's sense, the conventionality of the language of magic compels belief.[38] Only the force of society can insure that the conventional is believable, and in the conventions of kuchiyose in Tohoku, signs of trance are evidently not necessary to induce authentic effects: sobs, protestations of belief, action based on the dead's predictions.

In its overall movement, the repeated, formalized unintelligibility of the itako's chants thus effects a disassociation between signifier and signified: language is unbound as the chanting foregrounds itself as pure utterance, divorced from meaning. The form itself is emphasized; content is marginalized. Any signifier can refer to innumerable signifieds, and since there is no intrinsic connection between them, the force of language makes itself felt, compellingly.[39] It is in this milieu of inde-

---

38. Marcel Mauss, *A General Theory of Magic*, 117–27.

39. This is close to Lévi-Strauss's concept of zero symbolic value, which he uses in elucidating the concept of *mana*, the central organizing indeterminable of *A General Theory of Magic*. Mana is that concept which designates the compelling force of language as social convention. As Lévi-Strauss states: "Always and everywhere notions of this *(mana)* type intervene . . . to represent a value of indeterminate meaning *(signification)*, which being itself empty of meaning *(sens)* is therefore susceptible to the reception of any meaning . . . whatsoever. Its unique function is to make good a discrepancy between signifier and signified, or, more exactly, to draw attention to the fact that in certain circumstances . . . a relation of inadequacy exists between signified and signifier to the detriment of the anterior relation of complementarity." Lévi-Strauss, "Introduction a

terminate utterance that itako compel the dead to descend. The function of this moment of kuchiyose is not to present the dead as alive
again. On the contrary, its purpose is to establish the dead as "dead":
as somewhere else, as inhabiting another scene. It thus establishes the
dead person as recallable, retrievable.

The kuchiyose is not entirely unintelligible, however. There is instead a shift between incomprehensible, formulaic moments and understandable ones, between monologic chanting and dialogic exchange, between the medium and the dead as the ostensible
communicator. This shifting between levels divides the authority of
the speaker; there is no one source of speech, yet despite this shifting
the itako's voice qua voice does not change. The voice comes from the
medium's body, but the words come from somewhere outside the body,
from the dead. The unity of the voice and the presence of the person
behind it are thrown into question, as the speaking subject and the
subject of speech move away from one another.

In the chanted moments, the unity of signification is rent; the signifiers acquire an authority of their own. In the moments of dialogue,
this rent is restitched—there is a message here—but the message is
claimed to originate elsewhere: a second rift, between the medium and
the message, opens up. It is in this part of the kuchiyose that patterns
of speech appear which correspond to different kinds of spirits: grandparents, children, fathers, wives. In both moments something outside
the medium compels her speech: in the first case, language itself seems
autonomously authoritative; in the second, the dead person, not the
medium, becomes the source of speech.

There are thus two functions in kuchiyose. One is to establish the
dead as dead, as "not here," somewhere else from where they can be
recalled. An ensemble of repetitions, patterns, and unintelligibilities
embodying the force of language thus positions the dead as, indeed,
dead. Yet the other function of kuchiyose is to recall, literally, the dead
and through the voice to embody them, to establish them as "here."
This occurs when the itako starts speaking in the first person of the
dead, describing the after-death state and its insufficiencies.

What was striking to me in listening with the crowds to the kuchiyose (which, I should say, is clearly accepted; crowds of listeners indicate an effective itako), was the realization that the point of transference of voices—when the dead speak through the voice of the itako—

l'oeuvre de Marcel Mauss," xliv. Translated in David Pocock, "Foreword" to Mauss,
General Theory of Magic, 4.

is also the point when most of the questioners started crying, when mourning in the sense of the expression of grief began in cathartic earnest. To wonder why this particular moment empowers grief is to wonder further about the fraught relationships between memory and language energized at Mount Osore.

The dead person is still idealized—thus the role of the formulaic kata—and the dead speak as they should speak, according to their statuses.[40] Through this patterned description they retain their place as authoritatively dead, yet they speak directly to the questioner in the medium's voice: the subject of speech is different from the speaking subject. The idea is sometimes expressed that the silent dead borrow (kariru) the medium's voice, her body. There is thus an immediate and stunning difference here between the dead one's voice as remembered by family members and the voice of the medium, unlike other forms of possession where the strangely altered voice of the medium mimetically doubles the voice of the spirit. The itako do not attempt to imitate the timbre or pitch of the spirit's voice; there is no confusion between her voice and the remembered voice of the dead one. This would seem to be a moment of disillusionment, as it were, with the patent realization that the medium's words are *not* those of the beloved dead.

Yet this is the moment of grief, and I believe it is provoked not so much by a belief that the dead one is speaking, but precisely because of the realization that the dead one is *not* speaking, precisely because of the difference that is instituted through the itako's voice. Here is the moment of realizing the irretrievability of what is lost, signaled by the irresolvable gap between the voice of the medium and the dead person's remembered voice. Expressions of grief follow as much from the realization of this gap—of the impossibility of a communication—as from any simple belief that the dead have actually spoken. If mourning, as Freud said, has to do with the realization of loss—a process that must occur (at least, it seems, for many people in Europe, North America, and Japan) before the comforts of memorialization—then kuchiyose is a scene for encountering this bodily loss, this "hole in the real" that death institutes. A split between the body and voice of the

---

40. In Japan the notion of conforming to a status pattern is widespread and accepted. The notion of *rashisa* (likeness) and of performing according to an ideal typical model occurs in Japanese theater as well; thus, a female impersonator or a woman is *onnarashii,* "ladylike" or "like a woman," in accordance with Japanese conventions of ladylikeness. Kata are the performance conventions that produce conventional likenesses. That dead spirits should speak just as dead spirits should speak, repeatedly, is perhaps less of a cause for disbelief or skepticism than it might seem.

medium and that which is disembodied and voiceless thus effects a bodily recalling that exceeds the idealized status of the dead enframed by official memorialization.

Am I thus saying that the auditors don't believe that the dead are really speaking, and that this realization of impossibility inspires their grief? Not simply so. What occurs constitutes a phenomenon that cannot become an object of positive knowledge, as we have seen in the case of the uncanny (see chapter 3). There is, instead, a phantasmatic relationship to these phantasms. Again, the contours of fetishistic remembrance, of concurrent recognition and disavowal, come into view. The psychoanalyst Octave Mannoni described the formula for fetishism as "I know but nevertheless . . .": "I know that the dead do not speak, but nevertheless (I believe that they do)." It is this split between knowledge and belief that is sutured by the embodiments of the itako.[41] But the resolutions of such fetishistic remembrance are correspondingly precarious, suspended. Many of the people I spoke to at the site and at the temple hostel in Tanabu where I stayed did not express a strong belief that they had spoken to the dead. They instead talked about the comfort they had received through the attempt at communication, about which I shall say more later.

The movements between registers of language and the senses redouble those at other sites on the mountain. Like a ghost story, kuchiyose uncovers a difference between seeing and hearing. One does not see the dead in kuchiyose; one only hears them, and hearing itself is divided by the difference between the medium's voice and the remembered voice of the dead person. Yet the itako provides a visible source for the language of the dead, a source that is missing in reports of ghosts at Mount Osore. The itako embodies the split that ghosts imply: she provides the visible source of ghostly discourse. She embodies that difference between the dead and the living, the invisible and the visible. Her blind body becomes the sign of difference, of loss itself.

All the mediums at Mount Osore claimed to be blind or partially blind. Those who were fully blind had more customers than those who were not, suggesting that blindness was perceived as somehow allowing a more compelling access to the dead. In encounters with ghosts, the visual and the aural do not coincide. Yet this discrepancy is not a problem with the itako, because they cannot see. For them, voices never have a visual origin; voices always emanate from an invisi-

---

41. Slavoj Žižek discusses this formulation in *For They Know Not What They Do*, 245, cited in chapter 1.

bility. It is not simply that the itako "are blind and therefore they can see the invisible world," a logic of reversal that links blindness and insight. It is precisely because they are blind and *cannot* see the invisible world that they are enabled to hear the voices of the dead and become the visible form of the properly invisible.

Blindness is an image of primal loss, a bodily mark of something lacking. There is something missing in the itako, and what is missing is the imperative of sight to demand a visual origin for sound. This lack is supplemented by the itako's place as the visual and vocal point of origin for the speech of the dead; their status as women undoubtedly augments these images of privation and loss.[42]

No one expressed fear of the dead at the kuchiyose I witnessed. In kuchiyose the objective is to hear the itako voicing the words of the dead. It is a regulated setting for this hearing, an arranged transgression of the boundaries that the dead as ghosts unpredictably cross, and a commercial transaction. (It is important to remember that the itako usually refer to their activities with the prosaic Japanese word *shōbai*, "business.") Kuchiyose begins with the narrativized possibility of communication with the dead and constructs an encounter with a spirit; a ghost story's origin is found in an uncanny encounter with a dead person which it then narrativizes. Yet kuchiyose's encounter with the dead does not seem to lead to the fear that ghost meetings would provoke; kuchiyose seems to operate, rather, to make such an encounter regulated, predictable (if not thereby any less poignant).

This predictability is closely affiliated with another dimension of kuchiyose: the making of predictions. Kuchiyose does not stop with the processes of mourning, for many. It is equally important as a source of knowledge about the future, and that dimension is crucial in trying to understand the place of mourning. Several elderly women from Tanabu gathered around the itako's tents told me that the real reason for kuchiyose is to find out what to do in the future. Thus, remembering what is gone becomes the basis for foretelling what has not yet happened. Survivors must go through the process of recalling (which often leads to grief) before they can get predictions. And getting predictions is much of the impetus for requesting kuchiyose. The dead get something out of it (remembrance); the living get something out of it (foreknowledge). In calling up the past one learns about the future. Regrets

---

42. If one were to take a certain psychoanalytic logic further, blindness becomes the bodily mark of "castration" as the name for a primal loss. Women's bodies become the site for oedipal fantasies around the loss of the phallus: women as "castrated" men. A blind woman, then, becomes a doubly invested embodiment (and reminder) of loss.

and hopes, memories and predictions converge on the dead as the locus of wishfulness.

In telling the future, the skill of the particular itako becomes important. A woman from Aomori city told me that she used to have kuchiyose performed every year, but last year the itako was completely off the mark; this year she would forego it.[43] The dead are the ostensible sources of narratives of the after-death state; if so, there would seem to be no question that their words would be authoritative. The division between the itako's voice and the (remembered) dead one's leads to a certain gap across which mourning occurs, according to the imperatives of fetishistic disavowal. But when predictions are involved, the abilities of the itako become crucial, although the dead person is still ostensibly the source.

The predictions become the bit of extra knowledge motivating kuchiyose. Why should the dead be able to predict the future or give advice that bears upon the future? The status of the dead person presents one part of the answer. One's dead parent gives advice, just as when she or he was alive: the predictions are authoritative, in character. In a broader sense, any person who dies becomes authoritative by becoming ancestral. The authority of the dead person to back up predictive advice is augmented because it converges with the peculiar capacities of the itako. She in effect predicts encounters with the dead by recalling them; she has a general power of prediction. The status of a particular dead person (who retains the status he or she had within the family while alive), the general authority a person gains by mere virtue of being dead, and the itako's powers of prediction meet at the scene of kuchiyose. Yet the efficacy of the predictions is deferred, quite unlike the immediate consolations of mourning. It is only at a later date that one can check the truth-value of the dead's words, and that possibility of verification puts those presumably authoritative words of the spirits into the register of "knowledge" rather than "belief": the predictions are either on the mark or off. By shifting to the domain of experiential truth, the disturbing dynamic that links the authority of the dead with truthful words shifts, too. Now it is the itako's responsi-

43. The mediums make predictions and divinations (*uranai*) using other methods in their local business (*shōbai*). They use *zeichiku* (divining rods) and rosaries (*juzu*) in divining individual and household fortunes. They use the paired stick-dolls called oshira-sama to divine both village-wide and household fortunes. They also give advice and consultations, and are used as healers, now primarily as supplemental to established medical practices. Predictions at kuchiyose take their place among a range of other regulated methods and times.

bility, the itako's fault, if a prediction fails. It is now a matter of practical skill, a technology of prediction, that produces results not dependent on the dead themselves.[44]

The elderly women from the area see kuchiyose as kuyō, as an occasion for grief and as a source of knowledge about the future. It is repeatable, scheduled. Kuchiyose ends by redrawing the border between death and life that it worked to erase by recalling the dead; it thus operates as the "best kuyō," as the devotees from Shimokita would say. The desperate metropolitan visitors who come to Mount Osore expressly to contact the dead regard kuchiyose as an extreme measure, as a means to work through grief. In the first instance, the kuchiyose does contain the force of social convention, as kuchiyose has been a scheduled, almost necessary part of the household's relationship to the ancestors: the ancestors must be called at regular intervals, and these callings often require interhousehold cooperation. In the second, the urban visitors have no particular relationship to the itako and no long-standing group investment in kuchiyose.

Many people who travel long distances to Mount Osore to have an audience with an itako do so out of a sense of desperation; they approach the itako as a last resort. They cannot forget the dead person and are still driven by thoughts of the dead person as alive. They are still in a state of incomplete mourning and presumably the various resources of kuyō have not allowed them to relinquish their grief. They come to remember the dead (in the sense of memorialization: to remind themselves that those they remember are truly "dead") so that they can then forget the memories that haunt them.

I met two sisters, one from Tokyo, the other, older, from northeastern Japan. The older one told me this:

> My husband died last year. I wanted to come to Osorezan but
> I didn't want to come alone—that's why my sister came. My

44. Mori records the instance of a woman who came to Mount Osore from Tokyo to get advice from her dead father concerning the fate of her unmarried youngest daughter. She was in a state of confusion because her daughter had received two marriage proposals—one from Tokyo, one from Osaka—at the same time. Whom should she choose? When the dead father first spoke in the kuchiyose, he expressed surprise at having been called up. The woman reacted with surprise also, because she had not performed any sort of memorial service for her father in the twenty years since his death—wasn't it then natural that her father would express astonishment at having been so suddenly recalled? The father predicted that either the east (Tokyo) or the west (Osaka) would yield good matches for her daughter. The woman was reassured and went away with a "bright face." Mori records this incident as one of many in which he translated kuchiyose from the local dialect into standard Japanese for visitors to Mount Osore. Mori, *Reijō Osorezan monogatari*, 17–18.

husband got sick two years ago. He was really sick for one and
one-half years. Then he died. It's still so new, it's like he's still
alive. [The younger sister later said that he was *yōki* (spirited),
that he liked to drink and sing *enka* (Japanese popular songs).]
Somehow or other I understood some of what the itako was
saying. He said he had been returned [*modosareta*] to some
place, but when I asked where he was, he said he didn't know.
He said he was thirsty—for three months before he died he
was always hungry and thirsty, but he could hardly drink anything. So it was strange that he said he was thirsty. The itako
didn't have any particular recommendations. [The younger sister later said that she was told to give him water every day.]

I asked if the purpose of having kuchiyose done was to console the
dead spirit. She said, more than that, it was to be able to hear the
person once again. She said she did not know if she believed, but
somehow or other she was consoled. She felt she had to try to talk to
him again; there was much left unsaid, and that is why she wanted to
go and try to talk to him.

This woman's recounting of her reasons for coming to Mount Osore
and of her experience with kuchiyose was similar to others I heard.
The weight of words left unsaid compelled her to try to complete a
communication that was incomplete. She tried to fill this lack by calling the absent other into presence again. To try to hear the voice of the
dead just once more overrides the motive of consolation and propitia-
tion through remembrance—kuyō—that is also said to be a result of
kuchiyose. And it is the effort of communication that seems to offer
self-consolation, even though she is not sure whether the dead one has
really spoken: "I know but nevertheless . . ."

Dialect and Transgression

The widow from northeastern Japan noted that "somehow or other"
(*nantonaku*) she understood much of what the itako said. Yet on the
important matter of recommendations from the itako on how ritually
to take care of her late husband, she and her younger sister had
reached different understandings. This question of intelligibility is central to unraveling the efficacy of kuchiyose, because the itako speak in
a dialect barely, if at all, understandable to the vast majority of Japanese who retain their services at the festival. The itako use, as well, a
lexicon of taboo words (*imikotoba*) whose origins the itako themselves

do not comprehend.[45] Only the most experienced people from the locale can understand the itako, and even they run up against a modicum of unintelligibility; and they, as well, sometimes misunderstand the itako from other parts of northeastern Japan attending the festival.

People standing around the tents who had come in tour buses from Tokyo remarked that they could not understand a word. Others asked me how I could possibly understand anything, when "even we Japanese can't understand."[46] Some people carried tape recorders into the tents so that they could play back the itako's words later; sometimes the itako's attendants or one of the local old women who stayed in the tents through hours of others' kuchiyose would translate into standard Japanese. The unintelligibility of the dialect (usually Tsugaru, not Shimokita dialect) and the taboo words was further heightened by the style of the recitation, sometimes whispered, almost inaudible. The persistent calls of the sellers and the subdued talk of the crowds huddled outside augmented the difficulty of understanding for the customers in the tents. Often they would have to get as close to the mediums as possible in order to hear, asking the itako to repeat what she had said. There was a straining to hear, to understand what was unintelligible. For speakers of standard Japanese, then, kuchiyose is twice unintelligible. Not only is its ritual language incomprehensible, but the messages from the dead are as well. This incomprehensibility then requires a translator, a local person who will put the medium's words into standard Japanese. This person is a "secondary medium," yet another voice in a transmission conveying the words of the dead.

The question of dialect is vital here. The kuchiyose, and the words of dead spirits, are exotic, are outside the body of standard Japanese and standard understandings: the words are couched in an incomprehensible dialect (we are reminded again of Yanagita's inability to un-

45. Sakurai gives examples of these words, also called *idako kotoba* (itako words). A man is called *yumitori*, a woman *kagami* (mirror), a husband and wife, *ai no makura* (pillow of love), and a child, *takara* (treasure). The dead spirits descend through the use of these terms of address. In calling the dead person, then, the itako use formulaic substitutes that have no particular relationship to the person called at the point where one would use the normal term of address for a living person. He states that these words are almost all understood by the local clientele; they are not, however, generally understood by the one-time visitor to Mount Osore. Sakurai, *Nihon no shamanizumu*, 1:59.

46. For an increasingly standardized Japanese cultural landscape, a perceived internal exotic becomes problematic. Remaining dialects—of which there are many in Japan— become valorized as languages of difference within a much-valued culture of consistency. What is only marginally understood, from the standard perspective, becomes an exemplar of what is most traditional: the exotic and the traditional coincide at the farthest reaches of the Japanese national-cultural imaginary.

derstand Sasaki's dialect). Perhaps because of that they convey an even greater force to those that do not understand them, relaying, in a larger sense, a cultural difference at the same time that they speak of an intimate loss. Itako and their callings of dead spirits are supposed to incorporate what is most traditional about Mount Osore, itself an epitome of archaic Japan. Yet even though this voiced "tradition" is presented as quintessentially Japanese, it shows up in the guise of something ineluctably other.

"Tradition" implies an authoritative, conventional oral transmission. In the Japanese case, this transmission has a history of being legitimated ultimately by the ancestral dead. It is striking that this definition of "tradition" could describe kuchiyose itself: an authoritative oral transmission from the dead. But as we have seen, kuchiyose is also a figure for falsity, for theatricality, for obscurity, for unreliability, for what is scandalous and marginal from a certain contemporary perspective of national-cultural order. It becomes "traditional" *because* of these negativities. Thence the duplicity of "tradition" itself: a transmission that always contains the possibility of betrayal, of an arbitrary selection from the past.[47] Kuchiyose becomes the figure for tradition at the moment it is farthest removed from understanding.

An older world of orality becomes more "traditional" the more it is excluded from a modern scriptural economy and the closer it moves to a possible disappearance. And thus the evocation of that world— through forms of transmission archaically voiced—inevitably bears the marks of loss. Kuchiyose works with individual deaths but it works equally to situate national-cultural loss. Kuchiyose operates for locals and outsiders alike as a means to place themselves vis-à-vis this loss as it too ultimately participates in the impulse of memorialization. Not simply embodiments of the specific dead, the itako—and the practice of kuchiyose—have become larger markers for what appears to be vanishing. Their practices can even appear as acts of self-memorialization, as the itako themselves grow older, die, and are not replaced.

What makes kuchiyose a most poignant reminder of an entire spectrum of losses are the modalities of voicings and the registers of desire it embodies. The expansion of those possibilities of desire—such that kuchiyose has become a charged instance of a certain form of mourning work—are historically located within current Japanese interests. If all returns to the past are linked to returns to the voice, then the

47. Recall again Raymond Williams's discussion in *Keywords*, 268–69.

unintelligible voices of the itako become, through kuchiyose, both the promise and betrayal of this return.[48]

It is sometimes said that of all the classically sacred mountains remaining in contemporary Japan, only Mount Osore is "just like it used to be."[49] The logic that maintains it is "just like it used to be" surely discloses that it is *not* just like it used to be. Only from the position of loss can one assert that nothing has been lost; only when the seamless, unquestioned transmission of custom has been interrupted, does "tradition" emerge. The realization of loss is forestalled, denied, by an

48. Jacques Derrida is convincing in his efforts to erase the boundaries between speech and writing, by showing that speech—no less than writing in its narrowly construed sense—is a structure of iterability, a trace structure that affords no direct access to punctual presence. His work amply demonstrates the movement in philosophy and linguistics that locates presence in speech and regards writing as derivative, fallen, and somehow constitutively different than speech—a movement Derrida strenuously deflects and overturns with his wider notion of *écriture*. See his "Structure, Sign, and Play in the Discourse of the Human Sciences" and "Signature Event Context."

Two particular objections to his analysis could be made here in relation to the scene of speaking just described at Mount Osore. One is that Derrida seems not to address the effects of the voice in practice. This objection is linked to the second—that, from the historical perspective of power, it is speech—not writing—that is denied and reduced in the interests of an ever-burgeoning "scriptural economy," as Michel de Certeau would describe it. What role does the voice, and, in particular, older forms of the voice, older enunciations have in a world where enscripting is dominant? This question is one which haunted de Certeau in his attempts to move beyond a folklorism nostalgic for the simple presence of the voice of the folk.

Derrida of course makes a distinction between writing in the narrow sense and writing as a trace structure, which he would see as constituting spoken discourse no less than any other. But could it be that the very fact that "orality" and "nature" have been valorized and elevated over their fallen partners (writing, culture) in much of western philosophy is related to their historical subjugation? This valorization points directly to the concept of repression: "It becomes comprehensible that those objects to which men give their preference, that is, their ideals, originate in the same perceptions and experiences as those objects of which they have most abhorrence, and that the two originally differed from one another only by slight modifications." Sigmund Freud, "Repression," 108. Barbara Johnson astutely remarks on this reversal of effects: "While the critique of logocentrism undertaken by Derrida implies that Western patriarchal culture has always privileged the presence, immediacy, and ideality of speech over the distance and materiality of writing, this privilege has never, in fact, been unambiguous. An equal but more covert privileging of writing has also been operative. . . . The hidden but ineradicable importance of writing that Derrida uncovers in his readings of logocentric texts in fact reflects an unacknowledged, or 'repressed,' *grapho*centrism." Johnson, "Writing," in *Critical Terms for Literary Study*, 47. Johnson's essay thus expands the implications of Derrida's text for a consideration of speech in practice.

49. Mori, *Reijō Osorezan monogatari*, 16. Young travelers from Tokyo told me that Mount Osore was "unique" and had preserved its oldness (*furusa*) more than other sacred mountains. Recall here, also, the (dis)simulating logic of the "just like" discussed in chapter 2.

Iwasaki Toyo performing
kuchiyose for her customers

insistence that nothing is lost. It is denied by an idealization, a memorialization of place, a bracketing of practices, an assertion of continuity.

The mass media and tourist industries have played decisive roles in constructing the mountain as emblematic of a surviving Japanese past. At issue is a particular place that was a local object of awe and of particular beliefs about death, nurtured by long isolation and poverty. Replacing this specificity is a convertible, popular image of otherness, and of Osorezan as representative of this otherness. This move to monumentalize loss by replacing it with an image parallels the movement of memorialization at Mount Osore that brackets memories of the dead and turns them into representations of themselves. In each case, a certain nexus of authority—the temple and its Buddhist scenarios, the media and current fantasies of the Japanese folk past—operates to forestall the realization of loss. In national imaginings of Mount Osore, the mountain presents a homogeneous facade: it is the mountain in northeastern Japan where blind mediums summon dead spirits. Yet it is also a site of divisions and contentions inscribing a territory centered around the interplay of death and life, absence and presence, and the crossings between them: a heterogeneous space.

In describing Mount Osore during its summer festival, I have suggested allegorical parallels among processes of bounding and troping in language itself; the discourse of death and memorialization; and the modern monumentalization of the site as a representation of *extimité*. I have also described narrative activities, supplementary uses of the voice, and practices of mourning that trouble the distinctions these processes institute. But no simple rewriting of levels is sufficient, for there are differences of power and scope that skew the attempt. Memorialization at Mount Osore (even with the temple's assertions of authority and its four hundred years of managerial imperatives) is, in its entirety, endangered by the popularity of the itako (who themselves are dwindling in numbers) and by all the recuperations and problems of tourism.[50] By a movement of reversal that such recuperations bring, the itako, providers of an access to a world not subsumed by official

50. For a long time the temple at Mount Osore refused to allow itako to do kuchiyose within the temple grounds (other than at the time of the festival), fearing the vulgarization (*zokka*) of the mountain. The itako would perform for tourists and pilgrims at the rest house outside the temple grounds every Saturday and Sunday from April to October (the period when the mountain is open). But Mount Osore itself is located within a national park, and eventually the temple felt it could no longer resist the great demand for kuchiyose at Mount Osore proper; thus, since 1974 the mountain has entered a new stage of popularity. Now kuchiyose is performed any time for tourists within the temple grounds. Takamatsu, *Shimokita hantō no minkan shinkō*, 83. This influx of tourists with

memorialization have become the focal point for the idealization of the site. What was most provocatively threatening to order at Mount Osore has become the point of entry for a more comprehensive, central cultural ordering. Monumentalization at this level, though it parallels the logic of memorializing the dead, occurs on a scale that gives it the status of a master narrative. Within this narrative, Mount Osore becomes just another instance, however evocative, of the Japanese folk past. Outside this narrative and its burgeoning claims to encompass and account for the Japanese past, however, ghostly voices and cries of the living hauntingly trouble their enclosure. Although Mount Osore may no longer possess the sublime power to terrify, it retains the power to disturb.

---

money has inflated the cost of kuchiyose (to fifteen hundred yen in the mid-1980s), undermined its "simple" and "artless" (soboku) religious function for the local populace, and brought trouble (toraburu) to Entsūji (the temple), which is thinking of trying to return the mountain to its former state. Takamatsu, Shimokita hantō no minkan shinkō, 268.

CHAPTER SIX

Theatrical Crossings, Capitalist Dreams

Recalling the dead on Mount Osore enacts, through its transgressive figuration, a double displacement in the national-cultural allegory of Japanese modernity: kuchiyose (spirit recalling) becomes the figure for a scandalous falsity at the very moment it emerges as most powerfully authentic. That figure can trope the duplicities of tradition itself (duplicities that Raymond Williams has noted), as well as those of theatrical representation. That is, the very idea of theater emplots a difference between sign and referent that continually calls into question the status of representation and its effects. Terry Eagleton comments: "If representation is a lie, then the very structure of the theatrical sign is strangely duplicitous, asserting an identity while manifesting a division, and to this extent it resembles the structure of metaphor."[1] The divided identities that mediums embody in spirit recallings metaphorically recall, then, questions of representation. And the idea of theatricality becomes even more compelling when it is linked with the public status that stagings of spirit recallings at Mount Osore have attained in Japan since the 1960s. Little could be more intimate than the scenes of mourning that take place on Mount Osore, yet those scenes have become theatricalized in public ways that display intimacy as alienated.

The attractions of Tōno and Mount Osore operate in the folkloric register as they emblematize places marginal to metropolitan and middle-class stabilities, thereby attaining a certain unexpected cultural centrality. Yet there are other scenes, outside this dimension of the folk-

---

1. Terry Eagleton, *William Shakespeare*, 3–4.

loric, that are excessive in their troubling of the rationalities of contem porary Japan, other sites that throw into relief the workings of *extimité*, questions of public representation, voice and theatricality, modernity and marginality.

This chapter ethnographically encounters another mode of marginality, one that shares with folktales and spirit recitations a continuing reliance on vanishing practices of the voice: *taishū engeki*, small-scale, itinerant variety theater that had become extremely attenuated by the 1970s but experienced a surge of popularity in the mid-1980s. Performed by small traveling troupes that play one-month engagements in cramped theaters on the metropolitan fringes or in provincial hot springs hotels, taishū engeki has become in some quarters a fashionable, retro symbol of lower-class performative vitality. This vitality manifests itself in the direct interchange between audience and actors as well as through the widespread knowledge that the actors rely only peripherally on scripts: they learn hundreds of plays almost entirely through verbal instruction from the troupe leader. In the American idiom, taishū engeki evokes—both generically and figuratively—a cross between, say, small-time circus, 1920s vaudeville, amateur little theater, and fading Catskill comedy acts. It is an amalgam of what we might think of as largely superseded forms of public pleasure within earlier moments of modernity. In the Japanese idiom, taishū engeki's composite of vanishing modernities would include "samurai melodrama" (of which I will have more to say later), rock and roll combined with old-fashioned *enka* (Japan's populist song genre), the comic forms of *manzai* and *rakugo*, and so-called Japanese dance *(Nihon buyō)*. While some of these forms retain their popularity to a large degree (enka, for example), their inclusion in this particular assemblage, taishū engeki's "grand show" *(gurando shō)*, clearly places them outside the parameters of contemporary bourgeois respectability and current mass cultural success. Not only the particular assemblage but, it is crucial to remark, the itinerancy and class positions of the Japanese who perform it preclude taishū engeki from possessing the minimal tokens of respectable bourgeois life.[2]

As such, then, taishū engeki scandalizes in ways that are consonant with the practices at Mount Osore, particularly those of spirit recallings. Although the workings of desire are different at those two sites,

2. Dorinne Kondo is one of the only American anthropologists to have studied class problematics in Tokyo's shitamachi area. It should be stressed that itinerant theatrical performers are included within class frameworks only with difficulty, because they do not conform to the wage-earning imperatives of differential class memberships.

both play out phantasmatic scenarios of superseded modes of being, of encounters with the past, of temporal displacements. Kuchiyose is regarded by folklorists as pseudotrance, as a kind of "bad theater" that produces effects it, by all rights, shouldn't. Taishū engeki's stage plays produce spectacles that partake of what Peter Brooks has called the "melodramatic imagination," highly conventionalized presentations of good and evil, duty and love, what many critics would also regard as "bad theater" because of the stunningly binarized predictability of its narratives.[3] Yet night after night, regular theatergoers break into sobs at the same predictable denouements—the triumph of mother love or the sacrifice of family for duty, for example. A moment later, they are laughing, in the rapid and vast swings of emotion that only the excesses of melodrama can provoke. It is the very conventionality, then, of taishū engeki—its overcoded theatrical falsity as opposed to its realism—that produces the effects a certain modern sensibility would associate with authenticity, whether through realism in theater or verifiable trance in spirit recallings.

Max Horkheimer and Theodor Adorno wrote of the rationalized sleekness of the late liberal culture industry, which finds the seriousness of avant-garde art an embarrassment; only by transforming that art into approachable commodities can the industry come to terms with it. But even more unnerving, argue Horkheimer and Adorno, are unruly forms of amusement, of light entertainment, that cannot be fully subsumed under the totalizing and formulaic production processes of the culture industry: "The eccentricity of the circus, peepshow, and brothel is as embarrassing to it [the culture industry] as that of Schönberg and Karl Kraus."[4] That eccentricity is precisely what is at stake with taishū engeki, an eccentricity marked by the very terms of its existence. While in the televisual imagination, taishū engeki momentarily emerged as yet another vanishing species of folk performance (because of its primarily "oral" mode of transmitting knowledge) or as a suitable object of a neo-nostalgia that focuses on moments of modernity overcome, its eccentricity seems to embody an older world of speech, while the itinerancy and poverty of its practitioners mark it as sharply marginal to mainstream Japan.[5]

3. Peter Brooks, *The Melodramatic Imagination: Balzac, Henry James, Melodrama, and the Mode of Excess.*

4. Horkheimer and Adorno, "Culture Industry," 136.

5. This chapter is based on fieldwork done in the Tokyo area between 1983 and 1985, and in 1990. I attended some thirty taishū engeki performances, interviewed actors, and talked to theater owners and spectators about taishū engeki. I am indebted to Yamaguchi Masao for introducing me to this theater; he has written several articles about taishū engeki which are essential for any understanding of this performance genre.

Taishū engeki's very name embodies the contradiction that Horkheimer and Adorno, for example, explore so powerfully in their post-Holocaust anatomy of the coincidences of liberal mass culture and fascist practices of social control. The word *taishū*—which literally means "large groups of people"—can be translated as either "mass" or "popular." Although "mass culture" and "popular culture" are commonly used almost interchangeably, the difference between the two has long been a matter of debate within cultural studies. That is, "mass"—particularly in the way that Horkheimer and Adorno, for example, want to think about it—can "exclude from the outset the interpretation agreeable to its advocates: that it is a matter of something like a culture that arises spontaneously from the masses themselves, the contemporary form of popular art."[6] "Mass culture" would thus indicate culture as commodified and administered, pretargeted and produced for large numbers of consumers: the masses. "Popular culture" must be carefully distinguished from the culture industry's productions, if the popular is to retain any critical force or resistant grass-roots connection to the "people." If it is not distinguished as such, there is a danger of simply celebrating the ubiquitous products of advanced capitalism as genuinely and simply popular—of the people—without taking into account the interplay of persuasion, capital, and ideology at work in producing, say, a hit commodity (and at work in consuming it).

Taishū plays out in its very nomenclature a contradiction: that between the top-down, standardized power that *taishū*-as-"mass" implies; and the bottom-up, resistant prevalence that *taishū*-as-"popular" evokes. In thinking about the history of this contradiction—and the varieties of appropriation it has provoked in modern Japan—Kurihara Akira has written of a sequencing of three mass formations: "mass culture" *(taishū bunka)* as a truly communal popular culture (which he sees as a utopian horizon of cultural longing); mass culture as the classic modernist regime of movies, pop songs, magazines, and baseball, in which there is "ample room for the projection of desires and needs and for the exercise of the imagination"; and lastly, the dystopic eventuations of mass culture in advanced capitalism, in which social management, industrial culture, automation, consumption, and surveillance increasingly predominate (the world of video, TV commercials, electronic monitoring, and service industries).[7] Taishū engeki in the late twentieth century seemingly enacts the interplay of the first two formations of mass culture within the larger enclosure of the third.

6. Theodor Adorno, "Culture Industry Reconsidered," 12.
7. Kurihara Akira, *Kanri shakai to minshū risei: nichijō ishiki no seiji shakaigaku*, 30.

From the perspective of the information society (*jōhō shakai*, a concept first developed in Japan), there is something evanescently quaint about film and baseball, yet taishū engeki—flourishing in the interwar years along with the modern (*modan*) urban practices of movies and sports—is now even further removed, further superseded as it hovers near the horizons of a vaguely remembered and nostalgically recalled popular communality and neighborly immediacy. This very aura of the communal-popular, however, also recalls the ambivalent specter of privation: after the war, troupes often performed in ad hoc theaters, sometimes roofless shacks; when it rained, the spectators would watch while holding umbrellas. Taishū engeki plays out these contradictions for many in its audience, as its performers also harbor contradictory dreams about success and a popularity that can only evade them given the fundamental conditions of their theater.

Taishū engeki has often referred in very general terms to the various forms of so-called western-style light theater, comedy, or drama widely popular since the early twentieth century. The popular theater examined in this chapter, however, specifically designates only those small-scale itinerant performances whose repertoire features plays set in the Tokugawa period (focusing on themes broadly derived from kabuki), song shows, and dance segments. Other names applied to this sort of theater include *dosa mawari* and *inaka mawari* (barnstorming), *tabi shibai* (traveling theater), *zachō shibai* (theater led by a troupe head), and *sanryū kabuki* (third-rate kabuki). In fact, the term *taishū engeki* as applied to these small-scale itinerant troupes became common only within the last twenty years or so; many of the troupes appropriated it themselves, hoping thereby to widen their base of popularity and to articulate their more old-fashioned appeal with large-scale entertainment forms and variety shows. Far from truly mass in its appeal, however, taishū engeki succeeds in attracting only minute numbers of fans compared to such mega-attractions as rock concerts, baseball games, and televised spectacles. In that sense, it could not be further from the mass popularity of television, say, for which many taishū engeki actors ambivalently long.

Low-Budget Kabuki and Its Promises

If the taishū engeki discussed here is not the western-influenced light theater described in Japanese theater encyclopedias, what, then, is its content? Japanese television "samurai dramas" provide the most accessible parallel to taishū engeki themes. Its plays are set primarily in the Tokugawa period, with highly sentimental themes focusing on the classic conflicts between duty (*giri*) and human feelings (*ninjō*) and good and evil (*zen'aku*). Stock characters from historical drama (*jidai geki*) and kabuki repertoires often revolve around the figure of the *ya-kuza*, a traveling outsider—most often a criminal—at odds with the larger society of law and order. Again like television samurai dramas, there is plenty of sword fighting, or *chanbara*. Unlike the world portrayed on the TV screen, however, taishū engeki retains many more explicit elements of kabuki: *onnagata* (male players of female roles), *kata* (set forms of acting), and *mie* (stylized poses).

Taishū engeki actors themselves often refer to their performance as "third-rate kabuki." This perception of their art as a sort of low-budget kabuki stems from the historical basis of this itinerant theater. From at least the medieval period in Japanese history, *tabi geinin*—"traveling artistes"—wandered throughout Japan, fulfilling magico-religious functions as they visited communities periodically at festive occasions. Some groups formed their own settled communities and specialized in particular varieties of performance, such as doll theater. Many wanderers and communities of entertainers came to be viewed as outcastes. These artistes came to define in many ways the structural margins of settled agricultural communities; they formed the substratum for kabuki and allied entertainment forms in the seventeenth century. Forced to settle along riverbanks—undesirable land often forming the boundaries of villages and towns—they came to be known as *kawara kojiki*, or "riverside beggars."[8] Kabuki actors gradually attained spectacular prominence in the Tokugawa period, although actors and theaters were strictly controlled and segregated. A few major theaters and actors' dynasties emerged; actors with lesser names and less impressive credentials formed their own troupes, which played in theaters, large and small, in the urban centers. The very lowest ranks of these urban troupes and provincial actors formed the so-called dosa mawari, or barnstorming groups, which played at temple fairs and festivals throughout the countryside.

In the late Meiji and early Taishō (1912–1926) periods, actors started incorporating elements of European and American theater into their performances. Popular literature of the time created a whole new style of nihilistic sword hero, who became a major influence on the themat-

---

8. See chapter 5 for a discussion of the symbolism of the riverbank in Japanese folk religion.

ics of popular theater. Nakazato Kaizan's *Daibosatsu Tōge*, which began serialization in 1914, provided the prototype of this mode. In 1918, a western-style actor named Sawada Shōjirō consolidated these trends and formed a theatrical type he termed *shinkokugeki*, "new national theater."[9] Sawada wanted to make theater more accessible to the ascendant Japanese urban masses; his theater used the stories of Nakazato and others as the basis for a new brand of sword theater. The Taishō period witnessed the advent of the "chanbara age," with true-blue sword heroes predominating; the figure of the wandering yakuza came to the fore later, in the following Shōwa period. Shinkokugeki actors form the most immediate, recent influence on taishū engeki. The smallest and most impoverished of these shinkokugeki troupes became the direct precursors of today's taishū engeki practitioners.[10]

Chanbara and shinkokugeki had great popular appeal until the war years, when austerity measures kept them from flourishing. Occupation censors banned all swordplay from Japanese theater after the war, but the small troupes in the countryside could easily slip through the censorship nets; the period 1945 to 1953 was in fact a heyday for taishū engeki. Packed houses were the order of the day; theaters fronted almost every railway station on the main lines. Over seven hundred troupes toured Japan in the bitterly poor years after World War II; in the latter half of the 1950s, however, their popularity began to fade. The nadir came in the early 1970s, when many thought that taishū engeki might completely die out.

The troupes were extraordinarily poor—and getting poorer in the midst of Japan's accelerating affluence. Misato Eiji, now one of taishū engeki's greatest stars, recalled the near-starvation of his early childhood; his dreams of success centered not on theatrical stardom, but on having as much white rice as he could eat.[11] Hot springs resorts hired troupes to entertain guests during this period, but competition would push down the price until a whole troupe played a month's engagement for only eighty thousand yen. The decline in the number of theaters is equally telling: there were over fifty permanent and temporary theaters in Tokyo after the war; in 1960, nineteen remained; in 1976, only one was left. Shinohara Takamasa, the owner of the only two taishū engeki theaters in Tokyo described it this way in 1983:

9. Information about shinkokugeki taken from Takahashi Hiroshi, *Taishū geinō*, 149.

10. This information taken from Kata Kōji, Kizugawa Kei, and Tamagawa Shinmei, *Shitamachi engei nakiwarai*.

11. Ibid., 48–49.

The popularity of taishu engeki continued until the mid-50s, but when Japan entered into the period of "high economic growth," the entertainment halls were closed one after another with the waves of urban development. With the loss of customers due to TV, too, the theaters of Tokyo became lonelier year by year. . . . After the Kotobuki Theater in Senjū closed in 1975, it ended up that my place was the only one left in Tokyo. . . . The conditions were such that even though there were fifteen actors in the troupe, there would be only ten spectators in the audience.[12]

Why did taishū engeki decline so precipitously? The boom in property values forced owners of theaters in prime station locations to sell out. But television is inevitably cited, by actors and theater owners alike, as the single most important factor in the decline and near-demise of their tradition. Nonetheless, what TV takes away, it can give back—at least in reconstructed guises. In 1979, the first All-Japan Taishū Engeki Festival was held in Kyūshū, and Japan Broadcasting Corporation (NHK), those great discoverers of domestic exotica, produced a special on the festival. Since 1980, NHK has presented several taishū engeki specials, highlighting in particular the Umezawa Takeo Troupe and its dazzling female impersonator, Umezawa Tomio, otherwise known as Shitamachi no Tamasaburō. "Shitamachi" refers to the older, plebeian eastern quarters of Tokyo, where the merchant culture of the Tokugawa period—including kabuki—reached its apogee. "Tamasaburō" refers to Bandō Tamasaburō, currently the most stellar of all kabuki actors playing female roles. Combined, the two terms suggest an amalgam of lower-class spunk and sensuality with the refinement of higher culture. Umezawa Tomio, this most famous of taishū engeki female impersonators, has become both a cult figure and a star, with night-club appearances, guest spots on television shows (including a run in a 1982 TV series), records, and commercial endorsements. We can easily grasp the strains of this situation, in which a live theater decimated by the powers of television finds itself in the midst of a resurgence created by those same powers.

Tomio has thus been the single most important figure in pulling taishū engeki into the Japanese media spotlight and touching off the so-called taishū engeki boom of the mid-1980s, and the popularity of Tomio and the Umezawa troupe has prompted talk of a taishū engeki

12. Shinohara Takamasa, "Taishū engeki ni haru futatabi," 28.

renaissance. Shinohara Takamasa described the mid-80s resurgence in these terms:

> With the popularity of the Umezawa Takeo troupe providing the motive force, and with the efforts also of the theaters and troupes throughout the country, taishū engeki has taken a new turn for the better. In Tokyo and the surrounding area, there are two theaters. . . . If we include the little groups scattered here and there, then there are about eighty groups in Japan who are persisting.
>
> *Inaka shibai* [provincial theater], *tabimawari* [traveling theater], and taishū engeki have been despised, but the reason that they are now being reconsidered and enjoyed is undoubtedly because they afford an enjoyment which dissolves the differences between the stage and the audience. In the big theaters . . . it doesn't do to cry even if you feel like crying, and even if you want to yell out, you're hesitant about doing so. But in the little taishū engeki theaters nobody minds if you reveal your emotions from the tiny spectator area; and onstage, too, in the ad-libbing that goes on without any script, the actors are able to parry the whole range of the audience's emotions and respond to them.[13]

The appeal of communal emotions unleashed, of a return to the warmth of neighborhood solidarities, inspired the upswing of a new generation of taishū engeki fans. But it is clear that much of that resurgence was tied to the attractions of certain leading men, Umezawa Tomio first among them. As the tide inevitably receded in the latter half of the 1980s, however, most troupes found their status essentially unchanged. More Japanese may now know about taishū engeki, but not that many more actually go to see it. It has weathered the bleakest times of the 1970s, and now troupes eke out a meager existence, supported by cadres of loyal supporters in their home regions—often middle-aged women—and dependent on engagements at hot springs resorts and the few remaining taishū engeki theaters in Japan.

This theater still occupies a precarious position in Japan, but that very precariousness has made it an effective sign of marginality. To most contemporary Japanese, taishū engeki appears in newspaper and television reports as a nostalgic oddity, a fragment of another world strangely out of place. Some older people—those who grew up in the prewar period—remember going to neighborhood theaters during their childhood to see taishū engeki-like plays, often dragged along by

13. Ibid.

an ardent grandmother. But most of these same people would find it unthinkable to make the trek to one of the theaters in the seedier parts of Tokyo. The stable audience for the troupes tends to be older residents of the neighborhoods surrounding the theaters and middle-aged women. The recent, more evanescent audience for taishū engeki (for troupes lucky enough to attract attention) has been younger urbanites, particularly those in the media, entertainment, or academic businesses. Writers, advertising people, free-lance artists, and avant-garde dancers and actors have had a small-scale infatuation with this people's theater, finding a warmth and closeness lacking in the formalized high-theatrical traditions of Japan as they are performed today. Many of these same actors and artists are trying to achieve a populist ambience in their own work: for example, the late Terayama Shūji, with his extravagant mixing of motifs and images from Japanese history, and Kara Jūro, whose transient Red Tent *(aka tento)* theater creates a pastiche of objects drawn from the detritus of urban life.

Taishū engeki is, of course, far removed from the avant-garde affluence these artists represent. Employing conventions familiar to all Japanese through kabuki or television dramas, the theater nonetheless exceeds these conventions with its own particular mix, in which heightened corporeality and the significations of class predominate. One of the clearest markers of class position is the itinerancy of the troupes; troupes not only tour the countryside, but in many cases have no permanent homes whatsoever. They play one-month engagements in small theaters, health centers, *gurando hoteru* (grand hotels), and hot springs resorts, from Kyūshū to Hokkaidō.[14] Troupes play engagements every month of the year, seldom taking a day off. They commonly give two three-hour performances per day.[15]

Touring troupes bring all of their household goods, musical equipment, props, and costumes with them on the road. Even refrigerators, washing machines, and *butsudan*, the Buddhist household altars where the ancestral tablets are kept, accompany the groups on their circuits.

14. Kyūshū, Kansai, and Kantō are the three main regions for taishū engeki; permanent theaters do not exist outside these three regions.

15. My depictions of the life and structure of taishū engeki troupes are taken from conversations with troupe members, particularly Katsu Koryū of the Arashi Gekidan; from conversations with audience members and theater managers; and from readings in the small number of Japanese sources describing this theatrical stream. A Kyoto University graduate student, Ukai Masaki, spent over a year touring with the Ichikawa Hitomaru troupe. His description is one of the most revealing and complete records available of daily life with a taishū engeki troupe. See Ukai Masaki, "Taishū engeki no makuai: Nanjō Masaki no ichinen nikagetsu."

Although some troupes have one or two family members with homes, many do not; in either case, most groups are rarely able to return home. Children travel with them; school-age children attend the nearest school for one-month stints. In a land where compulsory, standardized education for all children forms the basis for national economic success and prestige, the itinerancy of children is perhaps the most unsettling reminder of the essential difference between taishū engeki actors and mainstream Japanese.

When troupes play theaters—as opposed to playing at hotels—they rent them out for a nominal fee, say, two hundred yen per day (in the 1980s). They then share the take from the performances with the theater; a split of 60 percent for the theater and 40 percent for the troupe is common. But the troupe's connection with the theater does not end with performing there; they actually set up house in the theater, living backstage for the month, cooking and washing in the gakuya, the "dressing room." They often spread mats on the stage, line up tables, and eat their meals onstage. In theaters that are covered with tatami (Japanese woven floor coverings)—such as the Shinohara Engeijō in Tokyo—the troupes sleep in the audience section. On the last day of the month's engagement, just after the late show, they pack up and leave, for the next afternoon a new troupe will open. Several members drive a truck filled with the troupe's belongings; the others follow by train. They arrive at the new site sometime in the morning, set up, and immediately start their next engagement.

Each gekidan or za (troupe) is headed by a zachō (troupe head), often the active male head of the family whose members comprise the majority of the group. Usually there is a designated fukuzachō (assistant head) and two or more actors whose names are listed on the playbill. Troupes commonly consist of fifteen to twenty members, of which more than half are considered kin (in the heyday of taishū engeki, troupes sometimes numbered over fifty). The Arashi Gekidan (Storm Troupe), which regularly played the two remaining theaters in Tokyo, is one such family troupe. The head, Katsu Koryū, is unusually young, in his mid-thirties; his elder brother Ryūji is a star player and takes most "handsome man" lead roles; another older brother plays comic roles. The zachō's wife occasionally appears onstage, and his mother— in her mid-sixties—is well known for her cameo roles. Children of the troupe also take their turns onstage.

Troupe headships are often inherited through the male line, going to the eldest son (the Arashi Gekidan is an exception). There are also some female troupe heads, including the veteran female leader of Gek-

idan Mama. In theory the zachō has complete control over the arrang-
ing and structuring of the performances; in practice this varies. Katsu
Koryū moved into the headship of Arashi Gekidan because it was
thought he would boost the troupe's popularity with his comic genius
and friendly manner. Nevertheless, his brother Ryūji—with his wider
knowledge of repertoire and deeper experience—remains the most
powerful member. In contrast, the most famous taishū engeki troupe,
the Umezawa Takeo Gekidan, keeps its star Umezawa Tomio in the
assistant head position; his older brother Takeo firmly retains official
leadership. Although the troupe leader is addressed by the ubiquitous
Japanese word for "teacher"—*sensei*—older troupe members are addressed by kinship terms, such as "elder brother" and "elder sister."

The life of a taishū engeki troupe becomes all the more remarkable
when one considers the special features of their art. They perform two
different plays for their noon performance, which lasts until 3:30 P.M.,
and repeat these plays for the 5:00 P.M. show. The next day, two completely different plays are performed. After the evening performance,
a visit to the public bath, and dinner, they practice (*keiko*), making tapes
for the next day and working on their individual song and dance numbers. The taishū engeki day usually lasts until two o'clock in the morning. This devotedly itinerant life, with its unending round of performances, is everything that contemporary middle-class Japan—with its
ideals of lifetime employment, affluence, and achievement—is not.
What gives taishū engeki its current appeal is undoubtedly linked to
the image of the itinerant. It is an image that has enduring appeal for
many Japanese, evinced by the seemingly eternal popularity of the
Tora-san series of films, featuring the pan-Japanese adventures and
romances of an itinerant peddler from shitamachi, the old "downtown" section of Tokyo. Itinerancy is itself repeatedly referenced in
taishū engeki plays, with the role of the traveling, marginalized yakuza
(in this case, a small-time outlaw); many, if not most, plays center
around such a character. And there is a continuing association in the
public mind between taishū engeki troupes and the underworld
(again, yakuza).

Spectators delight in the lightning-quick repartee and lengthy
monologues of taishū engeki troupes. Actors do not learn their lines
by memorizing a script in full, but instead through verbal instruction
known as *kuchidate keiko*. The troupe head teaches the members their
lines and actions directly, often only schematically indicating the plot
line and dialogue. The younger members take notes and then practice
on their own, but older, more experienced actors typically know hun-

dreds of plays by heart. The number of plays a zacho knows can range from one hundred to three hundred, although some claim to know as many as seven hundred. Only long years of practice and experience can enable one to know so many discrete plot lines.

This is not to imply, however, that no written scripts exist. Katsu Koryū told me that his father used to carry around a whole stack of script books, containing about three hundred plays. Plagiarism and copyright do not exist in this theater, and any written or verbal text is fair game. TV programs, movies, weekly magazines, the latest scandals, current crimes, elections—all are potential material for plays or gags. Often the zachō writes his own plays, but there is also a common fund of classic plays drawn from the domains of popular literature, western-style theater, and kabuki.

The taishū engeki repertoire thus is immense, particularly in proportion to the amount of time spent in rehearsal. Often only half an hour of practice precedes each one-hour play. What is the structure of this half-hour practice? The zachō first distributes the roles. Usually the actors have specialties—one always plays a lover (nimaime), another a hero (tateyaku), yet another a clown (sanmaime). The zachō goes over the play very rapidly, describing the setting, giving stage directions, reciting the dialogue.

The more experienced actors have done most plays several times throughout their lives, so they rarely need elaborate instruction. Younger actors, on the other hand, require repeated drilling; using tape recorders and notebooks, they rehearse as much as time and energy allow. The actors may also quickly rehearse the sword-fighting scenes, which form the backbone of taishū engeki as an "action" theater; others may get together and decide when and how to insert gags or manzai routines (comic dialogue).

To these actors, memorizing whole scripts would be impossible given the emphasis on change and extensive repertoire of their theater. Not only impossible, but unnecessary. What substitute for scripts are time and long experience, the ingredients necessary to assemble the components of the taishū engeki theatrical apparatus. What also enables kuchidate keiko to work is the structure of theatrical conventions and emotions within which taishū engeki occurs. These emotions and conventions are highly patterned and predictable, the stuff of melodrama. The moral economy of duty and human feelings, good and evil, mother love and filial piety; the setting—the Tokugawa period; the stock characters—evil landlord, dashing yakuza, hapless wife; and stylized modes of physical expression (kata) all combine to set up a

framework which encompasses innumerable small variations and opportunities for ad-libbing.

Although dialogues are not structured according to metrically formulaic principles, as in recited forms of epic poetry, taishū engeki is
deeply conventional and clichéd in its fund of characters and themes.[16]
In its stitching together of prefabricated motifs—both verbal and gestural—it resembles other forms of oral performance. Discussing the
remarkable powers of memory that preliterate poets possess, Walter
Ong notes:

> Formulas are ... somewhat variable, as are themes, and a
> given poet's rhapsodizing or "stitching together" of narratives
> will differ recognizably from another's. Certain turns of
> phrases will be idiosyncratic. But essentially, the materials,
> themes and formulas, and their use belong in a clearly identi-
> fiable tradition. Originality consists not in the introduction of
> new materials but in fitting the traditional materials effectively
> into each individual, unique situation and/or audience.[17]

Taishū engeki's relationship with "originality" is similar (although one
might question Ong's unproblematic assertion of "tradition"). But as
Ong implies, the notions of "orality" and "tradition" expressly imply
each other; in that sense, taishū engeki aligns itself along the axis of
tradition through its reliance on vocal modes of instruction and memo-
rization. Yet these "traditional" materials and forms are the marks of
the marginal in contemporary Japan.

Its performance modes have led many scholars to think of taishū
engeki as a folk performance (minzoku geinō), classifying it alongside
the storytelling genres and trance performances considered in earlier
chapters. Whereas the tales of Tōno and the spirit mediums of Mount
Osore speak of a folkic atemporality, taishū engeki's plays thematically
refer to the Tokugawa period, the last era before the incursions of the
West. They thus directly refer to a historical period that has become so
romanticized that it is as far removed from middle-class contemporary
Japan as the ghosts of Mount Osore—and as recuperable, through the
appropriate form of theatrical intervention. The performance context
of taishū engeki, however, refers to prewar urban Japan, with its flourishing entertainment districts filled with variety halls and small theaters. The 1920s and 1930s were a time when kabuki-derived little the-

16. See Ong, *Orality and Literacy*, for his discussion of Milman Parry's groundbreaking
work on the formulaic grounds of oral poetry.
    17. Ibid., 60.

ater flourished in both urban and provincial areas; the middle-aged women attending taishū engeki today usually cite a childhood spent in local theaters as the background for their continued interest. Taishū engeki performances thus already encompass two levels of historical reference: prewar modernity's nostalgia for Tokugawa premodernity and late modernity's nostalgia for the incipient communal mass culture of prewar modernity. The two, taken together now in the live theatrical setting, indicate contemporary modernity's incorporation of that historical displacement, becoming in the process a strangely appropriate locus for the neo-nostalgia discussed in chapter 2.

Taishū engeki, however, consists not only of low-budget, kabuki-derived plays set in the Tokugawa period. A taishū engeki performance is in fact a variety show—what many troupes call, not ironically, a "grand show." Not only two plays, but a separate song segment and dance performance, make up the show. While analyzing the plays themselves and the interaction of actors with the audience is essential for an understanding of taishū engeki, it is perhaps even more important to consider the overall structure of the performance—with its interruptions, digressions, and purely spectacular moments—in conjunction with a description of the theatrical setting itself.

The Grand Show

There has recently been an explosion of interest in the concept of the city in Japanese-language scholarship. Attention has been devoted, for example, to a binary division of the urban landscape into central and marginal areas: the city of light (*hikari no toshi*) and the city of darkness (*yami no toshi*).[18] The first is where political authority and economic distribution is the highest; the second is the locus of production and trade. Kurimoto Shin'ichirō, an anthropologist who developed this binary distinction, sees the yami no toshi as representing an entrance to the "other world," the same as the *takai* represented by Mount Osore and other mountains. Other analyses have sought to schematize the city in terms of the symbolism of the body.[19] Many Japanese works have taken Tokyo as their object, for Tokyo is the triple symbol of the urban in Japan: first as Edo, the great early modern metropolis; next as prewar Tokyo, the uncontested locus in Japan of the modern and

18. For example, see Kurimoto Shin'ichirō, "Hikari o kirisaku yami no Tokyo."
19. Yamaguchi Masao has undertaken this kind of analysis in an unpublished English-language essay entitled "Tokyo as a Cultural Text." He bases his analysis on Raymond Ledrut's *Les images de la ville*.

the western; and now as the fabulous megalopolis, largest in the world, and a premier example of what some critics call the postmodern city.

Tokyo's "city of darkness" is formed from the life of the peripheries, where actual spatial marginality doubles an economic and symbolic periphery. Much scholarly work on the city has focused on early modern Edo, where class and occupational differences were spatially demarcated, with special districts for prostitution, theater, punishment, and exchange distributed in an orderly manner throughout the city. In particular, a larger notion of theatricality has engaged many scholars as they attempt to account for the attractions of these marginal districts. Contemporary Tokyo, however, exists in a milieu where over 90 percent of all Japanese claim they are middle-class. While we might question the meaning of that statistic, it still indicates the power of middle-class norms: a milieu in which the margins are increasingly narrowed at the same moment that they are recuperated for mass-media consumption. It is thus a more difficult task to outline the conceptual margins of Tokyo today, although it is still possible to say that pockets of heightened poverty tend to coincide with the highly industrialized areas outside the main train loop of the Yamanote line, particularly in the northeast, and farther south, near Kawasaki and Yokohama.

Taishū engeki theaters are typically found in the boundary areas of cities—near bridges and rivers—or in industrialized areas of the city, commonly near lower-class shopping streets. Both the audience and, more markedly, the actors are excluded from what one author, referring to the industrial mainstream of enterprises and employees, has called the productive society (seisan shakai).[20] Regulars at taishū engeki are not only older women, but also the unemployed, the handicapped, and the poor. Until the recent surge of interest in taishū engeki and the glorification of the actors as the last upholders of a purer, more traditional theatrical aesthetic, troupes were commonly regarded as scandalous and vaguely criminal.[21]

The two remaining taishū engeki theaters in Tokyo lie in these mar-

20. Nishijima Tatsuo, "Katasumijinsei no kaihō-ku ima, taishū engeki wa shitamachi ni saku 'yami no toshi.'"

21. This is not to imply that taishū engeki actors are technically regarded as burakumin, a name originally applied to members of an outcaste status group first recognized by the Meiji government but since then more generally used to designate a larger group of discriminated-against people. But as much recent research in Japanese history and ethnology has revealed, wanderers and itinerant artistes of all sorts existed outside the bounds of settled agricultural society, and thus came to have the status of excluded persons (Emiko Ohnuki-Tierney's work examines the place of such "special status

gins: the Mokubakan is located in Asakusa, the classic early-modern and modern urban entertainment district now decidedly down at the heels; the smaller Shinohara Engeijō stands in a crowded residential and shopping area called Jūjō in northwest Tokyo. Asakusa had long been the epitome of the theatrical margins (a center of kabuki in the Meiji period, it later welcomed the first arrivals of western movies, vaudeville, and music reviews in Japan), yet its once legendary lineup of music halls has been replaced by decrepit movie theaters showing pornographic films. The symbolic center of Asakusa is the Sensōji temple (popularly known as Asakusa Kannon), a magnet for popular religious energies since the Tokugawa period. The approach to the temple—the famous aisle of shops called the *nakamise*—and the temple itself comprise one of the best-known scenes in all Japan; to most Japanese, Asakusa *is* Sensōji. This is the section of Tokyo that still seems to retain the ambience of shitamachi, an ambience that makes the temple an essential stop for all visitors, domestic or foreign, to Tokyo. It is the rare tourist, however, who wanders off course and explores side streets around the temple. These streets mark the area called the *okuyama*, the "interior mountain" of Asakusa, where a staggering array of entertainments, spectacles, and performances once took place in the shadow of the temple.

The Mokubakan (Rocking Horse Theater) stands as an obstinate reminder of the prewar variety of the okuyama, occupying part of a building shared by a *yose*, or "variety hall." The theater itself is a small, western-style auditorium with perhaps three hundred theater seats and an elevated stage. Yet the Mokubakan is one of the grandest venues for taishū engeki, for most remaining theaters are much smaller, poorer affairs: one large room covered with tatami mats, ceiling fans, and a tiny stage raised some three feet from the floor. The cramped scale of these neighborhood theaters—found in Kawasaki and here and there in Kyūshū, Osaka, and Yokohama—along with the mat-covered floor surface reproduces the Japanese domestic interior. It is this domestic intimacy and warmth that constitutes much of taishū engeki's appeal to its fans, neighborhood people who come to the theater to meet their friends and spend their evenings. Whether western-

---

people" within a structure of purity and pollution). Kabuki actors were regarded as "riverside beggars," were segregated in special sections of Edo, and were also subject to a range of restrictive regulations. Taishū engeki actors even today speak of being taunted with the epithet of riverside beggar. There are indications that taishū engeki troupes do have connections with the worlds of burakumin, Koreans, and criminals; these indications thematically arise in the plays themselves and in the composition of the audience.

style, like the Mokubakan, or smaller and more "authentic," like the Shinohara Engeijō, taishū engeki theaters are similar in several ways: in their facades, covered with posters and fronted by banners bearing the names of actors and troupes, in the manner of kabuki and sumō; in the low price of admission (typically eight hundred yen in 1985); and in the comfortably shabby condition of the facilities. This shabbiness reflects the socioeconomic status of most, although not all, of the patrons. Whether or not its audience is poor, however, taishū engeki reflects an older, vanishing aesthetic that is rooted in a conception of the taishū as down-home, lower-middle-class, and raised on the prewar ethics and aesthetics of samurai drama.

Avid fans begin arriving as much as an hour before a performance; in a theater like Shinohara Engeijō, patrons either rent or bring their own floor cushions and set up as close to the stage as possible. They typically bring their own food and drink, although the theater has a small concession stand selling snacks, soft drinks, and beer. On a weeknight the theater can be quite empty, with scattered clusters of people eating and smoking—despite prominent No Smoking signs flanking the stage; this was one of the few occasions where I witnessed Japanese openly disobeying a legal prohibition. Perhaps this breaking of a public, legal prohibition is made easier by the strongly domestic ambience of the theater, with spectators semireclining on mats in what resembles a huge Japanese living room.

On weekends, or during the performances of a popular troupe, the floor space can be packed beyond belief, with latecomers standing in the cement-floored entranceway in the back. The flexible capacity of the audience space is, in fact, an important element of the taishū engeki theatrical apparatus. On a busy night, one of the troupe members will cajole the audience from the stage, instructing them to crowd in closer, move over, or make way. The matriarch of the preeminent Umezawa Takeo troupe, for example, takes over this all-important function of packing the room, eliciting the active cooperation of the audience before the curtain rises. This participation of the audience is one of the features that aficionados say sets taishū engeki apart from what they feel is the static, elitist, and formalized atmosphere of kabuki. Theater scholars thus find in taishū engeki survivals of Tokugawa-period kabuki, with its dense crowds of spectators seated on mats, its profuse exchanges between the stage and audience, and its element of banquet.[22]

22. Yamaguchi Masao draws on Richard Schechner's work on the factor of banquet as important in the "selective inattention" that brings about a festive atmosphere at theatri-

Exchanges between stage and audience come in a variety of forms, occurring during the plays themselves as well as during the other sections of the grand show. Although interest in taishū engeki has tended to deal primarily with the plays (shibai), the sequence of rhetorical and visual strategies that comprise the entire show is equally important. The clearly demarcated performance segments follow an almost invariable order: first a play, then a song show, then another play, and last a lengthy dance segment; intermissions and greetings from the troupe head interrupt this four-part structure.

The curtain is pulled aside for the first play of the evening, the *mae kyōgen*, rhythmically punctuated by the wooden clappers that also announce the beginning of a kabuki play. Recorded music and sound effects accompany the opening. The first play is often the more tragic of the show's pair of plays, setting a somber, dramatic tone that, nevertheless, does not dominate the entire performance. Taishū engeki is characterized by swift transitions and multiple levels of emotion, characteristic, again, of melodrama. A typical first play might feature, for example, a brother's efforts to avenge a young man's murder; the tragic rejection of a suitor; a case of mistaken identity that leads to grave consequences; or a wandering criminal searching for his mother. These stock themes commonly appear in *jidai ninjōgeki* (historical melodrama), the staple fare of taishū engeki.

The opening curtain of a historical melodrama performed by the Arashi Gekidan reveals an outdoor scene, where preparations are taking place for a village festival.[23] A young woman (Ohana) innocently working in the fields is suddenly accosted by a roving tough. Luckily, the powerful local landlady walks by; she intervenes to stop the gangster and threatens him. He backs down, but later plots revenge with his fellow gang members: they plan to kill the landlady at the first opportune moment. Meanwhile, Ohana's betrothed, the landlady's younger brother Yūkichi, ambles in, unaware of the trouble. He and the landlady discuss the upcoming festival and plans for his marriage.

The scene changes to the landlady's house; the criminal gang bursts

---

cal performances. He notes, as have other scholars, that Tokugawa-period kabuki and sumō wrestling were filled with devices of selective inattention, including banqueting; he contrasts these performances with Noh, which excluded banqueting. In the taishū engeki context, I would substitute "picnic" for "banquet." Yamaguchi, "Tokyo as a Cultural Text," 9.

23. This play was performed by the Arashi Gekidan at Shinohara Engeijō on 16 March 1985.

in, murders her, after a dramatic exchange of swordplay, and flees the premises. In comes the younger brother as she is dying. In one of the extended death scenes so prevalent in historical melodrama, the landlady begs Yūkichi to keep silent; to take revenge would only destroy his chances for happiness with Ohana and spoil the long-awaited festival. In addition, their older brother is a former yakuza who has renounced his life of crime and "gone straight" (*katagi*). If he hears of her murder, he will undoubtedly seek revenge and meet his doom. Thus she implores him, with her dying breath, to remain silent about her murder.

The next scene occurs in the older brother's house. His young wife emerges from the kitchen into the front room, where he sits lost in thought. She happily announces *"Dekita!"* ("It's done!"), leading the Japanese audience to think that dinner is ready. The older brother, however, angrily interprets her announcement to mean that she has found a lover. But, no—she means that she is pregnant. This triple play on the meaning of *dekita*, to the chuckles of the spectators, is characteristic of the sort of punning comic relief that periodically interrupts the dramatic structure of taishū engeki. In the midst of the excitement over his wife's announcement, the brother plans a celebration. At that precise moment in walks Yūkichi, who says that there is something of great importance he must tell his older brother, something he cannot divulge in front of his wife. The older brother sends his wife to the back of the house to get sake and prepare food.

"What is it you can't talk to me about in front of my wife?" asks the older brother, and then the truth comes out: Yūkichi reveals the whole story of their sister's murder and begs his brother to join him in taking revenge. To his utter astonishment, however, the brother refuses. He explains that he has gone straight, that his wife is pregnant, and that he cannot risk destroying his life. He knows as well that his dead sister would want it his way; despite Yūkichi's entreaties, the brother steadfastly refuses to join in the vendetta. Finally Yūkichi gives up, sobbing as he leaves.

The wife walks in—she has overheard everything. She begs her husband not to join Yūkichi, not to destroy their happy home. He duly vows that he will not. He sends her out to buy more sake, and he is left alone. His solitude provides the occasion for the climactic moment of the play. Alone on stage, the brother begins a fiery monologue, declaring his undying hatred for his sister's murderers and vowing to avenge her. At the height of the monologue he strikes a heroic pose (*mie*) and abruptly pulls his kimono off his shoulders, revealing his tattoos—the mark of a yakuza. He exchanges his sober kimono for a flashy black and white satin one and digs out his long-unused swords, pulling them from their scabbards and testing their sharpness.

He makes his escape during his wife's absence and comes upon the murderers in an open field. The enemies clash in a blinding display of choreographed chanbara, extended until the brother has killed the last gangster. The mortally wounded gang leader, however, crawls to center stage and shoots the brother with a pistol.[24] In rushes younger brother Yūkichi, bent on joining the fray, but too late. The older brother expires onstage, accompanied by Yūkichi's paroxysms of grief.

This play ends on a tragic, if predictably tragic, note. Yet the real moment of catharsis occurs earlier, when the elder brother reveals his tattoos. Uncovering his tattoos is tantamount to exposing his criminal status; he thus announces his intention to give up domestic bliss and reenter the dangerous world of the yakuza. The revelation of the tattoo (the actor wore a special T-shirt silkscreened with a classic tattoo motif) occurs in the midst of his solitary struggle over giri and ninjō—"duty" and "human feelings"—the conflict of values that forms the dramatic core of taishū engeki plays. The uncovering of the marked body operates as the exposure of what could no longer remain hidden, as if the tattoos (once inscribed from outside the body) have inevitably somatized his criminality. The moment of bodily revelation also works to stop the narrative flow, as it counternarratively marks the instance of highest dramatic revelation (we now know, without further explanation, that he cannot relinquish his yakuza predilections). As such, the spectacle of the tattooed body creates effects very similar to other moments of counternarrative figurality in taishū engeki. His feelings toward his wife and his unborn child urge him to renounce vengeance; his duty as a man of honor compels him to embrace it. In Japanese historical melodrama, the resolution is never in question: duty wins out, inexorably, yet the conflict is not lessened thereby. The agony of the dilemma in and of itself forms the dramatic crux which here turns around the figure of the reformed criminal revealing the indelible marks of his criminality.

Doubled Crimes, Gendered Travesties

Taishū engeki is thus an arena in which a whole spectrum of semiotic richness is displayed in compensatory fashion, as if to supplement its

24. This was one of the few taishū engeki performances I saw where pistols were used. Guns are rather incongruous in plays set in the Tokugawa period.

Katsu Ryūji before the revelation
of his yakuza's tattoos

fundamental socioeconomic marginality. There is also a range of transcoding practices that shift between forms of desire (sexual, monetary) and structures of reification (gender, class) as they ultimately theatricalize all differences in the register of dream (*yume*), the recurrent trope of theater itself. The repetitive return, for example, to the figure of the yakuza is not unique to taishū engeki (one thinks of the contemporary yakuza film genre), but its repeated referencing of the world of the actors themselves indicates the kind of extradiegetic doubling that this theater incorporates, literally. The *tabigarasu* (bird of passage), the wandering criminal, is a substitute for the actors themselves, *tabiyakusha* (itinerant actors) who, because of their itinerancy and their profession, live outside the bounds of middle-class Japan. (During the dance segment of the performance I have just analyzed, one glimpsed a *real* tattoo on the shoulder of the actor who played the tattooed yakuza.) The audience is well aware of and appreciative of this doubled reference. The actors themselves often use stage names that refer to the world of the yakuza; in the Arashi troupe, the primary actors' names all contain the element *ryū* (dragon), a typical feature of underworld names: Ryūji, Ryūnosuke, Koryū (one of my Japanese middle-class friends first pointed this out to me). There is much talk about shady dealings in the taishū engeki world. In the greetings to the audience given by Umezawa Takeo, the troupe head, at an Umezawa performance I attended in January 1984, his litany of special performances, audience ratings, and recent NHK specials suddenly veered into a denial of yakuza connections—how he and Tomio (his star younger brother) had nothing to do with the yakuza, even though one of their siblings had joined a yakuza group: "The world of the yakuza is a separate world and we have no connection to it. My parents and grandparents are actors, and my brothers and sisters—except one. Two different worlds." He also insisted that they weren't afraid of the yakuza, and that nobody at the Shinohara Theater was, either. But he took the opportunity, as well, to explain that although yakuza figure prominently within the narratives of the plays, it's a "performance only" (*shibai dake*), whose only intent is to give pleasure to the audience.

It was a long series of denials; a year later, in March 1985, at the same theater, my neighbor during a performance told me that Tomio's mistress and Takeo's wife had been arrested for heading a prostitution ring; both women were now in jail, and the troupe was banned from performing at Tokyo's two taishū engeki theaters. Audience members at the Shinohara Theater pointed to the stage curtain: as regular performers at the theater, the Umezawa troupe's name used to be printed on the curtain; now it had been erased, although the shadowy outlines of the characters still remained.

The aura of scandal that accompanies theater was here expanded into the domains of outright criminality, an expansion that theater owners and other troupes wanted quickly to disown in the interest of their newly-found and precarious respectability for bourgeois audiences. Yet poverty and itinerancy, again, insure that taishū engeki can hardly attain stable middle-class status. Taishū engeki's grand show is replete, in its very attempts at grandiloquence, with markers of its failure to attain that status. Ethnic difference is one such marker, rare enough in contemporary Japan. The Amatsu Eijirō troupe from Osaka, which I saw in the larger Mokubakan Theater in Asakusa, sharply contrasted with other troupes with its heavily masculinized, rugged style (at the end of one play, the ghostly samurai avenger Yojimbō impales himself on a stake). Yet what was most striking was the display of Korean ethnicity: during the song show, the women wore long, pink Korean-style dresses. In a play performed by one of the best-known troupes from Kyūshū, the Mikaidō Shun troupe, an old ragpicker turns out to be the long-lost Korean father of a young woman who had been adopted by a Japanese family, thus precipitating a crisis in affection (should she stay with her adopted Japanese family or return with her Korean father?) that was all-too-evocative of the dilemmas of Korean ethnic identifications in Japan today. Two women in the audience across from me cried profusely; around the corner from the theater are a big Korean dry-goods store and a Korean pickle store (and it is said that the area's many shoe stores have Korean or burakumin—"outcaste"—associations). Actors, particularly in so-called traditional theatrical genres, have historically associated with outcaste groups or outsiders in general (Koreans are prominent in Japanese entertainment at all levels). The explicit theme of Korean ethnicity, largely absent in more dominant theatrical forms, and its relation to taishū engeki actors reduplicates the peripheral status of the troupes and many in their audience, in yet another stratum of referential doubling.

There is a consistent movement between the diegesis of the plays and extradiegetic reality, between stage and audience, that constantly calls the frame of theater into question. The very thematic conventionality of the plays operates as a kind of backdrop for the defamiliarizing interruptions, wordplay, counternarrative moments, and parodic overturnings that keep the audience expectantly surprised, as the predictable moral economy of the narratives and the gestural economy of its actors provide the spectacular display of emotional extremities. Audience members repeatedly told me they loved taishū engeki because they liked to "laugh, and then to cry": the pure dichotomization of affective polarities.

Configurations of surprise—what Peter Brooks refers to as the melodramatic "aesthetics of astonishment"—in taishū engeki are further amplified by the exhaustive transformations of gender roles onstage. Men dress as women, women dress as men, men play women playing men, women play men playing women: almost every conceivable variation on gender roles is carried out. Taishū engeki is more explicitly exhaustive in this play than either kabuki, which is limited to male actors, or the Takarazuka revue, the glitzy theatrical productions widely popular among young women (and others) in which women play all parts, male and female.[25] Like these two theaters, taishū engeki highlights cross-dressing; unlike them, it employs both male and female performers, and thus adds an additional layer of potential displacement to the varieties of representation enacted onstage.

Many troupes feature an *onnagata*, a male actor dressed as a woman. Dressed in a gaudy kimono, wearing white makeup and an elaborate wig, a taishū engeki onnagata particularly shines in the dance segment of the show (although they may appear during the plays as well). The Arashi troupe, for example, features one main onnagata; occasionally the troupe head will also play a comic female role. In one piece, an actress of the troupe played a male servant, while an actor took the role of a courtesan. When the (female) male servant tried to seduce the (male) courtesan, the audience howled at this broad reversal of roles. The Amatsu Eijirō troupe from the Kansai area is well known for its heavily masculinized plays, which emphasize swordplay and gory endings, with only a modicum of comic relief. In one performance at the Mokubakan, the troupe featured no onnagata whatsoever; instead, the dance show centered on women dressed as men. A group of three actresses dressed in male wigs and kimono engaged in a spirited round of swordplay; known as *onna kengeki* (women's sword theater), this form of female cross-dressing enjoyed wide popularity in the militaristic 1930s, although it is rarely practiced in taishū engeki today.[26]

25. See Jennifer Robertson's stimulating analysis of Takarazuka theater and modalities of cross-dressing in her "The Politics of Androgyny in Japan: Sexuality and Subversion in the Theater and Beyond."
26. Onna kengeki was a direct derivative from the kengeki (sword fighting dramas) that made up the most popular plays of shinkokugeki. There were two forms of onna kengeki: in one, women appeared as women wielding swords; in the other, they dressed as men. In either case, they would fight and defeat male enemies in sword fights. Takahashi, *Taishū geinō*.

The troupe's most impressive actress, Sakura Fubuki (literally, "Cherry Blossom Snowstorm"), made a foot-stomping appearance on stage as Sukeroku, the quintessential Edo dandy, one of the most famous figures in the kabuki repertoire. Her costume was complete down to the yellow *tabi* (Japanese socks) and "snake's eye" umbrella associated with Sukeroku. This particular troupe has chosen, then, to exaggerate "masculinity." Both the dances and the plays emphasize masculine martial virtues; the women also play displaced versions of tough men. Taishū engeki plays as a whole revolve around themes of male heroism and duty in feudal times, with explicit references in dialogue and song lyrics to the duties of an *otoko* (man). Even so, the Amatsu troupe is extreme in its stress on the macho aspects of the theater, with little softening from either comics or female roles.

The troupe that rings the most complex series of changes on the theme of gender is the Mikaidō Shun troupe. Mikaidō Shun, the troupe head, is one of the most handsome taishū engeki actors. Tall and slim with chiseled features, he would seem to make an unparalleled onnagata; strangely enough, however, he looks impossibly tall and angular on the taishū engeki stage, which is elevated only a few feet above the audience in the tiny theaters. A certain roundness is needed to give the onnagata the *iroppoi* (erotic) quality favored by taishū engeki fans. Much less handsome actors have made improbably seductive onnagata; Umezawa Tomio is one of those.

Mikaidō, however, is a talented actor and is able to pull off many transformations because of sheer good looks. In one drama he played the part of what was announced as a *gei bōi* (gay boy), wearing peach-colored lipstick and a purple satin kimono.[27] Using highly "feminine" Japanese, he tried to seduce the hero of the play: "I've always liked you so much. And now I hear you're going to get married to the boss's daughter and then inherit his position. Just because she's a woman!" The audience erupted into laughter when he began to unwind his *obi* (sash); the actors onstage laughed as well, in the sort of explicit recognition and sharing of the audience's pleasure (here, stemming from a normative heterosexuality) that is a large part of taishū engeki's appeal.

During the song show at the same performance, Mikaidō came on like a reverse caricature of a star in the Takarazuka theater, where selected actresses play "male roles" (*otokoyaku*). He wore an orange suit with a vest, his hair slicked back under a fedora, with points of rose makeup by his ears and pale lipstick; he sang a torch song written

27. 4 April 1984 at the Mokubakan.

from a woman's point of view. In this appearance, then, Mikaidō was a man playing a woman imitating a man. In the dance segment, the rather large and plain-looking actress of the troupe (Sakura Kaoru) danced a travel scene (michiyuki) in glittering white; although playing a woman, her bulk and large features made her look like an onnagata: a woman imitating a man impersonating a woman.

Conventionalized theatrical transvestism elaborated by both male and female performers adds a series of rich erotic overtones to the reduced binaries of male-female romantic love. During the narrative sections of the grand show, it is quite rare for a cross-dressed performer to appear in other than a comic role. That is, whether a man plays a female role or a woman plays a male role, they are almost invariably comic: their mere entrance onto the stage provokes laughter, as the performers stretch the parodic possibilities of gender transformation. In such moments, the familiar heterosexual valences are reinforced for and by the largely working-class, dominantly older female audience. It is as if the cross-dressed actor cannot become a serious (that is, nonparodic, noninterruptive) narrative operator within the theatrical scenario; similarly, the actor does not become the object of erotic identification in that role. The most famous of such taishū engeki cross-dressers—Umezawa Tomio—never appears in plays as an onnagata; instead, he appears as a bumbling clown figure who provides precisely the sort of quick repartee and extradiegetic winking that animates the performance. Where he does appear as an object of erotic cross-gendered attraction is in the dance show (buyō shō), the last, discrete part of the variety show that functions as a sheerly spectacularized display of eroticized bodies, open for an array of crossed identifications and objectifications. It is in that explicitly oneiric space that the nonnarrative possibilities of unbound desire are figured in the body of the male cross-dressed dancer, an unbinding accomplished by its differences from the absorptions of narrative theater.

Counternarrative and Figurality

Taishū engeki draws attention to itself as theatrical; that is, it makes no consistent attempt to pretend that it is depicting reality. Kabuki has been called a presentational theater rather than a representational theater, for it emphasizes spectacle and has a refined array of techniques to show itself off as spectacle. Taishū engeki derives from that kabuki aesthetic, but it also incorporates elements of western-style the-

atrical realism. It is the very smallness and intimacy of the performance space, however, that partially dictates taishū engeki's theatricality. When audience and actors face each other over a distance of only
five feet, it is very difficult to conceal the efforts at representation. Instead of subtle and finely drawn makeup, the audience sees thick lines
and edges: it is all too apparent that one is watching an actor. The
person in charge of the lights stands in the back of the theater in full
view; scene changes often take place in front of the audience. The exaggerated—grandiloquent and excessive—gestures and procedures
stem not only from the essentially melodramatic sensibility of the
troupes, but from the related consideration of scale: the actors move,
look, and act as if they were playing in a hall that holds five thousand
people rather than fifty. It is indeed a "grand show," and the insistence
on grand scale even in reduced circumstances is a mark of the form's
show-business aesthetic. Off-duty actors dress in black with gold
chains and diamond pinkie rings, inspiring comparisons to yakuza,
but perhaps more accurately representing the image of the successful star. Part of what taishū engeki represents is this hope of being
more than what it is—larger, grander, more popular. At the same
time its constraints assure that its limitations are its most precious
assets.

During performances, the audience often yells out to the actors, and
the actors yell back. For example, when a "bad guy" (akuyaku) comes
on stage, a spectator might shout, "Oh, it's you again! Why don't you
go back to the dressing room!" The actor might pause for a moment,
look out to the audience, and say, "Listen, Gramps. This is my job, so
I've got to do it. Please try to understand, OK?" In a play by the Umezawa troupe, the actor Tomio—as part of his dialogue—said he was
thirsty. Immediately a spectator ran to the front with a can of beer,
which Tomio accepted and started to drink onstage. There may be
snippets of gossip and shoptalk in the dialogue, and usually there is
some reference to the neighborhood or theater building itself in the
lines. This doubling can get labyrinthine at times, forming parallels
between different rivalries or relationships onstage and differences
among the audience. The Umezawa brothers constantly allude within
their plays to the structural contradictions of their real-life relationship:
the elder Takeo is the troupe head, but the younger Tomio is the star.
The two will often play brothers onstage, lacing their dialogue with so
many allusions to their offstage relationship that it is difficult to tell
where the purely dramatic ends and the offstage begins.

There is thus a movement back and forth between absorption into and alienation from the dramatic narrative. It is difficult to say if this movement attains the critical force of the "alienation effects" that Brecht desired for his own epic theater, but there is no doubt that there is a complexity as well as a profound pleasure found there.[28] The intrusion of moments of unexpected spectacle—whether comic, erotic, or both—into the conventional, highly coded narrative structure of the melodramas parallels the irruption of what Jean-François Lyotard has called the "figural" into the discursive process. While any number of related ideas could trope this irruption, such as that of the "material," the notion of figurality sharply foregrounds both the visual enframing of theatrical bodies in space and the allied possibilities of verbal figures or tropes. Lyotard calls the figural that which stems from the primary process (in Freudian terms), in which images, desires, and language circulate freely without bounds. The figural is thus the visible trace of this primary process; in other terms, it is the trace of the body.[29] Throughout taishū engeki, the figural intervenes to punctuate the temporal sequence of the narrative. Just as the frozen pose, the *mie*, occurs at the height of an anguished conflict, breaking the narrative flow with an instant that displays the body, the presence of both male and female transvestites also calls attention to the body. Similarly, punning, jokes, and double entendres could be considered verbal objects endowed with figurality. Into the ordered structure of language intrudes a form of discursive or rhetorical figurality which, by doubling the signified meaning, draws attention to the play of language itself, to its materiality.

These counternarrative devices within taishū engeki's formal plays account for much of the genre's pleasure and surprise, as do the shifts from theatrical reality to extratheatrical reality. Yet we would be wrong to thereby ignore the force of its narratives and standard roles. In a published interview, Umezawa Tomio and Takeo acknowledged that there is a degree of strategic calculation *(keisan)* in taishū engeki dramas, but said actors should not reveal it; they call it "showing calculation as uncalculated" *(keisan o keisan de naku miseru)*.[30] Roles should be

28. Yamaguchi Masao, "Taishū engeki no Burehito." Yamaguchi compares taishū engeki's use of gags and other theatrical devices to Brechtian alienation effects. Walter Benjamin wrote about the necessity, in Brecht's theater, for the audience to be in a state of complete relaxation—a condition certainly fulfilled in taishū engeki. Benjamin, "What Is Epic Theater?"

29. See J.-F. Lyotard, *Discours, figure.* Nakazawa Shin'ichi has employed Lyotard's insights in an analysis of Tokugawa-period spectacle *(misemono)*. Nakazawa Shin'ichi, "Shikaku no katasutorofu: misemonogei no retorikku to keishōsei."

30. Muramatsu Tomonori, Umezawa Takeo, and Umezawa Tomio, interviewed in "Shitamachi no Tamasaburō to wa nanimonoka," 63–73.

played exhaustively: a bad guy should be bad to the end, a good guy should be good. There should thus be a clear distinction between roles and also between the conventionalized modes of acting these roles, and it is this clarity that forms the basic integrity and interest of taishū engeki, unlike the moral vagueness of western-style theater (what they call *shingeki*, literally "new theater").

The actors compare their art with professional wrestling (*puro resu*), of which they are great fans. The postwar history of pro wrestling in Japan doubles the aesthetic development of taishū engeki, with one great difference: pro wrestling (including women's pro wrestling) is a successful prime-time spectacle; taishū engeki is not. Yet to the brothers Umezawa, the affinities between the two override their differences.[31] Both forms incorporate completely conventionalized characterizations and actions. Where then does the drama occur? It is not so much that the fans do not expect a particular outcome, but that the exact manner and timing of the outcome is in doubt. The audience tests its own calculations against that of the wrestlers; surprises occur when the audience's expectations are undercut. What is important is the clarity of the roles and the spectacular way they are embodied.

In the first essay of his *Mythologies*, Roland Barthes writes about the moral economy of wrestling in words that stunningly echo the cultural analysis of the two Umezawa brothers:

> Wrestling is not a sport, it is a spectacle. . . . The public is completely uninterested in knowing whether the contest is rigged or not, and rightly so; it abandons itself to the primary virtue of the spectacle, which is to abolish all motives and all consequences: what matters is not what it thinks but what it sees. . . .
>
> The spectator is not interested in the rise and fall of fortunes; he expects the transient image of certain passions. Wrestling therefore demands an immediate reading of the juxtaposed meanings, so that there is no need to connect them. The logical

31. It is telling that they do not compare taishū engeki to sumō, "traditional" Japanese wrestling. Sumō is the wrestling counterpart of kabuki: both were immensely popular urban entertainment forms of the Tokugawa period, both have contemporary prestige as traditional Japanese performances (although sumō attracts vastly larger crowds). The formal links between taishū engeki and kabuki are more direct than those between sumō and pro wrestling, which was imported from Europe and the United States in the postwar period. Yet both taishū engeki and pro wrestling present themselves as "mass" entertainment forms, distinctly lowbrow. Paralleling the fortunes of sumō, pro wrestling-as-spectacle has vastly outdistanced its theatrical cousin; it indeed attracts mass audiences, both live and on television; taishū engeki—"mass theater"—ironically does not.

conclusion of the contest does not interest the wrestling-
fan. . . . In other words, wrestling is a sum of spectacles. . . .
Wrestlers, who are very experienced, know perfectly how to
direct the spontaneous episodes of the fight so as to make
them conform to the image which the public has of the great
legendary themes of its mythology. A wrestler can irritate or
disgust, he never disappoints, for he always accomplishes
completely, by a progressive solidification of signs, what the
public expects of him.[32]

The complete accomplishment of expectations and total clarity (although not accomplished without overturnings and surprises) are the
marks of good taishū engeki as well, according to the Umezawa brothers. The exaggerated display of the conflict between duty and human
feelings takes precedence over the rewarding of good and punishment
of evil that dominates pro wrestling, whether in France or in Japan.
Yet the exhaustive, theatrical acting out of moral roles unites both the
worlds of wrestling and lower-class theater. Although both forms thus
present a mix of spectacle and moral narrative—or perhaps moral narrative *as* spectacle—taishū engeki differs in its explicit narrativity. It
is, after all, largely comprised of plays in which actors dramatize stories with dialogue and actions. This formal narrative structure thus
provides a background structure against which counternarrative moments emerge.

Yet the spectacle of taishū engeki is hardly limited to its plays; indeed, it would be difficult to understand its mobilizations of desire
and uses of bodies without placing its narrative moments against the
other frames of the performance. In the remaining two sections of the
grand show, other, more unmediated expressions of figurality make
their appearances. In the "song show," a hierarchy of voices, from skill-
ful to poor, is serially displayed; in the "dance show," the posed bodies
of the actors become spectacularized objects of desire.

Powers of Attraction

The *kayō shō* (song show) invariably comes second in the lineup of
entertainments at a performance, usually starting soon after the curtain
closes on the first play. Popular theater performances have only added
this separate song segment to their shows since the mid-1970s. Taishū
engeki used to mean exactly that: popular theater, and theater only,

32. Roland Barthes, "The World of Wrestling," 15–24.

**Taking revenge within the
moral economy of melodrama**

with no song or dance shows. In an attempt to keep up with changing times—to amuse in a manner consonant with the entertainments of television—the troupes have broken the purely theatrical continuum of their performance and added what are called the attractions (*atora-kushon*) of song and dance.

I still remember the shock I felt the first time I saw taishū engeki's song show. In the plays, actresses use period hairpieces and white makeup to complete the visual repertoire that signifies the Tokugawa period, yet in the song show they wear evening dresses or kimono and are wigless—a strange contrast to the dead-white face makeup they leave on in anticipation of the next play. Actors wear heavy pancake-style makeup, black eyeliner, and false eyelashes throughout the performance; as singers (or backup musicians) they put on either flashy, rock-star costumes or gaudy satin kimono. In contrast to the women, they wear wigs: short ones, often streaked with iridescent color.

The juxtaposition between the dramatically heavy stage makeup (which seems much too extreme for the distance from stage to audience, as if the actors were quoting themselves as actors, dramatically declaiming their status as actors) and hybrid costuming is startling. Even more startling, the curtain opens to reveal these strangely costumed figures—chalk-faced women in citations of cocktail dresses; younger men in black leather and earrings; older actors in satin kimono, false eyelashes, and headbands—in a rock and roll band complete with drums, guitars, amps, and electric keyboards. Part of the troupes' efforts to update their acts in the 1970s included live music, yet rock and roll instrumentation would not seem, on first consideration, the obvious choice for taishū engeki's audience: overwhelmingly middle-aged or elderly, female, and lower middle class. When I showed some slides of the song show to Keiō University graduate students in folklore, they burst into amazed laughter: these costumed figures seemed as startlingly improbable to younger Japanese as they did to me.

In fact, with few exceptions, the groups do not actually play rock and roll music. They instead play and sing enka, the staple fare of TV and karaoke bars, where patrons sing to prerecorded backup music. The themes of enka ballads are love and love lost; its poetic images are quintessential Japanese ones: tears, sake, falling blossoms. It is considered the musical repository of essentially Japanese sentiments. Syrupy strings combine with *shamisen* and western clarinet in enka's minor-keyed melodies, accompanying the distinctive vibrato-laden style of enka singers. With a popularity that largely transcends generational or class divisions, enka is Japan's prototypical mass song form. Neverthe-less, with Japan's current affluence and cosmopolitanism, it has lost its appeal for many of the young and educated, whose musical obsessions cover the entire range of world musics. For many of them, enka re-mains the outdated sonic preserve of the masses—downtrodden office workers, factory laborers, farmers. Yet enka has shown remarkable staying power. Much like country and western music (to which it is often compared), enka encompasses a universe of sentiment outside the bounds of cosmopolitan pretensions.

Enka is the invariable musical accompaniment to taishū engeki. Re-corded enka greets the audience on its arrival, plays during intermis-sions, forms the background for dances, and wafts over the crowd as it leaves the theater. Taishū engeki is unthinkable without this song form; its themes permeate and redouble those of the plays. And all actors and actresses learn a large repertoire of standard (and not-so-standard) enka. Enka, then, is what the song show is all about and what the audience expects. (Several women at the performances told me that they listened to no other music but enka; one woman said she had a stack of enka records "this high," as she lifted her arm about three feet off the floor.) It creates the musical milieu of the theater; it is comforting and comfortable, what the audience knows best.

Yet in a taishū engeki show, enka is sung to the backing of loud, raucous, untuned rock and roll. Most of the players cannot even make the basic, predictable chord changes that structure enka. As one troupe head told me, he plays the guitar and all the rest is just *bonchan bon-chan*—banging around on the instruments. What makes this doubly strange is that the audience is composed of seventy-year-old grand-mothers and grandfathers, not the usual audience for loud, out-of-tune rock and roll. Yet not once did I hear a negative comment about the loudness of the music. I asked a woman sitting next to me at a perfor-mance why the song show was so loud. She replied, "Taishū entertain-ments are always loud. That's because all the grandmas and grandpas in the audience can't hear." Her pragmatic explanation calls into ques-tion any theory that would attempt to account for the band's volume sheerly in terms of aesthetic choices.

Yet musical dissonance, too, somehow eludes comment: out-of-tuneness seems not to be a matter of concern for taishū engeki regulars (again, because they are hard of hearing?). Rather than impaired hear-ing, however, I think their lack of concern reflects a notion of the song show that differs radically from the perspectives of younger, outside spectators, whether American or Japanese. For theater regulars, the

troupe members' efforts represent not music as an aesthetic category—
something that can be judged as good, bad, out of tune, or painfully
loud—but rather an exposure of collective sentimentality. To sing is to
reveal one's feelings—the act itself is most important, not the sonic
quality of the result. Aesthetic judgments are not the point here. The
point is to applaud, equally, the display of the troupe member's efforts.
Thus the audience rarely comments during the show on the quality of
the performances themselves, whether the singing was good or not. It
is expected that some of the singers will be bad, and some good; there
is a hierarchy of voices, a display of types. Everyone in the cast sings—
the good, the bad, and the mediocre—with recorded backing alternat-
ing with the live band. The worst singer (often the youngest) goes first
in this hierarchy, the troupe head near the end (the troupe leaders invariably have trained voices).

One could argue, in fact, that the performers are not really "singing,"
in the way some Americans, for example, might define it; similarly, the
troupes' efforts at playing instruments perhaps should not be construed as "music." Instead, the sounds, both instrumental and vocal,
produce primarily a social, not an aesthetic, effect. Singing in taishū
engeki is similar to the function of singing in karaoke bars, where ine-
briated office workers take vocal turns at the microphone. There are
also innumerable song contests on Japanese television, where the point
seems less to determine the greatest talent than to show that everyone,
no matter how talentless, should sing. Any guest who has attended a
Japanese wedding party or celebratory banquet can attest to the importance of singing: everyone is required to sing a song, without exception. Group harmony, predicated on the assumption of a hierarchy of
differences, is musically enacted in these scenes.

Taishū engeki differs, however, from these common Japanese scenes
by maintaining a barrier, permeable as it is, between performers and
customers. Never do the players actually invite spectators to come onstage and sing; the taishū engeki scene is *not* the actual equivalent of
a karaoke bar. It is, after all, paid professional entertainment. Rather,
the singers enact a vocal representation of status differences with
which the audience identifies. This is not to say that special excellence
goes unnoticed. There are indeed brilliant singers in taishū engeki,
some of whom attract fans. Audience members avidly discuss the mer-
its of one actor as compared to another, or of troupes from eastern
Japan versus troupes from the west. A star like Umezawa Tomio induces swoons in his female coterie when he appears as a female

dancer; women sometimes travel hundreds of miles to see a favorite, and some attend every daily performance to watch a particular actor. Fans give money, flowers, and gifts of all sorts to their favorites; they take photographs during the performances and keep scrapbooks. The most coveted recognition of their adulation is to be invited backstage for a drink. There is thus a star system with celebrity status in taishū engeki.

But I heard little, if any, *criticism* of the performers from regular customers. The special excellence of a performer might be remarked upon, but rarely the defects. When entertainment—a movie, a play, a concept—is paid for, there is usually a feeling that one has the right to be critical, to comment on the performance. Taishū engeki, however, works to trouble, if not erase, the boundaries between stage and spectators. This troubling works to negate the critical distance separating actors and audience, particularly in the nonnarrative sections of the performance—the added attractions of song and dance. The taishū engeki audience is thus not a critical audience. It instead functions as an almost unanimously supportive group, and the very lack of commentary and criticism indicates the degree of identification between the audience and the performers.

The song show also marks that segment of the performance when exchanges across the stage boundaries intensify. During a particularly comic and lively opening play, spectators and actors might engage in repartee. Yet it is usually in the song show (and later, during the dancing) that the audience begins to play a more active role.

The song show is hosted by a master of ceremonies, frequently one of the comically gifted troupe members, who announces the songs, introduces the singers, and tells jokes. He also talks directly to the audience; this was the part of the performance when I, as the lone foreigner, would be addressed from the stage. The master of ceremonies would often try to engage American me in conversation; inevitably he would ask if I was married or where my husband was. His remarks indicated the vector of much of taishū engeki's comedy: sexual humor, although rarely does it shade into the truly explicit.

Yet it is the audience that initiates the most direct contact with the performers during this part of the show. For example, a fan will sometimes throw a streamer to a singer, who will hold one end of it while the adoring fan holds the other, thus maintaining a tangible, physical contact throughout the song. Audience members sometimes walk up while a particular singer is performing and leave gifts—cigarettes,

Electric guitars
in the song show of
the Arashi troupe

clothes, imported whiskey, boxed candy—on the stage. They often give flowers to singers, waiting until the end before presenting the bouquet. In every case, the singers give stereotypically profuse thanks for the presents, even though such gift giving is a predictable and almost formal part of the performance. The giving of presents to the performers cements the relationship between patron and artiste, allowing the givers to feel decisively included in the larger world of taishū engeki.

Such giving of gifts of appreciation (called *ohana* or *goshugi*) was an established part of theater and performances in earlier periods but has publicly faded from the large, established theatrical scenes of today. Occasionally one can still witness spectators at outdoor shrine performances throwing twisted pieces of paper onto the stage. Called *ohineri*, the papers contain coins: condensed expressions of audience appreciation, token amounts of money hidden by paper coverings, as is customary when giving money in any form. Shinohara Takamasa, the owner of the Mokubakan and head of the Tokyo Taishū Engeki Association, has written that in the early postwar days, when there was a real scarcity of material goods, everyday commodities far outranked gifts of money in frequency and importance. Soy sauce and white rice were standard gifts, and he states that "some people made it difficult for the actors to perform by strewing the stage with hard-to-get cigarettes." [33]

The giving of commodities as goshugi—particularly in the postwar period—points to the culture of poverty shared by audience and actors alike: displays of generosity became all the more important. Poverty is still the implicit context; even if the taishū engeki audience is now more diversified, the troupes still remain in dire financial straits. Yet the entire theatrical apparatus of taishū engeki operates to create a space of luxury, of excess, of splendor and plenty. Fans no longer bring soy sauce or rice up to the stage; instead they give luxury goods (although cigarettes retain a certain cachet). Yet the best goshugi, the one that has largely replaced material things in the symbolic economy of taishū engeki, is money. Money has become the more powerful sign of wealth in an age of material affluence, as well as the object of media curiosity.

Although fans may sometimes bring up objects during the plays in response to dialogue—for example, if one of the actors asks for a smoke, someone may throw him a pack of cigarettes—only in the "added attraction" segments does gift giving occur. The song and dance shows foreground individual performers divorced from the nar-

---

33. Shinohara, "Taishū engeki ni haru futatabi," 28.

rative and mimetic constraints of drama. Within a succession of framed moments, the players hierarchically display their talents, which in no small part consist of displaying the body. These parts of the show provide occasions for particular spectators to reward particular performers. If the song show functions explicitly as a staged enactment of hierarchical social harmony, the dance show relies even less on a notion of talent, instead presenting the more unmediated attraction of the posed body.

Another play, called the *kirikyōgen*, follows the song show. This play tends to be longer than the first, and is often funnier. After the kirikyōgen, the troupe head comes out, kneels in front of the curtain, and gives his formal greetings to the audience; these greetings are called the *kōjō noberu*. He may take the opportunity to talk about the day's performance, to reveal inside information about the workings of the theater, to make jokes about the weather, or to advertise the next day's program. The kōjō noberu thus works, alongside the extratheatrical references found in many plays, to demystify the theater as theater by including the audience within a conspiratorial framework.

It also serves as a prelude for the climax of the whole performance: the *buyō shō* (dance show), the last added attraction. Here each actor takes a solo turn, dancing in modified and simplified "Japanese dance" (Nihon buyō) style to, again, enka music (this time, however, recorded enka). The dance show marks the appearance of the long-awaited onnagata dancers. Although onnagata may appear in some of the plays, they usually do so in a comic mode; rarely do they appear as seductive objects of desire (some troupes feature highly comic special performances in which all the actors dress up as women). Again, the most famous female impersonator in taishū engeki, Umezawa Tomio, never portrays a woman during a play; only in the dance show does he star as an onnagata. The onnagata represent the pinnacle of taishū engeki's claims to artistry and beauty; if a troupe is lucky enough to have a young and good-looking onnagata, its chances for success are greatly enhanced. The female impersonators have also proved the most intriguing part of taishū engeki to outside observers, just as the willowy Bandō Tamasaburō has pulled in hordes of new fans for kabuki.

The dance show—particularly moments when onnagata or handsome male dancers appear—is also the scene where the conjunction of money and sexuality is the most sharply revealed. Fans are more likely to give gifts during the dance show than the song show, and while the song show does not usually elicit gifts of money, the dance show does.

In this last phase of the taishū engeki performance, enka and Japanese dance combine to produce an effect of the pose. The melodic phrases of enka are sharply defined; at the end of each phrase, the dancer strikes a pose, and the audience applauds at the precise moment when a phrase is complete, when the pose peaks. This aesthetic of the pose is similar to kabuki, where spectators clap at the execution of a technical effect or at a frozen dramatic moment. As Earle Ernst observes, it is as if western audiences were to clap every time a pianist completed a difficult passage during a concerto performance, rather than at the end of the work (what Ernst did not note is the very similar applause following, say, a guitar solo in a blues performance).[34] In taishū engeki these effects are a good deal less technical than the spectacular, sculptural poses of kabuki actors, from which they are derived, yet they nonetheless effectively delineate the body in space, carving out moments when form is detached from other considerations. More than any other part of the taishū engeki performance, the dance show presents the body as an object of visual contemplation.

The gaze of the spectators is directed, then, solely towards the figure of the dancer, dressed in a Japanese kimono, usually a particularly ornate and gorgeous one. The great majority of the dances, set to romantic enka, feature flirtatious smiles and glances cast toward the audience; a few, however, accompanied by the martial strains of marches, present the male body in a heavily masculinized idiom: clenched fists, grimaces, samurai swords. Theatrical swordplay and its surrounding dramatic themes, we should not forget, really constituted the core of taishū engeki until recent days, and swordplay numbers still show up in the taishū engeki dance repertoire.

Just as comedy has displaced the tragic essence of taishū engeki (serious plays used to make up most of the repertoire, while comedy was merely supplemental), lighter, romantic dance pieces have replaced the heavier, martial dance numbers. That the accent now falls on creating a space of dreams (yume) and beauty during the dance show has much to do with the ascendancy of the onnagata figure—and, I should add, with the dominance of older women in the audience; in the theater's heyday, as many men as women attended. Rather than stirring the audience with exaggerated postures of male valor and vigor, today's taishū engeki dancers often prefer to lure spectators with doubled signs of theatrical femininity: not only is the so-called feminine accented, but it finds its strongest expression in men disguised as women.

34. Earle Ernst, *The Kabuki Theater*, 76–77.

Why should a man dressed as a woman prove so alluring to taishū engeki fans, particularly female fans? Innumerable critics have pondered this question in considering the powers of transvestite theater. Roland Barthes boldly (and with residual orientalist confidence) proclaims that "the Oriental transvestite does not copy Woman but signifies her: not bogged down in the model, but detached from its signified; Femininity is presented to read, not to see: translation, not transgression."[35] Barthes was referring to the refined female impersonators of the kabuki stage; he could just as easily have been referring to Noh actors who, with masks and costumes, soberly portray a startling range of female types. Onnagata could indeed be viewed as parodically transgressive, however. In the extended sense that Linda Hutcheon has developed, parody implies "difference within repetition" and a "coded transgression" of a previous work or text; there is always the implicit referencing of a previous work on which the parodic one leans (unlike postmodern pastiche).[36] Transvestism itself implies this sense of parody in its extended sense: repetitive difference from the encodings of sex, gender, sexuality, and their socially approved markers. Gender and sex—and the coherence of what they imply for other registers of the social—pull apart in the transvestite's guise. When this crossing becomes explicitly enacted in the space of theater difference becomes additionally metaphoricized; the very possibility of such costumed incoherence doubly enacts the powers of the theater itself as a space of dreams, of oneiric crossings of all kinds.

Anne Herrmann, in her studies of theatrical transvestism, claims that such crossings operate "as a dramatic device to figure historicized forms of social transgression. Such transgression never takes the form of travesty itself; that is, cross-dressing as such is not coded as violation. Rather, the vacillation between masculine and feminine serves as a metaphor for a particular social contradiction."[37] That is, transvestism figured dramatically is as much about other kinds of social contradiction as those transparently revealed by gendered bodies; far from leading to a kind of androgynous undecidability, transvestism often works to proliferate contradictions on any number of levels, rather than to resolve them. Taishū engeki parodically cross-proliferates the contradictions of class position, of gender and sexuality, of different formations of modernity, of the culture industry and the question of

35. Roland Barthes, *Empire of Signs*, 53.
36. See Linda Hutcheon, *A Theory of Parody: The Teachings of Twentieth-Century Art Forms.*
37. Anne Herrmann, "Travesty and Transgression: Transvestism in Shakespeare, Brecht, and Churchill," 295.

the popular. One of the ways it achieves this proliferation is indeed through travestied figurations.

Taishū engeki makes the (now) "high-class" kabuki specialists in female roles the object of distancing by transforming them into third-rate representations and thereby foregrounding their relationship to region and class: playbills expressly highlight their star onnagata as plebeian copies of Tamasaburō: Shitamachi no Tamasaburō, but also—in an explosion of local place names—Naniwa no Tamasaburō, Genkai no Tamasaburō, Ginza no Tamasaburō. A host of would-be Tamasaburōs fill the taishū engeki stages, with their down-home, voluptuous, regional versions of Tamasaburō's cool, central perfection. Barthes admired the subtlety and mobility of the signifier in the Japanese empire of signs, yet in taishū engeki, onnagata resemble western drag queens as much (or as little) as oriental ciphers of femininity. They not only translate women into signifiers of difference (as kabuki actors do), they then translate that translation into a travesty of kabuki transvestism. In so doing, they proliferate the contradictions between the class status of their own third-rate kabuki and that of the first-rate version.

Yet the powers of desire are not yet figured into these possibilities of travesty, powers that make a few of the male crossed-dressed dancers (*not* simply as actors, it should be remembered) the objects of the intense interest of female fans. It is true that only onnagata who approach a kind of kabuki-inspired beauty really become these objects of desire. Fat, buck-toothed, or old onnagata might be admired for their skills, but are not erotic attractions. They might continue to fascinate if they appear during plays, but when they dance they do not inspire the adoration of female spectators. The closer a dancer comes to a more centrally defined notion of handsomeness or beauty, however, the less a burlesque atmosphere prevails and the more a scene the audience considers beautiful *(kirei)* unfolds. When this beauty finally emerges, then, alongside the other compelling attractions of the taishū engeki performance, erotic attraction becomes foregrounded as the question of narrative recedes. Yet the articulation of differences is perhaps most marked during the dance shows, when gifts of money emerge to intensify this attraction.

Ephemeral Gifts

Gifts of money are highly acceptable in polite Japanese society. Money is given for weddings and funerals, for birthdays and graduations. In the case of weddings and funerals, the amount of the monetary gift is recorded by the recipient's family, which then sends a return gift (*not* of money) of an appropriately corresponding worth. There is nothing wrong, then, with the transformation of money into the form of a gift; indeed, it is the only acceptable gift in many social situations in Japan. The money, however, is almost always presented in hidden form; that is, it is enclosed in an ornately decorated envelope or wrapped in paper. This wrapping indicates its status as a gift; ideally, money should not be given in its unadorned state. In fact, many purely fiscal transactions in Japan treat money as if it were *not* money by placing it in envelopes. There is something vaguely scandalous about money in its uncovered state, and Japanese refer to unwrapped money as "naked" (*hadaka*).

To give money in its unmediated form, or even to pick up money lying on the ground, is vulgar in Japanese society. Yet in the dances of taishū engeki, restrictions on the display of money are transgressed with great flair. Moreover, money itself becomes an object—a decorative object—alongside the figures of the dancers. Not only does money signify all that money can buy, but it also becomes figural, arrestingly material. With the culminating appearance of a popular dancer, money emerges as part of the performance. Women go on stage and drape leis made of ten-thousand-yen notes over his neck (ten thousand yen is worth almost eighty U.S. dollars); they cover both sides of big dancing fans with bills, or hang notes from the ribs of a parasol. An actor may thus receive thousands of yen on a single night. Even with the appearance of a less popular dancer, modest displays of bills punctuate the end of a performance.

Money thus becomes a signifier not only of exchange value, but of exchange value transformed into ornament or artifact: into aestheticized use value. The strange coincidence here of use and exchange value in the body of money itself bears displaced witness to its origins in the commodity form. Yet in another mode of display, money is not used to construct or embellish a material object; instead, ten-thousand-yen notes are thrown into the air and showered over the body of the dancer. The dancer is literally inundated with money. This technique bypasses even the slight pretension of domesticating money that the leis, fans, and umbrellas of bills disclose. Money now becomes almost a pure sign, powerful because of its sheer quantity, its excessiveness matched only by the erotically charged figure of the dancer. In the vast majority of performances I saw, only modest gifts or envelopes of money were presented to dancers. Yet with the appearance of a taishū engeki star, money—profuse and undisguised—works to reinvest the erotic valence of the dancer, to reemphasize, literally, the possibilities of attraction within the dancer's (often cross-dressed) body.

I have never observed or heard of money tossed over a male dancing as a male. Only when a man plays a woman (and not just any woman, but a femme fatale) is money literally "thrown away." I believe that throwing money over an onnagata's body is particularly charged for several reasons. First, as I have suggested, money in its "naked" form is highly marked in Japanese society; how much more so is the display of an abundance of bills. The money is not only thrown, however. The dancer also picks it up from the floor, transgressing yet another polite convention. Both parts of the action (giving and receiving) constitute an exchange which travesties the gift giving that forms such an important part of Japanese convention.

It must be remembered, however, who gives and who receives in this exchange. Female fans (hiiki kyaku) are the ones who give money; they are the ones who often travel hundreds of miles to watch a favorite actor. In giving money to male dancers, these fans reverse the assumed order of things, in which men give money to women. And in giving money in such a spectacular fashion—by throwing money at the performer—the women invert the scenario of subjugation even more powerfully.

This scenario shows, however, not a woman subjugating a man, but a woman subjugating a man playing a woman. Women in the audience are thus able to make a *double* identification, both with the female patron—now in a position of power—and with the seductive recipient, male yet female. They are able to identify with the female devotees who, by giving money, occupy the dominant position of the male, and with the passive role of the dominated—a woman outwardly, a man in reality. Women patrons I talked to spoke repeatedly of how "beautiful" their chosen recipient was; they claimed that giving money made them feel closer to their idol.

The conjunction of money and the cross-dressed dancer intensifies a dialectic of desire and a reversal of gendered valences. Both are signifiers of literal excess, of that which goes beyond the boundaries—of gender roles, of class positions, of national-cultural conventions. And such excess itself is again the mark of the primary process, the figural. These moments of pure spectacle, of figurality unbound and repressions lifted, point to a world of desires fulfilled, if only fleetingly.

For an audience and for actors that are not wealthy, the simultaneous display of so much money has a force that goes beyond the energy released by breaking a taboo. It is no wonder, again, that actors refer to taishū engeki (and the dance show, in particular) as a space of dreams, by no means an arbitrary image. Dreams designate precisely that state of being in which desire is unbound and wishes fulfilled, where excessive linkages proliferate and all is possible. Dreams are commonly contrasted with the demands of reality testing, as a domain in which (as Freud would say) the "no" does not exist. Dreams thus become an apt metaphor for the theater itself.[38] With its crossings of dream, wealth, and desire, taishū engeki's theater of dreams (to reiterate the title of one of Umezawa Tomio's songs, "Yume no shibai") overturns the ethics and aesthetics of advanced Japanese capitalism, even as it discloses the longings of the margins to partake more fully of the affluent realities that it offers.

Taishū engeki thus reinfiltrates contemporary Japanese society, particularly in its evocations of the specter of class. Taishū engeki's very name declares its class position; it evokes something cheap, something anyone can afford. It thus immediately refers to money, and one of the great sources of pride for taishū engeki theater owners and troupes is the rock bottom price of admission and the three or four hours worth of performative variety one gets for that price. There is indeed much going on in taishū engeki, as if it had to compensate for its cheapness by providing an almost exhaustively rich grand show.

By Japanese middle-class standards, of course, taishū engeki is anything but grand, the breadth of its appeal the opposite of mass—contradictions that are repeatedly played out within the theater. Having proclaimed itself as taishū, the theater seems to have set itself the task of constructing a fantasy of cheapness, almost to parody Japanese middle-class conceptions of tawdry bad taste. On more than one occasion the well-bred Japanese women I dragged to taishū engeki looked on in disbelief at the scenes unfolding on stage..When I asked an older affluent Japanese couple if they thought taishū engeki was vulgar (*gehin*), they replied no, not really, it was probably just *hade* (gaudy or showy). Yet such showiness is precisely the hallmark of lower-class aesthetic vulgarity.

Taishū engeki embodies this aesthetic of hade, which it interprets as gorgeousness.[39] Through this excessive aesthetic it appeals to and ful-

38. In invoking the metaphor of the dream, taishū engeki practitioners are also referring to high classic Japanese aesthetic theories, in which the notion of the dream (yume) plays an important part.

39. It has derived much of this spectacular aesthetic from kabuki, now of course the epitome of a refined showiness that is the static aesthetic reflection of Tokugawa-period merchant culture.

fills its audience's expectations for theatrical luxury. Through its complex gender transformations, its variety of performances, its dissolution of the boundaries between stage and spectators, its figurality, its emphasis on the voice, and its endless reworkings of an older narrative economy, taishū engeki overturns current middle-class consumer modes of aesthetic appreciation as it exceeds the boundaries of bourgeois good taste. One could hardly think of a more perfect representation of lower-class aesthetics: if taishū engeki holds forth a dream of gorgeousness to its regular audience, it is a fulfillment of urban middle-class nightmares of what the lower class must be—that lower class which, according to the results of countless Japanese opinion polls, hardly exists in what has been termed a virtually classless society. At venues like the Mokubakan, however, the poor return in hauntingly full force to disturb the common wisdom about classlessness.[40]

Yet as the public television specials, magazine articles, and young new audience members indicate, taishū engeki simultaneously appeals to a Japanese longing for an aesthetic lushness stubbornly marginal to contemporary Japanese notions of good taste. Taishū engeki could easily clean up its act and more closely approximate standard norms of aesthetics, refinement, and acceptability. The famous Umezawa troupe has tried just that, with sell-out appearances at the ritzy Honda Theater in one of the fashionable sections of Tokyo. Not surprisingly, those performances failed to re-create the world of the theaters precariously surviving on Tokyo's fringes, where signs of wealth and accumulation—elaborate costuming, sexual excess, the display of money—are juxtaposed against signs of poverty and insufficiency: crude sets, scratched records, cramped quarters, shabbily dressed fans. This juxtaposition upsets the balance achieved in postindustrial Japan between the rational use of wealth and a standardized middle-class culture: taishū engeki eschews the middle in all things.

Japanese mass media have found in taishū engeki yet another potential fetish object: a reminder of performative possibilities past, of the narrative romance of the Tokugawa period, that at the same time sustains vanishing (but not yet vanished) forms of modernity. Its thematic

40. Thus, many observers state that the middle class as such no longer exists in Japanese society; instead, they point to the emergence of a vast "middle mass" which subsumes previous class differentiations. More recent studies have called attention to the fragmentation of the middle mass into fragmented masses (bunshū) or micro masses (shōshū) based on new patterns of consumption. See, for example, Murakami Yasusuke, "The Age of New Middle Mass Politics: The Case of Japan." On the fragmented and micro masses see Fujioka Wakao, Sayōnara taishū: kansei jidai o dō yomu ka, and Hakuhōdō Seikatsu Sōgō Kenkyūjo, ed., "Bunshū" no tanjō.

Katsu Koryū and the aesthetics of intimacy

references are cross-cut by its implicit referencing of the apogee of its precursors' urban popularity, the prewar modern period itself. Sometimes classified as a variety of folk performance, taishū engeki—like storytelling or trance—appears to carry on an unarguably Japanese knowledge. Through its itinerancy, its restricted venues, and its reliance on oral modes of knowledge, it is thus treated as a potential marker of loss, a loss that is transmuted into a vibrant guarantee of the continuity of presence. Yet in performance taishū engeki rescinds that guarantee as it proffers, instead, this ephemeral gift: the possibility of exceeding the containments of desire, if only for a moment.

Afterwords on Repetition and Redemption

National culturalism and its relationship to the uncanny; the contradictory longing for superseded forms of being—the premodern, the "traditional," the irrational—and the recurrence of those forms in commodified guises; the desire for origins and for unmediated practices of the voice: all bespeak a condition of modernity-in-common (of common modernity). The difference in Japanese modernity, however, might subsist not in the cultural uniqueness of its inflections (what culture, if we are to retain that concept, is not unique?), but in the historically specific experiences of a nation-state bearing the imperatives of an originally Eurocentric modernity. Rey Chow, writing about "oriental modernity," has noted that "'Western things' . . . are never merely dispensable embellishments; their presence has for the past century represented the necessity of fundamental adaptation and acceptance. It is the permanence of imprints left by the contact with the West that should be remembered even in an ethnic culture's obsession with 'itself.'"[1]

The varieties of cultural self-obsession that I have discussed—with practices of the voice, with a time when the dead could speak, with communal spaces of performance—can be read as a longing for a premodernity, a time before the West, before the catastrophic imprint of westernization. Yet the very search to find authentic survivals of premodern, prewestern Japanese authenticity is inescapably a *modern* endeavor, essentially enfolded within the historical condition that it would seek to escape. Thus, that search speaks also of the denials of

1. Chow, "Seeing Modern China," 27.

modernity's ruptures. These denials have often led (both in everyday Japanese life and in Japanological analyses) to forms of essentialism that place Japan in a sort of exceptionalist limbo, where the continuities of culture are commonly invoked to deny the dislocations of history.

Yet to assert Japanese modernity is not an unambiguous task. Correlated with the historically located transformations that have accompanied the rise of capitalism and nation-statehood in the twentieth century, modernity implies a structure of consciousness and subjectivity with a peculiar relationship to temporality, one in which continuity (the continuity of "tradition," for example) can never be taken for granted within the upheavals of capitalist commodity relations. Places of origins, displaced, subsist as traces of loss that reinfiltrate modernity's present, in Japan as elsewhere. In doing so, these losses emerge as actively troublesome to rationalized orders of things. In modern regimes of knowledge, their excluded status cannot easily be left as simply that; indeed, such residues demand an accounting in the present—either through active forgetting or efforts at rememoration.

This book has also, then, tried to evoke a sense of the recurrent yet elusive forms of absence that haunt the historical present of that place called Japan. The vanishing tremble on the edge of dissolution, but never move completely to the side of disappearance (or appearance). Phantasmatic subjects slip past the resolutions of simple presence (or absence). Figured materialities interrupt the ordered progressions of narrative. The notion of marginality, too, operates excessively: the margin is both inside and outside, both included and excluded from the text itself, undermining oppositions of center and periphery, recuperation and resistance.

In Japan, as elsewhere (although one could argue that the process is highly accelerated in Japan), the residues of modernity are efficiently taken up by culture institutions and circulated as citations of difference. When the marginal is temporally inscribed within the nostalgic register as the vanishing, it then functions as a special, and fetishized, guarantor of social stasis. Fetishized, in the sense that the vanishing is never allowed actually to disappear, but is kept hovering, with anxiety and dread, on the edge of absence. We have seen, for example, how Japanese nativist ethnology, in its attempts to rescue disappearing worlds of narrative and practice from oblivion, rehabilitated them in the guise of the folkloric. Such an endeavor offers the reassurances of knowledge, even of knowledge that radically troubles the premises of modernity.

This book has followed the contradictory operations of loss and its phantasmatic recoveries through various efforts, whether disciplinary (as in nativist ethnology), institutional (Japan National Railway's tourism campaigns), or civic (Tōno). At the same time, it has indicated ways in which particular sites, practices, and people exceed these recoveries, forming reserves of pleasure and loss within the national-cultural topography of contemporary Japan. Tenuous lines of escape move through practices of the voice and rhetorical overturnings: the parodic performances and word play of taishū engeki, the incomprehensibility of trance language and the rumors of ghosts on Mount Osore, the dark narratives and remnant dialect of Tōno. In the midst of domestication, these places and practices continue to disturb; they are not what they are imagined to be. They exist as ghostly reminders, as potentially scandalous presences that, by all rights, should not be there—yet which *must* be there, vanishing, to act as constitutive reminders of modernity's losses.

Taishū engeki and its excessive dream rhetoric, for example, reiterate a return to the dynamic of the phantasm that has shaped Japanese encounters with modernity. That taishu engeki should parody, and in many senses exceed, the phantasmagoria of advanced capitalism, in its *own* theater of dreams is perhaps only fitting. It was the German critic Walter Benjamin, particularly in his Arcades Project (the *Passagen-Werk*), who named the peculiar situation of capitalist phantasmagoria, with its disorienting swirl of outmoded objects and novel commodities, archaic texts and Hollywood movies, messianic Marxists and prophetic dandies. This phantasmagoria was simultaneously crossed with nostalgia for the obsolete and fascination with the new. If the modern Parisian that obsessed Benjamin (and his model was Baudelaire) was filled with both the ennui and detachment of the disenchanted city dweller, he (and perhaps she) was also perpetually seeking to refind a relationship to those objects that modernity had superseded. In the ruined cityscapes of Europe, Benjamin found the allegorical potential—hidden in the profusion of commodities and in the modalities of distraction and interruption that mechanical reproduction assured—for a paradisiacal modernity. Ever alert to "dialectical images," images that could wrest the moment from an objectified past, Benjamin uncovered the little politics embedded in the commodity detritus of everyday life and in the material moments of that life: dialectical images had political potential because they unsettled the phantasmagoria, momentarily allowing new possibilities to emerge.

In revealing capitalism as dream, then, Benjamin also spoke of awak-ening—not atavistically, to a precommodified world (in what he called a repetition of the past), but to a new recognition of the present in all its commodified and unjust profligacy. Attention to the present itself would yield a certain fidelity to the past and to the dead (the mode he called a redemption of the past). For Benjamin, the seemingly struc-tural interdependence of disavowal and desire (such as is found, again, in fetishization) became politicized within the temporality of moder-nity as the relationship between commodification and redemption.[2]

To return to taishū engeki, the class mimesis it effects is unsettling for everyday occupants of the capitalist dreamworld. Its thematic rep-resentation of the social relations of the Tokugawa world—a *premodern*, precapitalist Japanese past—alongside its reproduction of the commu-nal performance conditions of an earlier moment within modernity—the *prewar*, when an urban working-class culture might have existed—unfolds a layering, an imbrication of different moments of modernity. It proffers, then, theatrical comforts for those disillusioned with Japan's current postprosperity condition: the performance of times when the calibration of duty with human feelings was unquestioned, when spec-tators were neighbors, when TV had yet to colonize the space of view-ing. These comforts can slide over into the domain of the sheerly nostalgic, into the sphere of the repetition of the past and its ob-jectification. Yet in its most redemptive, or utopian moments, taishū engeki performances yield, in some senses, a revelation of modernity's potential for a classless society. That is, even as it exposes the class conditions that are so often obscured in bourgeois societies, taishū en-geki's space of dreams (if yet less dreamlike than the mass cultural world outside) describes an ephemeral setting where antinomies of class are resolved, but only transiently, within the realm of its dream logics.

I am not wholly comfortable with Benjamin's language of redemp-tion; neither am I satisfied with a rhetoric of resistance that could be

2. The interimplication of reification and utopia, of objectification and resistance, was always recognized and theorized by critics such as Theodor Adorno, who is nevertheless often accused of having an irremediably negative view of mass culture. Such accusations overlook Adorno's remarkable recognition of the "promise of happiness" that even the most cynical products of the culture industry embody. Fredric Jameson takes up this theme in his "Reification and Utopia in Mass Culture." Benjamin's thought-world was taken up with the promise of happiness within modernity's catastrophes, and thus with the utopian potential within the reification of life that he saw increasing with the domi-nance of the commodity form under capitalism.

deployed to encompass the marginal practices I have addressed. Neither redemption nor resistance seems unambiguously available within the repetitions of consumer capitalism. Yet, I circle back to the figure of the fetish once more. For if we have seen the way contemporary Japanese fetishize, and thus reify, certain emblems of identity (and what could be more emblematic of the fetish than the commodity form itself?), that process also reveals the presence of a wish: the wish to reanimate, not simply fix, the past at the moment of its apparent vanishing. That wishfulness could be located within a larger space of rememoration, such that, for example, the spirit recallings on Mount Osore might indeed actively mourn the losses of the nation-culture, as they mourn the dead. Mount Osore would then work as a dialectical image, allegorically revealing the enlivening wish that the fetish, for all its seeming fixity, nevertheless discloses.

No doubt the most visible dialectical image to have emerged in recent years into the tenebrous light of national consciousness was the death of the Shōwa emperor in 1989, a moment when the imperial fetish shimmered briefly on the edge of historical exposure. For Hirohito, as the metonym of World War II, perpetually forced Japanese to recall the enormous losses of that war; his death, marking a moment when the question of loss and violence could reemerge from its contemporary irrelevance, brought into question once more the very meaning of Japanese history. As Norma Field has revealed, that moment was indeed all too brief, allowed to coalesce only for an instant before the restitution of the routines of everyday late-modern life. Nevertheless, as she also shows, forgetfulness is not total; and it is to specific people and their renunciations of the emperor system that she turns in outlining an enlivening politics of remembrance.[3]

The instances and practices I record do not have the clarity of resistant rememoration that Field uncovers. They pass over the enormity of the war in their attempts to find a Japan existing unchanged before modernity's incursions. (The fragile exception to this absence might be the mourning practices on Mount Osore, which do include the aged spirits of the war dead.) In doing so, they avoid encountering the literal trauma of the war. Yet, through allegorical readings, they all stand as revelatory instances of modernity's losses.

The accelerating attenuation of even these reminders, these elegiac resources—and what seems to be their increasing irrelevance in the

3. Field, *In the Realm of a Dying Emperor.*

late twentieth century—has led many observers, Japanese and non-, to speak of Japan as a chillingly evacuated critical space. In what has been called the postmodern aesthetic of contemporary Japanese—and particularly Japanese youth—there is a loss of nostalgia itself, a double removal: not only has the imagined object of loss vanished, but even the sense of loss itself. All voices and forms of language seem equally present, equally homogeneous. Within this mass-mediated space, the very possibility of complex dialectical images is thus foreclosed.

Yet others insist that Japan's affluence has given rise to a new series of discourses, of multiple voices, within the mass media. Some speak of a liberation of desire and playfulness within consumption, of an expansion of the possibilities only money can buy, of new forms of individuality and sociality unthinkable outside the particular en-ablements of advanced capitalism. Even further, these critics would ask if this sort of liberation is not in itself a form of resistance to the imperatives of historical reason, to the demands of social control. There is no doubt that Japan today contains vast cultural reserves, as shown by the interpretive energies perpetually reconstituting forms of the authentic through texts, images, and disciplines. It remains to be seen whether these energies and the possibilities set free by advanced consumer capitalism constitute new openings for the heterogeneous, or if in fact they are merely more efficient means of recuperation. One suspects the latter, but of course the very framing of the dilemma of recuperation and resistance is made unstable by the phantasmatic im-peratives and instances presented here. The layering of forms of mo-dernity—the high modern notions embedded in nostalgic travel or alongside the arguably postmodern erasure of nostalgia proper—cor-relate and coexist with generational differences, with class slippages, with movements across the boundaries of dialect and region, such that a totalized characterization of Japan as postmodern misses this point: that the very gap between concurrent forms of modernity and their associated modes of production lends differential energy to the possi-bility of working through (if not redeeming) the national-cultural past in Japan, as elsewhere.[4] Despite the expanding domains of consump-tion, transnational corporations, and video simulation, that possibility ensures that Benjamin's dream of transformative modernity is not yet obsolete, not quite. Perhaps his not quite obsolete vision of modernity is taking its place as one more instance of the vanishing, along with its

4. The differences between those forms indicates what Ernst Bloch referred to as "non-synchronicity," a gloss on Marx's "uneven development."

objects. Yet suspended at the moment of disappearance, both visions and objects still linger in a world now suffused with the particular dreams of Japanese modernity. Those dreams move through the entwined temporalities of Japan and others, as they return, once again, to inscribe the uncertain fates of the vanishing.

BIBLIOGRAPHY

Adler, Judith. "Origins of Sightseeing." *Annals of Tourism Research* 16, no. 2 (1989): 8–11.

Adorno, Theodor. "Culture Industry Reconsidered." *New German Critique*, no. 6 (Fall 1975): 12–29.

———. "Valéry Proust Museum." In Adorno, *Prisms*, 173–85. Translated by Samuel and Shierry Weber. Cambridge, Mass.: MIT Press, 1981.

Amino Yoshihiko. *Muen, kugai, raku: Nihon chūsei no jiyū to heiwa*. Tokyo: Heibonsha, 1978.

Anderson, Benedict R. O'Gorman. *Imagined Communities: Reflections on the Origin and Spread of Nationalism*. London: Verso, 1991.

Appadurai, Arjun. "Disjuncture and Difference in the Global Cultural Economy." *Public Culture* 2, no. 2 (1990): 1–24.

———. "Introduction: Place and Voice in Anthropological Theory." *Cultural Anthropology* 3, no. 1 (1988): 16–20.

Apter, Emily, and William Pietz, eds. *Fetishism as Cultural Discourse*. Ithaca: Cornell University Press, 1993.

Bakhtin, M. M. "Discourse in the Novel." In Bakhtin, *The Dialogic Imagination*, 259–422. Edited by Michael Holquist. Translated by Caryl Emerson and Michael Holquist. Austin: University of Texas Press, 1981.

———. "The Problem of Speech Genres." In Bakhtin, *Speech Genres and Other Late Essays*, 60–102. Edited by Caryl Emerson and Michael Holquist. Translated by Vern N. McGee. Austin: University of Texas Press, 1986.

Balibar, Etienne. *Race, Nation, Class: Ambiguous Identities*. London: Verso, 1991.

Barthes, Roland. *Empire of Signs*. Translated by Richard Howard. New York: Hill and Wang, 1982.

———. *The Grain of the Voice: Interviews 1962–1980*. Translated by Linda Coverdale. New York: Hill and Wang, 1985.

———. "Rhetoric of the Image." In Barthes, *Image Music Text*, 31–51. Translated by Stephen Heath. New York: Hill and Wang, 1977.

———. "The World of Wrestling." In Barthes, *Mythologies*, 15–25. Translated by Annette Lavers. New York: Hill and Wang, 1972.

Baudrillard, Jean. *For a Critique of the Political Economy of the Sign.* Translated by Charles Levin. St. Louis: Telos Press, 1981.

Befu, Harumi. "Nationalism and *Nihonjinron.*" In *Cultural Nationalism in East Asia: Representation and Identity,* edited by Harumi Befu, 107–35. University of California Institute of East Asian Studies Research Papers and Policy Studies, no. 39. Berkeley, 1993.

Benjamin, Walter. "What Is Epic Theater?" In Benjamin, *Illuminations,* 147–54. Edited by Hannah Arendt. New York: Schocken, 1969.

Berlant, Lauren. *The Anatomy of National Fantasy: Hawthorne, Utopia, and Everyday Life.* Chicago: University of Chicago Press, 1991.

Bestor, Theodore C. *Neighborhood Tokyo.* Stanford: Stanford University Press, 1990.

Bhabha, Homi. "Of Mimicry and Man: The Ambivalence of Colonial Discourse." *October,* no. 28 (Spring 1984): 125–33.

Blacker, Carmen. *The Catalpa Bow.* London: George Allen & Unwin, 1975.

Blanchot, Maurice. *The Space of Literature.* Translated by Ann Smock. Lincoln: University of Nebraska Press, 1982.

Boon, James A. "Why Museums Make Me Said." In *Exhibiting Cultures: The Poetics and Politics of Museum Display,* edited by Ivan Karp and Steven D. Lavine, 255–77. Washington, D.C.: Smithsonian Institution Press, 1991.

Brooks, Peter. *The Melodramatic Imagination: Balzac, Henry James, Melodrama, and the Mode of Excess.* New York: Columbia University Press, 1985.

Buck-Morss, Susan. *The Dialectics of Seeing: Walter Benjamin and the Arcades Project.* Cambridge, Mass.: MIT Press, 1989.

Castoriadis, Cornelius. *The Imaginary Institution of Society.* Cambridge, Mass.: MIT Press, 1987.

Chakrabarty, Dipesh. "Postcoloniality and the Artifice of History: Who Speaks for 'Indian' Pasts?" *Representations,* no. 37 (Winter 1992): 1–26.

Chatterjee, Partha. *Nationalist Thought and the Colonial World: A Derivative Discourse.* London: Zed Books, 1986.

Chow, Rey. "Seeing Modern China: Toward a Theory of Ethnic Spectatorship." In Chow, *Women and Chinese Modernity: The Politics of Reading Between West and East,* 3–33. Minneapolis: University of Minnesota Press, 1991.

Clifford, James. "Notes on Travel and Theory." *Inscriptions,* no. 5 (1989): 177–88.

———. "Objects and Selves—An Afterword." In *Objects and Others: Essays on Museums and Material Culture,* edited by George W. Stocking, Jr., 236–46. Madison: University of Wisconsin Press, 1985.

———. *The Predicament of Culture: Twentieth-Century Ethnography, Literature, and Art.* Cambridge, Mass.: Harvard University Press, 1988.

Crapanzano, Vincent. "Hermes' Dilemma: The Masking of Subversion in Ethnographic Description." In *Writing Culture: The Poetics and Politics of Ethnography,* edited by James Clifford and George Marcus, 51–76. Berkeley: University of California Press, 1986.

Crary, Jonathan. *Techniques of the Observer: On Vision and Modernity in the Nineteenth Century.* Cambridge, Mass.: MIT Press, 1990.

Dale, Peter N. *The Myth of Japanese Uniqueness.* New York: St. Martin's Press, 1986.

Daniel, E. Valentine. Review of *A Crack in the Mirror: Reflexive Perspectives in*

Anthropology, edited by J. Ruby (Philadelphia: University of Pennsylvania Press, 1982). *Urban Life* 14, no. 2 (1985): 247–48.

de Certeau, Michel. *Heterologies: Discourse on the Other.* Translated by Brian Massumi. Theory and History of Literature, vol. 17. Minneapolis: University of Minnesota Press, 1986.

———. *The Practice of Everyday Life.* Translated by Steven F. Rendall. Berkeley: University of California, 1984.

———. "Psychoanalysis and Its History." In de Certeau, *Heterologies: Discourse on the Other,* 3–16. Minneapolis: University of Minnesota Press, 1986.

de Certeau, Michel, with Dominique Julia and Jacques Revel. "The Beauty of the Dead: Nisard." In de Certeau, *Heterologies,* 119–36.

Derrida, Jacques. *Of Grammatology.* Translated by Gayatri Chakravorty Spivak. Baltimore: Johns Hopkins University Press, 1976.

———. "Signature Event Context." In Derrida, *Margins of Philosophy,* 307–30. Translated by Alan Bass. Chicago: University of Chicago Press, 1982.

———. "Structure, Sign, and Play in the Discourse of the Human Sciences." In Derrida, *Writing and Difference,* 278–93. Translated by Alan Bass. Chicago: University of Chicago Press, 1978.

———. "'This Strange Institution Called Literature': An Interview with Jacques Derrida." In Derrida, *Acts of Literature,* 33–75. Edited by Derek Attridge. New York: Routledge, 1992.

Dirks, Nicholas B. "History as a Sign of the Modern." *Public Culture* 2, no. 2 (1990): 25–31.

Dolar, Mladen. "'I Shall Be with You on Your Wedding-Night': Lacan and the Uncanny." *October,* no. 58 (Fall 1991): 5–23.

Dreyfus, Hubert L., and Paul Rabinow. *Michel Foucault: Beyond Structuralism and Hermeneutics.* 2d ed. With an Afterword by and an Interview with Michel Foucault. Chicago: University of Chicago Press, 1982.

Eagleton, Terry. *William Shakespeare.* Oxford: Basil Blackwell, 1986.

Ernst, Earle. *The Kabuki Theater.* Honolulu: University of Hawaii Press, 1974.

Fabian, Johannes. *Time and the Other: How Anthropology Makes Its Object.* New York: Columbia University Press, 1983.

Fernandez, James. "Andalusia on Our Minds: Two Contrasting Places in Spain as Seen in a Vernacular Poetic Duel of the Late Nineteenth Century." *Cultural Anthropology* 3, no. 1 (1988): 21–35.

"Fetish." Special issue. *Princeton Architectural Journal,* no. 4 (1992).

Field, Norma. *In the Realm of a Dying Emperor: Japan at Century's End.* New York: Random House, Vintage, 1993.

Figal, Gerald. "The Folk and the Fantastic in Japanese Modernity: Dialogues on Reason and the Imagination in Late Nineteenth and Early Twentieth Century Japan." Ph.D. dissertation, University of Chicago, 1992.

———. "From *tengu* to *senzo:* The Hidden World in the Writing of Yanagita Kunio." Paper written for the 39th annual meeting of the Midwestern Conference on Asian Studies, Bloomington, November 1990.

Fischer, Michael M. J., and Mehdi Abedi. *Debating Muslims: Cultural Dialogues in Postmodernity and Tradition.* Madison: University of Wisconsin Press, 1990.

Foucault, Michel. "Afterword: The Subject and Power." In *Michel Foucault: Beyond Structuralism and Hermeneutics,* by Hubert Dreyfus and Paul Rabinow, 208–26. Chicago: University of Chicago Press, 1982.

————. "The Discourse on Language." In Foucault, *The Archaeology of Knowledge*, 215–37. New York: Harper Colophon, 1976.

————. "Nietzsche, Genealogy, History." In Foucault, *Language, Counter-Memory, Practice: Selected Essays and Interviews*, 139–64. Edited by Donald F. Bouchard. Translated by Donald F. Bouchard and Sherry Simon. Ithaca: Cornell University Press, 1977.

————. *The Order of Things: An Archaeology of the Human Sciences*. New York: Vintage Books, 1973.

————. *Power/Knowledge: Selected Interviews and Other Writings, 1972–1977*. Edited by Colin Gordon. Translated by Colin Gordon et al. New York: Pantheon, 1980.

————. "Theatrum Philosophicum." In Foucault, *Language, Counter-Memory, Practice:* Selected Essays and Interviews, 165–96. Edited by Donald F. Bouchard. Translated by Donald F. Bouchard and Sherry Simon. Ithaca: Cornell University Press, 1977.

Freud, Sigmund. "Fetishism." In *The Standard Edition of the Complete Psychological Works of Sigmund Freud*. Translated by James Strachey, with Anna Freud, Alix Strachey, and Alan Tyson. 1927; London: Hogarth Press, 1955.

————. "Mourning and Melancholia." In Freud, *General Psychological Theory*, 164–80. Edited by Philip Rieff. 1917; New York: Macmillan, 1963.

————. "Repression." In Freud, *General Psychological Theory,* 104–15. Edited by Philip Rieff. 1915; New York: Macmillan, 1963.

————. "The 'Uncanny.'" In Freud, *Studies in Parapsychology*, 19–60. Edited by Philip Rieff. 1919; New York: Macmillan, 1963.

Frow, John. "Tourism and the Semiotics of Nostalgia." *October*, no. 57 (Summer 1991): 123–51.

Fujii, James. "Culture, Political Economy and Japan's Discourse of Internationalization." Paper presented at the Third Walter H. Shorenstein Conference in East Asian Studies, Center for East Asian Studies, Stanford University, 13–14 May 1993.

Fujioka Wakao. *Kareinaru shuppatsu: jisukabā Japan*. Tokyo: Mainichi Shinbunsha, 1972.

————. *Sayōnara taishū: kansei jidai o dō yomu ka*. Tokyo: PHP Kenkyūjo, 1984.

Fujioka Wakao and Nakai Kōichi. *Jisukabā Amerika: Amerika no kankō kyanpein.* Tokyo: Marunouchi Shuppan, 1968.

Fujitani, Takashi. "Japan's Modern National Ceremonies: A Historical Ethnography, 1868–1912." Ph.D. dissertation, University of California, Berkeley, 1986.

Fukuda Ajio. "Nihon minzoku kenkyūshi nenpyō." *Kokuritsu Rekishi Minzoku Hakubutsukan Hōkuku*, no. 2 (March 1983): 41–81.

Fukutomi Tōru. "Genchi no hōkoku: 'hojokin no tengoku' o yuku." *Bungei shunjū*, May 1980, 118–27.

Garber, Marjorie. *Shakespeare's Ghost Writers: Literature as Uncanny Causality.* New York: Methuen, 1987.

Geertz, Clifford. "Religion as a Cultural System." In Geertz, *The Interpretation of Cultures: Selected Essays*, 87–125. New York: Basic Books, 1973.

Gekkan Akurosu Henshū Shitsu, ed. *Ima, chōtaishū no jidai*. Tokyo: Parco Shuppan, 1985.

Gluck, Carol. *Japan's Modern Myths*. Princeton: Princeton University Press, 1985.

Godzich, Wlad. "Foreword: The Further Possibility of Knowledge," in *Heterolo gies*, by Michel de Certeau, vii–xxi. Minneapolis: University of Minnesota Press, 1986.

Gorai Shigeru. "Yūkai to junrei." In *Nihon no tabibito*, edited by Asahi Karuchā Sentā, 5–42. Asahi Karuchā Bukkusu 21. Osaka: Osaka Shokan, 1983.

Gordon, Colin. Afterword to *Power/Knowledge: Selected Interviews and Other Writings*, by Michel Foucault, 229–59. New York: Pantheon, 1980.

Haga Noboru. *Sōgi no rekishi*. Tokyo: Yūzankaku Shuppan, 1980.

Hakuhōdō Seikatsu Sōgō Kenkyūjo, ed. *"Bunshū" no tanjō*. Tokyo: Nihon Keizai Shinbunsha, 1985.

Hane, Mikiso. *Peasants, Rebels, and Outcastes: The Underside of Modern Japan*. New York: Pantheon, 1982.

Harootunian, H. D. "Disciplinizing Native Knowledge and Producing Place: Yanagita Kunio, Origuchi Shinobu, Takata Yasuma." In *Culture and Identity: Japanese Intellectuals during the Interwar Years*, edited by J. Thomas Rimer, 99–127. Princeton: Princeton University Press, 1990.

———. *Things Seen and Unseen: Discourse and Ideology in Tokugawa Nativism*. Chicago: University of Chicago Press, 1988.

———. *Toward Restoration: The Growth of Political Consciousness in Tokugawa Japan*. Berkeley: University of California Press, 1970.

———. "Visible Discourses/Invisible Ideologies." In *Postmodernism and Japan*, edited by Masao Miyoshi and H. D. Harootunian, 63–92. Durham: Duke University Press, 1989.

Hayami Tasuku. *Jizō shinkō*. Tokyo: Hanawa Shinsho, 1975.

Herf, Jeffrey. *Reactionary Modernism: Technology, Culture, and Politics in Weimar and the Third Reich*. Cambridge: Cambridge University Press, 1984.

Herrmann, Anne. "Travesty and Transgression: Transvestism in Shakespeare, Brecht, and Churchill." In *Performing Feminisms: Feminist Critical Theory and Theatre*, edited by Sue-Ellen Case, 294–315. Baltimore: Johns Hopkins University Press, 1990.

Hobsbawm, Eric, and Terence Ranger, eds. *The Invention of Tradition*. Cambridge: Cambridge University Press, 1983.

Hori Ichirō. *Folk Religion in Japan: Continuity and Change*. Edited by Joseph M. Kitagawa and Allan L. Miller. Chicago: University of Chicago Press, 1968.

———. *Nihon no shamanizumu*. Kōdansha gendai shinsho, vol. 256. Tokyo: Kōdansha, 1971.

Hori Ichirō and Yanagita Kunio. "Watashi no ayunde kita michi." *Denki* 1:5–6.

Horkheimer, Max, and Theodor W. Adorno. "The Culture Industry: Enlightenment as Mass Deception." In Horkheimer and Adorno, *Dialectic of Enlightenment*, 120–67. Translated by John Cumming. New York: Seabury Press, 1972.

Huntington, Richard, and Peter Metcalf. *Celebrations of Death: The Anthropology of Mortuary Ritual*. Cambridge: Cambridge University Press, 1979.

Hutcheon, Linda. *A Theory of Parody: The Teachings of Twentieth-Century Art Forms*. New York: Methuen, 1985.

"Ima mo senshisha o yobu hitobito." *Nagasaki shinbun*, 6 January 1986.

Inoue Hisashi. *Shinshaku Tōno monogatari*. 1976; Tokyo: Shinchōsha, 1980.

Irokawa Daikichi. *The Culture of the Meiji Period*. Translation edited by Marius B. Jansen. Princeton: Princeton University Press, 1985.

———. "The Survival Struggle of the Japanese Community." In *Authority and the Individual in Japan: Citizen Protest in Historical Perspective*, edited by J. Victor Koschmann, 250–82. Tokyo: University of Tokyo Press, 1978.

Ivy, Marilyn. "Critical Texts, Mass Artifacts: The Consumption of Knowledge in Postmodern Japan." In *Postmodernism and Japan*, edited by Masao Miyoshi and H. D. Harootunian, 21–46. Durham: Duke University Press, 1989.

———. "Formations of Mass Culture." In *Postwar Japan as History*, edited by Andrew Gordon, 239–58. Berkeley: University of California Press, 1993.

Iwamoto Yoshiteru. *Mō hitotsu no Tōno monogatari*. Tokyo: Tōsui Shobō, 1983.

Jameson, Fredric. "Postmodernism, or the Cultural Logic of Late Capitalism." *New Left Review*, no. 146 (September/October 1984): 53–92.

———. "Reification and Utopia in Mass Culture." *Social Text*, no. 1 (Winter 1979): 130–48.

Jay, Martin. "Scopic Regimes of Modernity." In *Vision and Visuality*, edited by Hal Foster, 3–28. Seattle: Bay Press, 1988.

Kamata Hisako. "*Tōno monogatari* no shitazome." *Iwate nippō*, 24 February, 1975.

Kamishima Jirō. "Intabyū: kokyō sōshitsu no genzai kara." *Dentō to gendai*, no. 55 (November 1978): 8–14.

Kamishima Jirō, ed. *Yanagita Kunio kenkyū*. Tokyo: Chikuma Shobō, 1973.

Karatani Kōjin. *Nihon kindai bungaku no kigen*. Tokyo: Kōdansha, 1980.

———. "One Spirit, Two Nineteenth Centuries." In *Postmodernism and Japan*, edited by Masao Miyoshi and H. D. Harootunian, 259–72. Durham: Duke University Press, 1989.

———. *The Origins of Modern Japanese Literature*. Translation edited by Brett de Bary. Durham: Duke University Press, 1993.

———. "Ri no hihan: Nihonshisō ni okeru puremodan to posutomodan." *Gendaishi techō*, May 1986, 36–47.

Karp, Ivan, and Steven D. Lavine, eds. *Exhibiting Cultures: The Poetics and Politics of Museum Display*. Washington, D.C.: Smithsonian Institution Press, 1991.

Kata Kōji, Kizugawa Kei, and Tamagawa Shinmei. *Shitamachi engei nakiwarai*. Tokyo: Shinshindō, 1984.

Katō Hidetoshi and Yoneyama Toshinao. *Kitakami no bunka: shin Tōno monogatari*. Tokyo: Kyōyō bunkō 416, Shakai Shisōsha, 1963.

Kelly, William W. "Japanese No-Noh: The Crosstalk of Public Culture in a Rural Festivity." *Public Culture* 2, no. 2 (1990): 65–81.

———. "Rationalization and Nostalgia: Cultural Dynamics of New Middle-Class Japan." *American Ethnologist* 13, no. 4 (1986): 603–18.

Kikuchi Teruo. *Tōno monogatari o yuku*. Tokyo: Dentō to Gendaisha, 1983.

Kitagawa, Joseph. *Religion in Japanese History*. New York: Columbia University Press, 1966.

Kōda Rohan. *Rohan zenshū*. Vol. 10. Tokyo: Iwanami Shoten, 1929.

Kodansha Encyclopedia of Japan. S.v. "meisho zue," "urban planning."

Kōjien. 2d ed. S.v. "Shūsakujin," "furusato."

Komai Hiroshi. "Tan'itsu minzokushugi wa koerareruka: Nihon ni okeru tabunkashugi no kanōsei." *Sekai*, September 1992, 88–96.

Komatsu Kazuhiko. *Kamigami no seishinshi*. Tokyo: Dentō to Gendaisha, 1978.

———. "The Meaning of the Stranger in Japanese Folk Culture: Stranger-Killing Legends and Their Transformation." Paper prepared for the international symposium "Symbolism Through Time" of the Wenner-Gren Foundation for Anthropological Research, Fez, Morocco, 12–21 January 1986.

Komatsu Kazuhiko, ed. *Kore wa "minzokugaku" de wa nai: shinjidai minzokugaku no kanōsei*. Tokyo: Fukutake Shoten, 1989.

Kondo, Dorinne K. *Crafting Selves: Power, Gender, and Discourses of Identity in a Japanese Workplace*. Chicago: University of Chicago Press, 1990.

Kosaka Shūhei, ed. *Nyū Japanorojii*. Tokyo: Satsukisha, 1985.

Koschmann, J. Victor. "Folklore Studies and the Conservative Anti-Establishment in Modern Japan." In *International Perspectives on Yanagita Kunio and Japanese Folklore Studies*, edited by J. Victor Koschmann, Ōiwa Keibō, and Yamashita Shinji, 131–64. Ithaca: Cornell University China-Japan Program, 1985.

———. "Nihonjinron in Postwar Japanese History." Paper presented at Annual Meeting of the Association for Asian Studies, 1988.

Krauss, Rosalind. "Nostalgie de la Boue." *October*, no. 56 (Spring 1991), 111–20.

Kristeva, Julia. *Desire in Language: A Semiotic Approach to Literature and Art*. Edited by Leon S. Roudiez. Translated by Thomas Gora, Alice Jardine, and Leon S. Roudiez. New York: Columbia University Press, 1980.

Kurata Hisako, comp. "Nenpyō" (Chronology). In *Tōno monogatari*, by Yanagita Kunio, 214–26. Tokyo: Kadokawa Shoten, 1982.

Kurihara, Akira. *Kanri shakai to minshū risei: nichijō ishiki no seiji shakaigaku*. Tokyo: Shin'yōsha, 1982.

Kurimoto Shin'ichirō. "Hikari o kirisaku yami no Tokyo." In Kurimoto, *Taishū bunka ron*, 229–36. Tokyo: Kōbunsha, 1985.

Kusunoki Masahiro. "Osorezan shinkō." In *Tōhoku sangaku to shugendō*, edited by Gakkō Yoshihiro, 20–47. Tokyo: Meicho Shuppan, 1979.

Kuwabara Takeo. "Tōno monogatari kara." In *Yanagita Kunio kenkyū*, edited by Kamishima Jirō, 123–30. 1937; Tokyo: Chikuma Shobō, 1973.

Lacan, Jacques. *Écrits: A Selection*. Translated by Alan Sheridan. New York: Norton, 1977.

———. *The Four Fundamental Concepts of Psycho-Analysis*. Edited by Jacques-Alain Miller. Translated by Alan Sheridan. New York: Norton, 1978.

Laplanche, J., and J.-B. Pontalis. "Fantasy and the Origins of Sexuality." In *Formations of Fantasy*, edited by Victor Burgin, James Donald, and Cora Kaplan, 5–34. London: Methuen, 1986.

———. *The Language of Psychoanalysis*. Translated by Donald Nicholson-Smith, with an Introduction by Daniel Lagache. New York: W. W. Norton, 1973.

Ledrut, Raymond. *Les images de la ville*. Paris: Edition Anthropos, 1973.

Lefort, Claude. "Outline of the Genesis of Ideology in Modern Societies," in Lefort, *The Political Forms of Modern Society: Bureaucracy, Democracy, Totalitarianism*, 181–236. Edited by John B. Thompson. Cambridge, Mass.: MIT Press, 1986.

Lévi-Strauss, Claude. "Introduction a l'oeuvre de Marcel Mauss." In Mauss, *Sociologie et anthropologie*. Paris: Presses Universitaires de France, 1950.

———. "The Sorcerer and His Magic." In Lévi-Strauss, *Structural Anthropology*, 161–80. Translated by C. Jacobson and B. Grundfest Schoepf. New York: Doubleday, 1963.

Lyotard, Jean-François. *Discours, figure*. Paris: Klincksieck, 1971.

————. *The Postmodern Condition: A Report on Knowledge.* Minneapolis: University of Minnesota Press, 1984.

MacCannell, Dean. *The Tourist: A New Theory of the Leisure Class.* New York: Schocken, 1976.

Marcus, George. "Past, Present, and Emergent Identities: Requirements for Ethnographies of Late Twentieth-Century Modernity Worldwide." In *Modernity and Identity*, edited by Scott Lash and Jonathan Friedman, 309–30. Oxford: Basil Blackwell, 1992.

Marcus, George E., and Michael M. J. Fischer. *Anthropology as Cultural Critique: An Experimental Moment in the Human Sciences.* Chicago: University of Chicago Press, 1986.

Mattelart, Armand. *Advertising International: The Privatisation of Public Space.* Translated by Michael Chanan. London: Routledge, 1991.

Mauss, Marcel. *A General Theory of Magic.* Translated by Robert Brain. New York: W. W. Norton, 1975.

"Minzokugaku to Iwate: shinshun seidan." *Iwate nippō*, 1 January 1953.

Mishima Yukio. *Shōsetsu to wa nanika.* Tokyo: Shinchōsha, 1972.

————. "Tōno monogatari." In *Yanagita Kunio kenkyū*, edited by Kamishima Jirō, 197–99. 1970; Tokyo: Chikuma Shobō, 1973.

Miyoshi, Masao. *Accomplices of Silence: The Modern Japanese Novel.* Berkeley: University of California Press, 1974.

————. *Off Center: Power and Culture Relations between Japan and the United States.* Cambridge, Mass.: Harvard University Press, 1991.

Miyoshi, Masao, and H. D. Harootunian, eds. *Postmodernism and Japan.* Durham: Duke University Press, 1989.

Moeran, Brian. "Individual, Group and *Seishin:* Japan's Internal Cultural Debate." *Man* 19, no. 2 (1984): 252–66.

————. *Lost Innocence: Folk Craft Potters of Onta, Japan.* Berkeley: University of California Press, 1984.

Mori Yūo. *Reijō Osorezan monogatari.* Mutsu-shi: Namioka Shoten, 1975.

Moriya Takeshi. "Geinō o enzuru hitotachi." In *Enja to kankyaku*, edited by Obayashi Tarō, 237–60. Tokyo: Shōgakkan, 1984.

Morris-Suzuki, Tessa. *Beyond Computopia: Automation and Democracy in Japan.* London: Kegan-Paul International, 1988.

Morrow, Lance. "Japan in the Mind of America." *Time*, 10 February 1992, 16–21.

Morse, Ronald. "Yanagita Kunio and the Modern Japanese Consciousness." In *International Perspectives on Yanagita Kunio and Japanese Folklore Studies*, ed. J. Victor Koschmann, Oiwa Keibo, and Yamashita Shinji, 11–28. Ithaca: Cornell University China-Japan Program, 1985.

Murakami Yasusuke. "The Age of New Middle Mass Politics: The Case of Japan." *The Journal of Japanese Studies* 8, no. 1 (1982): 29–72.

Murakami Yasusuke, Kumon Shunpei, and Satō Seizaburō. *Bunmei toshite no ie shakai.* Tokyo: Chūō Kōronsha, 1981.

Muramatsu Tomonori, Umezawa Takeo, and Umezawa Tomio. "Shitamachi no Tamasaburō to wa nanimonoka." *Kōkoku hihyō*, no. 52 (September 1983): 63–73.

Nakazawa, Shin'ichi. "Shikaku no katasutorofu: misemonogei no retorikku to keishōsei." In *Misemono no jinruigaku*, edited by Victor Turner and Yamaguchi Masao, 224–43. Tokyo: Sanseidō, 1983.

Nihon Chiiki Kaihatsu Sentā, ed. *Tōnopia puran: jiritsu toshi Tōno kara no hōkoku* Tokyo: Seibunsha, 1982.

Nihon minzoku jiten. S.v. "Gion matsuri," "goryō," "itako," "Jizō-kō," "Jizō shinkō," "kappa," "kappa komahiki," "somin shōrai," and "tennō matsuri." Tokyo: Kōbundō, 1972.

Nishijima Tatsuo. "Katasumijinsei no kaihō-ku ima, taishū engeki wa shita-machi ni saku 'yami no toshi.'" *Asahi shinbun* (evening edition), 29 May 1985.

Oda Tomihime. "Shokōhon *Tōno monogatari* no mondai." *Kokubungaku* 27, no. 1 (1982): 72–78.

Ohnuki-Tierney, Emiko. *Illness and Culture in Contemporary Japan: An Anthropological View.* Cambridge: Cambridge University Press, 1984.

———. *The Monkey as Mirror: Symbolic Transformations in Japanese History and Ritual.* Princeton: Princeton University Press, 1987.

Ong, Walter. *Orality and Literacy: The Technologizing of the Word.* London: Methuen, 1982.

Ōtō Tokihiko. "Kaisetsu" (Commentary) to *Tōno monogatari,* by Yanagita Kunio, 196–213. Tokyo: Kadokawa bunko no. 1295, Kadokawa Shoten, 1982.

Pemberton, John. *On the Subject of "Java."* Ithaca: Cornell University Press, 1994.

Plutschow, Herbert, and Fukuda Hideichi, trans. *Four Japanese Travel Diaries of the Middle Ages.* With Notes by Plutschow and Fukuda and Introduction by Plutschow. Cornell University East Asia Papers, no. 25. Ithaca, 1981.

Poster, Mark. *The Mode of Information: Poststructuralism and Social Context.* Chicago: University of Chicago Press, 1990.

Robertson, Jennifer. "The Culture and Politics of Nostalgia: *Furusato* Japan." *International Journal of Politics, Culture and Society* 1, no. 4 (1988): 494–518.

———. *Native and Newcomer: Making and Remaking a Japanese City.* Berkeley: University of California Press, 1991.

———. "The Politics of Androgyny in Japan: Sexuality and Subversion in the Theater and Beyond," *American Ethnologist* 19, no. 3 (1992): 419–42.

Rosaldo, Renato. "Grief and a Headhunter's Rage: On the Cultural Force of Emotions." In *Text, Play, and Story: The Construction and Reconstruction of Self and Society,* edited by Edward M. Bruner, 178–95. Washington, D.C.: American Ethnological Society, 1984.

Ross, Andrew. *No Respect: Intellectuals and Popular Culture.* New York: Routledge, 1980.

Said, Edward. *Orientalism.* New York: Vintage, 1979.

Sakai, Naoki. "Modernity and Its Critique: The Problem of Universalism and Particularism." In *Postmodernism and Japan,* edited by Masao Miyoshi and H. D. Harootunian, 93–122. Durham: Duke University Press, 1989.

———. "Return to the West/Return to the East: Watsuji Tetsuro's Anthropology and Discussion of Authenticity." *Boundary 2* 18, no. 3 (1991): 157–90.

———. *Voices of the Past: The Status of Language in Eighteenth-Century Japanese Discourse.* Ithaca: Cornell University Press, 1991.

Sakurai Tokutarō. "Minkan shinkō to sangaku shūkyō." In *Sangaku shūkyō to minkan shinkō no kenkyū,* edited by Sakurai Tokutarō, 27–32. Tokyo: Meicho Shuppan, 1976.

———. *Nihon no shamanizumu.* 2 vols. Tokyo: Yoshikawa Kōbunkan, 1974.

Sakuta Keiichi. "The Controversy over Community and Autonomy." In *Author-*

ity and the Individual in Japan: Citizen Protest in Historical Perspective, edited by J. Victor Koschmann, 220–49. Tokyo: University of Tokyo Press, 1978.

Santner, Eric L. *Stranded Objects: Mourning, Memory, and Film in Postwar Germany*. Ithaca: Cornell University Press, 1990.

Sasaki Kizen. *Tōno no zashikiwarashi to oshirasama*. Tokyo: Hōbunkan, 1977.

Sasaki Shun'ichi. "Banpaku to jisukabā Japan." *Gekkan kankō*, no. 153 (June 1979), 25–27.

Seidensticker, Edward. *Low City, High City: Tokyo from Edo to the Earthquake*. New York: Alfred A. Knopf, 1983.

Shimazaki Tōson. "Nochi no Shinkatamachi yori." In Shimazaki, *Tōson zenshū*, 6:200–201. Tokyo: Chikuma Shobō, 1967.

Shinohara Takamasa. "Taishū engeki ni haru futatabi." *Nihon keizai shinbun*, 26 January 1983.

Siegel, James T. "Images and Odors in Javanese Practices Surrounding Death." *Indonesia*, no. 36 (October 1983), 1–14.

Silberman, Bernard. "The Bureaucratic State in Japan: The Problem of Authority and Legitimacy." In *Conflict in Modern Japanese History: The Neglected Tradition*, edited by Tetsuo Najita and J. Victor Koschmann, 226–57. Princeton: Princeton University Press, 1982.

Silverberg, Miriam. *Changing Song: The Marxist Manifestos of Nakano Shigeharu*. Princeton: Princeton University Press, 1990.

———. "Constructing the Japanese Ethnography of Modernity." *Journal of Asian Studies* 51, no. 1 (1992): 30–54.

———. "Remembering Pearl Harbor, Forgetting Charlie Chaplin, and the Case of the Disappearing Western Woman: A Picture Story." *Positions: East Asia Cultures Critique* 1, no. 1 (1993): 24–76.

Smith, Robert J. *Ancestor Worship in Contemporary Japan*. Stanford: Stanford University Press, 1974.

———. *Japanese Society: Tradition, Self, and the Social Order*. Cambridge: Cambridge University Press, 1983.

Stewart, Kathleen. "Nostalgia—A Polemic." *Cultural Anthropology* 3, no. 3 (1988): 227–41.

Stewart, Susan. "Notes on Distressed Genres." In Stewart, *Crimes of Writing: Problems in the Containment of Representation*, 66–101. New York: Oxford University Press, 1991.

———. *On Longing: Narratives of the Miniature, the Gigantic, the Souvenir, the Collection*. 1984; Durham: Duke University Press, 1993.

Stocking, George W., Jr., ed. *Objects and Others: Essays on Museums and Material Culture*. History of Anthropology, no. 3. Madison: University of Wisconsin Press, 1985.

Takahashi Hiroshi. *Taishū geinō*. Tokyo: Kyōikushiryō Shuppankai, 1980.

Takamatsu Keikichi. *Shimokita hantō no minkan shinkō*. Tokyo: Dentō to Gendaisha, 1983.

Tanaka Hisao. "Jizō shinkō to minzoku." In *Bukkyō minzokugaku*, 244–57. *Kōza Nihon no minzoku shūkyō*, vol. 2. Edited by Gorai Shigeru, Sakurai Tokutarō, Ōshima Takehiko, and Miyata Noboru. Tokyo: Kōbundō, 1980.

Tanaka Kakuei. *Building a New Japan: A Plan for Remodeling the Japanese Archipelago*. Translated by Simul International. Tokyo: Simul Press, 1983.

Tanigawa, Ken'ichi. "Kaioetou" (Commentary) to *Tōno monogatari*, by Yanagita Kunio, 245–66. Tokyo: Yamato Shobō, 1972.

Taussig, Michael. "With the Wind of World History in Our Sails." In Taussig, *Mimesis and Alterity: A Particular History of the Senses*, 70–87. London: Routledge, 1993.

Tōno-shi. *Tōnopia puran III: shizen to rekishi to minzoku no hakubutsukōen toshi kensetsu kōsō*. Tōno: Tōno-shi, 1975.

Tōno-shi Kikaku Zaisei-ka, ed. *Tōno shisei sanjūnen no ayumi*. Tōno: Tōno-shi, 1984.

———. *Tōno-shi sōgō keikaku*. Tōno: Tōno-shi, 1981.

Treat, John Whittier. "Yoshimoto Banana Writes Home: *Shōjo* Culture and the Nostalgic Subject." *Journal of Japanese Studies* 19, no. 2 (1993): 353–87.

Trumpener, Katherine. "The Voice of the Past: Anxieties of Cultural Transmission in Post-Enlightenment Europe." Ph.D. dissertation, Stanford University, 1990.

Tsumura Takashi. "Gendai Nihon in ariuru fuashizumu wa nanika." *Shisō no kagaku*, May 1981, 49–57.

Twine, Nanette. "The Genbunitchi Movement: A Study of the Development of the Modern Colloquial Style in Japan." Ph.D. dissertation, University of Queensland, 1975.

Uchino, Tatsurō. *Japan's Postwar Economy*. Tokyo: Kodansha, 1978.

Ukai Masaki. "Taishū engeki no makuai: Nanjō Masaki no ichinen nikagetsu." *Aruku miru kiku*, no. 208 (June 1984): 4–40.

Van den Abbeele, Georges. *Travel as Metaphor: from Montaigne to Rousseau*. Minneapolis: University of Minnesota Press, 1992.

Volosinov, V. N. *Marxism and the Philosophy of Language*. Translated by Ladislav Matejka and I. R. Titunik. Cambridge, Mass.: Harvard University Press, 1973.

Whisnat, David E. *All That Is Native and Fine: The Politics of Culture in an American Region*. Chapel Hill: University of North Carolina Press, 1983.

Williams, Raymond. *Keywords: A Vocabulary of Culture and Society*. New York: Oxford University Press, 1976.

Yamaguchi Masao. "Kingship, Theatricality, and Marginal Reality in Japan." In *Text and Context*, edited by Ravindra K. Jain, 151–79. Philadelphia: Institute for the Study of Human Issues, 1977.

———. "Taishū engeki no Burehito." In *Kabuku: taishū gekidan no sekai*, edited by Minami Hiroshi, Nagai Hirō, and Ozawa Shōichi, 149–60. Tokyo: Shiromizusha, 1982.

———. "Tokyo as a Cultural Text." Typescript. n.d.

Yanagita Kunio. "Genbun no kyori." *Bunshō sekai* 4, no. 14 (1909): 167–72.

———. *The Legends of Tōno*. Translated by Ronald Morse. Tokyo: Japan Foundation, 1975.

———. "Saihan oboegaki" (Preface to second edition, 1935). In *Tōno monogatari*, 59–61. Tokyo: Yamato Shobō, 1972.

———. "Shasei to ronbun." *Bunshō sekai* 2, no. 3 (1907): 30–32.

———. *Tōno monogatari*. 1910; Tokyo: Yamato Shobō, 1972.

Yoneyama, Lisa. "Hiroshima Narratives and the Politics of Memory: A Study of Power, Knowledge, and Identities." Ph.D. dissertation, Stanford University, 1992.

Yoneyama Toshinao. "Yanagita and His Work." In *International Perspectives on Yanagita Kunio and Japanese Folklore Studies*, edited by J. Victor Koschmann, Ōiwa Keibō, and Yamashita Shinji, 29–52. Ithaca: Cornell University China-Japan Program, 1985.

Yoshida Teigo. "The Stranger as God: The Place of the Outsider in Japanese Folk Religion." *Ethnology* 20, no. 2 (1981): 87–99.

Yoshimoto Takaaki. *Kyōdō gensōron*. 1968; Kadokawa bunko no. 5014, Kadokawa Shoten, 1982.

Yoshino Kosaku. *Cultural Nationalism in Contemporary Japan: A Sociological Enquiry*. London: Routledge, 1992.

Žižek, Slavoj. "Eastern Europe's Republics of Gilead." *New Left Review,* no. 183 (September/October 1990): 50–62.

———. *For They Know Not What They Do: Enjoyment as a Political Factor*. London: Verso, 1991.

INDEX

Page numbers in italics refer to illustrations.

261